THE INNS OF
GREECE & ROME

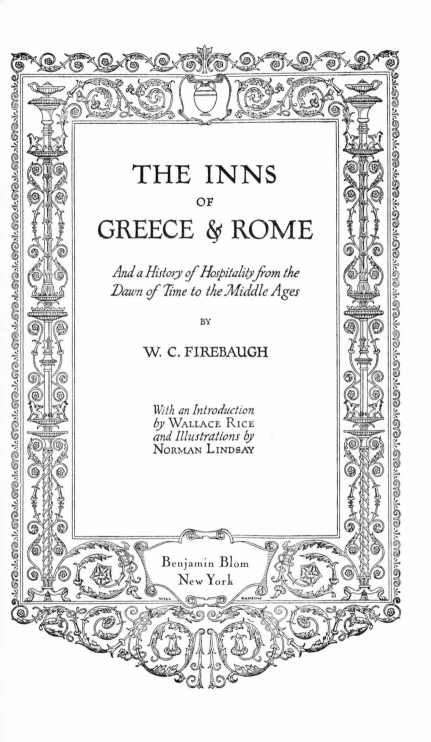

THE INNS

OF

GREECE & ROME

*And a History of Hospitality from the
Dawn of Time to the Middle Ages*

BY

W. C. FIREBAUGH

*With an Introduction
by* WALLACE RICE
and Illustrations by
NORMAN LINDSAY

Benjamin Blom
New York

First published Chicago, 1928
Reissued 1972 by
Benjamin Blom, Inc.
New York, N. Y. 10025

Library of Congress
Catalog Card Number 76-175878

Printed in the
United States of America

ILLUSTRATIONS

INTRODUCTION

Surely there is fitness in having a man born and reared in the best hotels of his time, of which his father was proprietor, write a brief introduction to this interesting account of the best, and worst, inns of antiquity. For to most of us life outside the home, whether stately or humble, is an abnormal and too often a subnormal state of being, fully met when the only home one has known in early life is itself an inn.

Reading of the hostelries of Greece and Rome as disclosed in the classic and post-classic writings of these lands, where the good old tradition of hospitality was often so grossly abused, one is left to wonder if it was not after all the exception that secured attention, if the honest keeper of the clean tavern, with its warmest welcome and savory food, was not in all ages performing his pious duty to his guests, simply and unostentatiously and unmentioned, while his ill favored competitor with his tricks of misrepresentation, adulteration, and secret theft caught the attention of poet and prose writer, who justly found him guilty of an inhumanity which stands forth as a sacrilege to the race.

For giving shelter from the storm, drink to the thirsty, and food to the hungry has been at all times and places a fundamental duty; and men, however unable to attain their own ideals whether simple or lofty, have always been dutiful. The debt owed by host to guest was sacred and until lately has so remained in all stages of society, even those of savagery in which the stranger is perforce an enemy. Means of securing not mere immunity from plunder and attack but all the rites of hospitality have been noted by travellers in every continent where taverns had not yet been demanded by the numbers of sojourners. The sacredness of the wanderer's goods and person has been willingly conceded, even to the formation of a permanent bond between the provider of bread and salt and him who partakes thereof. May we not rightly assume, therefore, that even when the inns of antiquity are shown at their worst there were still countless hosts, respecters of the gods and worshipful of the rites of guestship, who welcomed the coming, rejoiced the staying, and sent good luck with the parting guest?

But in modern days a more subtle danger threatens the ancient spirit, however maintained through the ages. The devil of industrialism has invaded the hotel, and even the revival of the roadside tavern in response to motor travel has been contaminated by the desire to make money first and allow the guest's comfort and pleasures to become a mere secondary consideration.

Here I recall my father's sitting in the corridor down which his guests must depart, his spacious pockets filled with little flasks of choice liquor, with his own hands bestowing these upon the men who slept under his roof, not as an advertisement, not to secure their return thereto, but because they had enabled him to discharge a duty blest by the gods, for which he was duly thankful.

Happy picture of a bygone age in these United States, and happy memory of a good man, best perhaps because so genial a host, now gone to his reward a long generation ago, having preserved into our own time the good and ancient tradition so vividly set forth in this entertaining volume.

WALLACE RICE.

THE INNS OF GREECE & ROME

CHAPTER I.

Inns and Taverns of Antiquity—A Nation's Inns an index to its roads and methods of transportation—Inns of the great routes of Egypt —Beer a National beverage—Vintage Wines in the time of Rameses— Tavern Songs—Drinking and conviviality among students—Method of making wine—Cabarets of Alexandria—Athenaeus the glutton— Drunkenness among women—Juvenal's accounts of the debaucheries of the Egyptians.

One whose habits of mind prompt him to seek diversion amongst company more select than that brought together by chance in some inn or tavern may deem such a subject unworthy of consideration and may even find fault with the writer for presuming to invite him upon such a ramble, for it will be a ramble, and along the little known byways of culture. In fact, a history of hospitality can not be less than a contribution to the most interesting chapter in anthropology: the chapter which deals with Survivals in Culture. Let us then remind him of the cellar of the Auerbachs, and the legends which have grown up around it: the ventas and posadas of the Spain of Cervantes, of many an enchanting passage in the Letters of James Howell, of the Wild Boar's Head kept by Mrs. Hurtig, in Eastcheap, of the Tabard Inne of Chaucer, and last, but not least, of the Mermaid Tavern, where Ben Jonson gained inspiration for much of his finest work!

The inns and taverns of antiquity were not lacking in scenes which deserve to be reanimated and preserved. It is true that such establishments occupied a lowly station

1

and that the calling of the innkeeper was looked down upon, and even despised, but fortunately, the subject has an interest aside from the poetic, an interest which justifies the most minute treatment in detail. The nature of this interest will begin to make itself felt when we give thought to our inns and palatial hotels and the conditions which brought about such development. The institutions of our day fill a double purpose; they minister to the comforts and needs of their patrons, and they cater to the amusement and social needs of the public. That interchange of ideas which, more than any other factor, has refined and broadened civilization, and contributed to refinement in taste and standards of comfort, has its origin in three primary causes: wars of conquest, travel, and commerce, and the last named has contributed more than the other two. The greatest progress in the modern world has been made in the direction of overcoming space, whether by telephone, airplane, ocean greyhound, or luxurious transcontinental trains, and the impetus behind all these is commerce.

If, then, we examine the public houses of the ancients with closer attention, is it not in fact the same as though we were to dissect their civilization for purposes of contrast with our own?

Are not a nation's inns an index to its roads and methods of transportation, as well as a true reflection of the national character?

With this in mind we shall collect the scattered notices upon the subject and attempt to bring it together into a connected whole. For the present, we shall devote our principal efforts to the inns and taverns of Egypt, the Levant, Greece, and Rome; though in the future we hope to pursue the subject through the Dark Ages, and deal with the refectories and monastic orders which took upon themselves the burden which a dying commerce could no longer support. The growth of gilds in France, Italy, the Low Countries, and England slowly rehabilitated commerce and the monastic orders were gradually relieved of their burden as we reach the age of Chaucer.

With the most primitive ages we have no concern, for where traffic and commerce do not exist, where individuals do not travel, and the wild hordes wandering in search of spoil and pasturage are the only wayfarers, there is no necessity for an inn.

The Heroic Age, however, furnishes us with an entirely different picture and one infinitely more beautiful and agreeable. Following an age of chaotic social relations we are confronted with a rude culture which finds its closest parallel in the writings of the Old Testament. It has been well said that the two great literary works which bear the closest resemblance to one another are the works of Homer and the Old Testament. This, on its face, is a startling assertion, but a little reflection will make the conviction stronger. These two collections of writings are emphatically the productions of two opposed civilizations which had progressed to about the same stage of development. In both we have wars and rapine; both are largely poetic and poetry is older than prose as a literary medium. In both we find a realistic description of practically the entire circle of life down to its smallest details: might begins to yield the palm to wisdom and guile, but hospitality is still a duty and an obligation. Even in that age individual traveling was by no means common. Save in the instances of Egypt, Tyre, and Sidon, and probably Cnossos, commercial intercourse was of little importance: it was carried on almost exclusively upon the water and at its best was but little removed from piracy. The urge to go out into the world to gain knowledge, that divine dissatisfaction from which all progress comes and which, in the ages to follow, was to inspire the works of Herodotus and Rutilius, had not yet awakened. A few, perhaps, visited relatives or friends living near at hand, or some vagrant may have fled from the scene of his crime of passion. Yet even in that age, and before it, we know of the sack of Cnossos, and read of the wanderings of Ulysses. He, however, was an unwilling traveler and was driven by powers beyond his control.

In the early heroic age there were no special establishments designed to profit from the necessities of strangers. An arrangement nobler and more beautiful served as a substitute, and a general hospitality, founded upon religion, custom, and obligation, was practised.

Taking our subject in order, we will begin with Egypt, whose monuments have preserved more than one scene in wineshop and tavern, and whose festivals are the very stuff of which the purest hospitality (purissimae impuritatis) was made.

"No people," says Brugsch, in his Historie d' Egypt, "could be gayer, more lively, or of more childish simplicity, than those old Egyptians who loved life with all their hearts and found the deepest joy in their very existence. Everybody was fond of enjoyment, sang, drank, danced, and made excursions into the country."

"They loved the flowing cup when work was done," remarks Arnold, in his History of Beer and Brewing, "and perhaps, sometimes, when work was not yet done. Thus the hieroglyphics tell us, and thus, too, do their ancient literature, their imperishable monuments, their inscriptions, their papyri, nay, even their temples and their tombs."

"Beer was the national beverage of the Egyptians, and it was perhaps with them first of all, prior to the Babylonians and Assyrians, that barley was grown and beer made. Beer was as intimately interwoven with Egyptian life as it is with that of any modern European country

where the vine is not grown in abundance. Four thousand
years ago the Egyptian peasant and landowner drank it,
as did the craftsman, the soldier, the merchant, the priest,
and the king. They brewed beer and they drank beer
down to the very last of the Pharaohs, under the
Ptolemies, as under the Roman rule. Even today, the
poverty-stricken fellah drinks his old fashioned Egyptian
beer, just as his ancestors did under Senefru or Thothmes,
or Rameses, and he is still bearing the same yoke they did,
thousands of years ago, and as much imposed upon and as
much tyrannized over as they were. But he does not
alone DRINK his beer in the same fashion, HE ALSO MAKES
IT IN THE SAME WAY."

Maspero, in his "Sketch from Life in an Ancient
Egyptian City," has combined and condensed an immense
amount of material from original sources into a connected
and lucid description which we hasten to quote:

The scene is probably laid in some Egyptian city of
the New Empire, circa 1300 B. C., in the time of Rameses
II. In our wanderings through the streets of this city we
come at length to a beer-house or tavern.

"The reception-room has been freshly lime washed,"
says Maspero. "It is furnished with mats, stools, and
armchairs, upon which the habitual customers sit side by
side, fraternally drinking beer, wine, palm brandy (*shodu*),
cooked and perfumed liquors, which would probably seem
detestable to us, but for which the Egyptians display a
strong taste. The wine is preserved in large amphorae,
pitched outside, and closed with a wooden or clay stopper,
over which some mud is laid, painted blue and then
stamped with the name of the owner or the reigning
Pharaoh. An inscription in ink, traced upon the jar,
indicates the origin and the exact date of the wine: THE
YEAR XXIII, IMPORTED WINE; THE YEAR XIX, WINE OF
BOUTO, and so on.

"There is wine of every variety, white and red; wine from Mareotis, wine from Pelusium, wine of the Star of Horus, Master of Heaven, native growths from the oases, wines of Syene, without counting the wines of Ethiopia, nor the golden wines which the Phoenician galleys bring from Syria.

"Beer has always been the favorite beverage of the people. It is made in a mash-tub of barley steeped in water, and raised by fermented crumbs of bread. When freshly made it is soft and pleasant to the taste, but it is easily disturbed and soon turns sour. Most of the vinegar used in Egypt is made from beer. This defect is obviated by adding an infusion of lupine (?) to the beer, which gives it a certain bitterness and preserves it.

"Sweet beer, iron beer, sparkling beer, spiced beer, perfumed beer . . . cold or hot, beer of thick sticky millet like that prepared in Nubia and amongst the negroes of the Upper Nile. The beer-houses contain stores of as many varieties of beer as of different qualities of wine.

"If you enter, you are scarcely seated before a slave or a maid-servant hastens forward and accosts you: 'Drink unto rapture, let it be a good day, listen to the conversation of thy companions and enjoy thyself.' Every moment the invitation is renewed: "Drink, do not turn away, for I will not leave thee until thou hast drunk.' The formula changes, but the refrain is always the same . . . drink, drink, and again, drink. The regular customers do not hesitate to reply to these invitations by jokes, usually of the most innocent kind: 'Come now, bring me eighteen cups of wine with thine own hand. I will drink till I am happy, and the mat under me is a good straw bed upon which I can sleep myself sober." (The remarks of the drinkers are taken from a scene of a funeral meal in the tomb of Ranni, at El-Keb. I have paraphrased them to make them intelligible to modern readers.)

VINTAGE EXPERTS

They discuss together the different effects produced by wine and beer. The wine enlivens and produces benevolence and tenderness; beer makes men dull, stupefies them, and renders them liable to fall into brutal rages. A man tipsy from wine falls on his face, but anyone intoxicated by beer falls and lies on his back. The moralists reprove the excesses, and cannot find words strong enough to express the danger of them. "Wine first loosens the tongue of man, even wresting from him dangerous words, and afterwards it prostrates him, so that he is no longer capable of defending his own interests. Do not, therefore, forget thyself in breweries; be afraid that words may come back to thee that thou hast uttered without knowing that thou hast spoken. When at last thou fallest, thy limbs failing thee, no one will help thee, thy boon companions will leave thee, saying: 'beware of him, he is a drunkard!' Then, when thou art wanted for business, thou art found prone upon the earth, like a little child. Young men especially should avoid this shameful vice, for beer destroys their souls. He that abandons himself to drink is like an oar broken from its fastening, which no longer obeys on either side; he is like a chapel without its god, like a house without bread, in which the wall is wavering and the beam shaking. The people that he meets in the street turn away from him, for he throws mud and hoots after them until the police interfere and carry him away to regain his senses in prison."

Thus has Maspero given us an intimate picture of Egyptian life under Rameses II, enabling us to glance back over the centuries.

We shall probably be greeted with song and laughter in the next tavern we enter. The company will be jolly and bent on festivities and both string and wind instruments will contribute to the occasion. While we are catching up with the rest of the party and sampling the

stock in trade, singers will entertain us with something
like the following:

> Let sweet odors and oils be placed for thy nostrils,
> Wreaths of lotos flowers for thy limbs
> And for the bosom of thy sister (mistress), dwelling in thy heart,
> Sitting beside thee.
> Let song and music be made before thee.
> Cast behind thee all cares and mind thee of pleasure,
> Till cometh the day when we draw towards the land
> That loveth silence.*

The Horatian philosophy of Carpe Diem was thus not
original with the Augustan.   Why should they not make
merry:

> "Whether your term of life drags on in sorrow,
> Or in some grassy nook you forget tomorrow,
> Dallying and idling at your leisure
> Wooing with Falernian your pleasure,
> While Youth and Fortune grant you power,
> While yet the Sisters' threads endure. . . .

and the Egyptian, fatalist and almost Epicurean, withal,
goes on to say:

> For no one can take away his goods with him,
> Yea, no one returns again who has gone hence.†

Every now and then there is mention of students'
private drinking bouts with doubtless all the con-
comitants of a successful party, for it was not the
Egyptian custom to deprive the women of the social
indulgences in which the men took such delight. Abste-
miousness was no part of the creed of Egyptian woman-
hood, as is easily seen from tomb decorations, frescoes, contemporary literature, and the like, and the gilded youth
of the day took its pleasures where it found them even as

*Duemichen, Hist. Insc. II, 40.
†Harris 500 Pap. Maspero Etud. Egypt.   I.

our own today. In proof of this statement we have the evidence of a letter written by some teacher or tutor to his pupil who "did forsake his books," and "did wander from street to street."

> Thou art caught as thou dost climb upon walls,
> And dost break the plank,
> The people flee from thee,
> And thou dost strike and wound them."*

Yes, even in that dark age the college boys were enlightened enough to have acquired a taste for beer, wine, palm brandy, or other ardent spirits: "every evening, the smell of beer, the smell of beer (that) drives men away." Our rah-rah boy of long ago was also "instructed how to sing to the flute, to give a monologue to the accompaniment of the pipe, to intone the lyre, to sing to the harp."

Another budding genius, who probably found the cost of high living totally out of all proportion to the allowance granted him by his father, is advised by that worthy man "to content himself with two jugs of beer and three loaves of bread."†

Nor are drinking and conviviality the only subjects allied to hospitality upon which antiquity has commented. As there was a cause, so also was there an effect and we learn quite a little about that famous "pulling of the hair," that morning-after-the-night-before feeling. The Egyptians used a very simple and popular remedy to cure it; a remedy which, since the discovery of the bromide pick-me-up, has become obsolete in the so-called western civilizations, but one which the writer has often seen used when the guests of some Chinese mandarin were a trifle heavy and lumpy in spots after undergoing a

---

*Pap. Anastasi, in Sel. Papyri.
†Sallier Papyri.

course of sprouts at the august table. Athenaeus also
mentions the same specific, and the English translator of
his work has put the verses into English rhyme:

> Last evening you were drinking deep,
> So now your head aches, go to sleep;
> Take some boiled cabbage, when you wake
> And there's an end of your headache.

And, fortifying his position still further, he runs on,
"and Eubulus says, somewhere or other,"

> Quick, wife! Some cabbage boil of virtues healing,
> That I may rid me of this seedy feeling.

Some idea of the amount of wine and beer available in
Egypt (its population probably did not exceed some seven
and one-half millions) may be gained from the Great
Harris Papyrus, a document one hundred and thirty-
three feet in length, in which are recorded the endowments
of Rameses III, during a reign of about thirty-one years.
The amounts of wine and beer granted by him to the
temples were:

> Jars of Wine.............256,460
> Jugs of Beer.............466,303

The capacity of the beer jugs is not known to us, but,
judging by their bulk in proportion to the human figures
in the frescoes, they must have held more than one
gallon, and we thus arrive at the conclusion that the
average annual contribution of beer for sacrificial purposes was about fifteen thousand gallons, and, of wine,
probably about nine thousand five hundred gallons. Nor
should we assume that these beer and wine endowments
were in the form of a levy upon the people. They probably came direct from the royal treasury and are set down
as regular expenses for the sacrificial fund. "There can
be no doubt that the department for the management of

the royal domains, that is, in this case, the royal brewery, made the beer."[*]

From what has gone before we can infer that the taverns of old Egypt were no less popular there than elsewhere, and we have the testimony of Strabo, the geographer, to the conditions which in his day prevailed at Canopus.

"They sail by this canal to Schedia," says mine author, "to the great river, and to Canopus, but the first place at which they arrive is Eleusis. This is a settlement near Alexandreia and Nicopolis, and situated on the Canopic Canal. It has houses of entertainment which command beautiful views, and hither resort men and women who are inclined to indulge in noisy revelry, a prelude to Canopic life, and the dissolute manners of the people of Canopus."[†]

Nor is this the only passage in which Strabo makes mention of the taverns and cabarets of that joyous clime:

"But remarkable above everything else is the multitude of persons who resort to the public festivals, and come from Alexandreia by the Canal. For day and night there are crowds of men and women in boats, singing and dancing without restraint, and with utmost licentiousness. Others, at Canopus itself, keep hostelries, situated on the banks of the Canal, which are well adapted for such kinds of diversions and revelry."[‡]

The theory of decantation as a preservative and ripener was well known to the Egyptians, who taught it to the Hebrews. According to Strabo the Mareotic vintage was very highly esteemed after having ripened and aged, the process being aided by decantation. The Egyptians had several methods of pressing the grapes.

[*]Arnold, supra cit. p. 77.
[†]Lib. XVII, Chap. I, No. 16.
[‡]Lib. XVII, Chap. I, No. 17.

Sometimes they trod them under foot in stone troughs but
their more general practice seems to have been as follows:
they would weave an osier weir, enclose the grapes therein,
as though in a hammock of fine meshed net, and then have
recourse to torsion by means of bars to press the juice and
permit it to flow into a vessel placed to receive it.
Wilkerson has produced a bas-relief in which this process
is illustrated.

In the age of the Ptolemies, wine had come to be
regarded as one of the sources of wealth and one of the
glories of that sensual land. Athenaeus has transmitted
much information concerning the vintages, indicating
their respective claims to excellence, as, for example, their
color, their headiness, their excellence, their bouquet, taste,
and so on. That of Coptos is light and an aid to digestion, and was prescribed to patients with fevers. The
Mareotic was an excellent white wine, with an exquisite
bouquet, diuretic, and as it destroyed neither co-ordina-
tion nor lucidity, it was little likely to give one that
morning-after-the-night-before feeling. Another there is
called by some Alexandrine the best, but the finest of
all was the wine which was produced on that tongue of
land between the sea and the lake, which was called the
Taeniotic, the ne plus ultra of the Egyptian wines, and
it was of a dark yellow color.

Athenaeus, always the glutton whom he professes to
be, omits, nevertheless, a number of vintages which ought
to be included. Far be it from us to reproach him for
having omitted to mention the wine of Libya, a detestable
beverage which the proletariat at Alexandria drank and
guzzled whenever anything but water or beer came its
way. "It is bad," says Strabo. "One is likely to discover
more sea water than wine in one of those casks, which,
along with their beer, is the drink of the commoners at
Alexandria. One is reminded of the smuggling conven-

tions on the China coast, when, if one were to substitute
counterfeit coin on the Chinese bootlegger who was good
enough to supply the needs of the enlisted personnel of the
Navy, his successor was certain to have as many bottles
of sea water as there were counterfeit coins in the original
order. And this, at five Mexican dollars per head, notwithstanding the peril of hauling such contraband cargo
up the side of a white ship with a white pack thread,
there was always the danger that some officious officer
might look overside and beat the bottle to its destination
before the prospective owner could cache it and himself.
But the elegant gastronomer and refined host and entertainer should not have failed to mention the Sebennytici
vini which were derived from the mixture and blending of
the juices of three different grapes, whose slips came from
three different parts of Greece, and which the gluttons at
Rome set such store by.

"The Sebennytici," says Pliny, "come from three
varieties of grapes called Thasian, Oethalus, and Peuce."
It would only be just, then, should Athenaeus, in speaking
of the wine that abounded under the name of *Arsinoite*,
and which came from the oasis of that name, to pay
tribute to it. Lastly, Athenaeus, in editing his list of the
wines of Egypt, should not have passed over in silence the
wine of Meroe, which is often confounded with Mareotic,
its pale rival, more especially as Lucan, in a passage no
less bombastic than eloquent, has taken the trouble to
distinguish between these two exquisite vintages. The
passage occurs in his description of the banquet of Caesar
and Cleopatra, and is one of the finer points in Egyptian
wine making:

"Many birds and wild beasts did they set before them,
the Gods of Egypt; and crystal supplied the water of the
Nile for their hands, and capacious bowls studded with
gems received the wine, but not of the grape of Mareotis,

but noble Falernian, to which, in a few years, Meroe had
imparted maturity, compelling it, otherwise full of
maturity, to ferment."*

The immoderate thirst of the drunkards of Egypt
could not have been assuaged by anything short of that
abundance of liquors of exquisite savor, nor could the
unbridled passion for drunkenness which the women
manifested have been sated otherwise. The bas-reliefs and
tombs furnish peremptory evidence of this devouring
passion, and, among a host, one illustration is often cited,
in which two women are represented, one of them paying
her dues to nature, being full of drink, while the other
holds her head and renders her kind service. The orgies
of Memphis and Alexandreia have been perpetuated by
pictorial art as well as by literature, and the scenes in
Pierre Louys' Aphrodite are by no means an exaggeration.
On the contrary, they are well within the limits of art and
are, if anything, less than realistic. A slave, holding a
basin whilst her mistress discharges the bile from a
stomach which can endure no more, is also an illustration
well known to the Egyptologist, and in still another bas-
relief we see two slaves supporting their master, who is
dead drunk, on his precarious voyage home from the com-
messatio. Joseph, therefore, had reason on his side when
he remarked that of all people in the world, the Egyptians
were the most debauched, and there is little of hyperbole
in the statements of Strabo, quoted above, or in the
terrible passage from Juvenal which follows. A passage
that seethes with energy and contempt, with sarcasm and
satire, a banquet at Tentyra or Canopus or Ombi, the
brawling and fighting which are the inevitable sequelae,
more especially when the same city limits contained the
revelers and their enemies. The passage occurs in Satire
XV, lines 33 to 83.

*Pharsalia, Lib. X, 159-165.

"Between the neighboring towns of Ombi and Tentyra there burns an ancient and long cherished feud and undying hatred, whose wounds are not to be healed. Each people is filled with fury against the other because each hates his neighbors' gods, deeming that none can be held as deities save its own. So when one of these peoples held a feast, the chiefs and leaders of their enemies thought good to seize the occasion, so that their foe might not enjoy a glad and merry day, with the delight of grand banquets, with tables set out at every temple and every crossroad, and with night-long feasts, and with couches spread all day and all night, and sometimes discovered by the sun on the seventh morn. Egypt doubtless is a rude country, but in indulgence, so far as I myself have noted, its barbarous rabble yields not to the ill-famed Canopus. Victory, too, would be easy, it was thought, over men steeped in wine, stuttering and stumbling in their cups. On the one side were men dancing to a swarthy piper, with unguents, such as they were, and flowers and chaplets on their heads; on the other side a ravenous hate. First come loud words as preludes to the fray; these serve as a trumpet to arouse their hot passions; then, shout answering shout, they charge. Bare hands do the fell work of war. Scarce a cheek is left without a gash; scarce one nose, if any, comes out of the battle unbroken. Through all the ranks might be seen battered faces, and features other than they were; bones gaping through torn cheeks, and fists dripping with blood from eyes. Yet the combatants deem themselves at play and waging a boyish warfare because there are no corpses to trample. What avails a mob of so many thousand warriors if no lives be lost? So, fiercer and fiercer grows the fight; now they search the ground for stones, the natural weapons of civic strife, and hurl them with bended arms against the foe; not such stones as Turnus or Ajax flung, or like that with

which the son of Tydeus struck Aeneas on the hip, but
such as may be cast by hands unlike to theirs, and born in
these days of ours. For even in Homer's day the race of
man was on the wane; earth now produces nothing but
weak and wicked men that provoke such gods as see them
to laughter and loathing.

"To come back from our digression, the one side, rein-
forced, boldly draws the sword, and attacks with a
shower of arrows; the dwellers in the shady palm groves
of the neighboring Tentyra turn their backs in headlong
flight before the Ombite charge. Hereupon, one of them,
overafraid and hurrying, tripped and was caught; the
conquering host cut up his body into scraps and morsels,
that one dead man might suffice for everyone, and
devoured it, bones and all. There was no stewing of it in
boiling pots, no roasting upon spits—so slow and tedious
they thought it to wait for a fire that they contented
themselves with the corpse uncooked."

Wine, however, not only intervened in the affairs of
the Egyptians and Hebrews, Phoenicians and Assyrians,
to arouse them to violence and cause such bloody affairs
as that described above, it also played an important part
in the settlement of disputes and business difficulties
everywhere. It was one of the principal sinews of commerce and credit through all antiquity, and, incidentally,
the one means by which a contract was sometimes
concluded. Among the Romans, and among our own
forefathers of the Middle Ages, no affair of importance
was disposed of without taking a drink upon it, and it is
so today, in the countries still fortunate enough to be free
from the propaganda of zealots and bigoted reformers,
whether it be the little intrigue of some artizan or the
vital concern of some cabinet minister, whether the pledge
be red zinfandel or some rare brandy, the ratification
(rata fiat) is never complete without this last formality.

And it was the same amongst the Phoenicians, and after them with the Hebrews, for they derived many of their business usages from the merchant princes of Tyre and Sidon. When a bargain had been struck, and a satisfactory understanding reached they shook hands, and ordered a drink called "Chopen," that is to say, metaphorically, the wine of the land, to drink to celebrate the treaty. The French word *chopine* is said to have come from this custom. It is not impossible, but it is certainly very ingenious, if true, or, in our newspaper parlance, interesting if true.

We have said above that beer was the drink most in demand in Egypt, and Diodorus Siculus has credited Osiris with the invention of it. "Wherever a country did not permit the culture of the vine, there he (Osiris) taught the people how to brew the beverage which is made of barley, and which is not greatly inferior to wine in odor and potency."*

*Lib. I, 20.

CHAPTER II.

Assyrian and Babylonian inns conducted by women—Laws regulating inns—Drinking led to most unbridled extremities—Entire city of Nineveh in different degrees of intoxication—Aromatic wines—Hebrew conception of hospitality—The inn at Bethlehem where Joseph and Mary were forced to take shelter in the stable in which Jesus was born—O'Donovan's description of the caravanseraei at Kuchan.

In closing our account of the professional hospitality amongst the Egyptians we should bear in mind that they regarded the affairs of everyday life, whatever their tenor, as of little importance; on the other hand, they lavished untold wealth and meticulous care upon their tombs as the places of eternal silence and the sanctuaries to which they withdrew themselves to sleep out time. In these tombs the character of the Egyptian, king or noble, was accurately mirrored, and a sense of dignity, aloof and impersonal, was probably as deeply imbedded in his character as the desire for life itself.

Our information as to Assyrian and Babylonian inns and taverns is necessarily limited because of the fact that their ruins were buried deep below the surface of the country as it is today. Until a relatively recent period we knew little of their records and experienced the greatest difficulty in deciphering such of their inscriptions as had come to light. Now, however, clay tablets, sherds, and tiles have begun to give up their information and the picture is becoming more and more distinct, though they are still far from complete. In the code of Hammurabi (B. C. circa 2225) we have a few facts from which we may infer with reasonable certainty that wine and beer were vended and drunk upon the premises. The ownership of such beer-houses, wine-shops, or taverns, as were conducted in

Nineveh and Babylon seems to have been vested in the hands of big merchant princes who installed women as managers, and these women actually conducted the resorts. Payment seems to have been made in grain, the price of which was fixed by statute. Patrons were given credit and the score was paid after the harvest. Women conducting such places were forbidden by law to demand money, as this might have caused the customer embarrassment or inconvenience, and the establishment would also have profited if, after the harvest, there had been a fall in the price of grain. Each evasion or contravention of this law was punishable with death. The paragraphs vital to our subject follow:

No. 108. If any of the wine-selling women have not accepted grain in lieu of money, but have insisted upon money in ordinary coin, and thus have assisted in lowering the price of drink and grain, she shall be summoned and thrown into the water.

No. 109. If rebels have assembled in the house of a wine-selling woman, and she has not seized upon them and led them to the fortress, she has forfeited her life.

No. 110. If a priestess who does not reside in the convent have opened a dram shop, or if she have entered there with the purpose of drinking, she shall be burned.

It is of interest to note that the huge block upon which the laws were inscribed had been erected in the temple at Esagil, which was the temple of Bel Merodach, in Babylon. It was discovered in 1901-2 by De Morgan, French archaeologist, and a Dominican monk named Scheil, in the acropolis at Susa. Evidently it had been removed from Babylon by the Elamites. Its contents prove an astonishing degree of civilization in early Babylon and only recently it was invoked as a precedent by a jurist in St. Louis, Missouri.

In addition to the native products, such, for example, as the wines made from palms and dates, caravans also transported the choice vintages of neighboring countries. Drinking was almost universal. Royal banquets were always heavily provided with wine, as both Daniel and Curtius Rufus testify, and the daily fare of the upper classes would have been ill esteemed without the benign and cheering influence of the spirit of the grape. In the houses of the wealthy, fruit juices were fermented and mead and cordials were common. Curtius Rufus, in his history of Alexander the Great, states that in Babylon drinking was an out and out vice, and that in many instances it was carried to the most unbridled extremes and led to excesses such as even the court of Rome knew but infrequently.

As to Assyria, Maspero has drawn the following picture from original sources:

"The Assyrian is sober in ordinary life, but he does not know how to stop if he once allows himself any excess. Wines of Assyria and Chaldaea, wines from Elam, wine from Syria and Phoenicia, wines from Egypt, amphorae and skins are emptied as soon as opened, without visibly quenching the universal thirst. After one or two days no brain is strong enough to resist it, and Nineveh presents the extraordinary spectacle of an entire city in different degrees of intoxication. When the festival is over several days are required before it resumes its usual aspect. Whilst the people are becoming tipsy outside, Assurbanipal feasts the leading chiefs and the ministers of state within the palace. They are seated on double chairs, two on each side of a small table, face to face. The chairs are high, without any backs or footstool upon which the guests can rest either elbows or feet; the honor of dining with the king must always be paid for with some fatigue.

"The tables are covered with fringed cloths, upon which the dishes are placed by the slaves. Unlike the common people, the nobles eat little, so that few dishes of meats are placed before them, but cakes and fruits of different kinds; grapes, dates, apples, pears, and figs are brought in continued relays by long lines of slaves.

"On the other hand, they drank a great deal—with more refinement, perhaps, than the common people, but with greater avidity. Upon this occasion, the king has distributed the most precious vases in his treasury, cups of gold and silver, the majority of them moulded or chased in the form of a lion's head. Many of them were formerly sacred vessels which the priests of vanquished nations used in their sacrifices; some are from Babylon or Carchemish, some were taken from Tyre or Memphis, whilst others belonged to the temples at Samaria and Jerusalem. By using them for a profane occasion, the Assyrians insult the gods to whose service they belong, so that to the pleasure of drinking is added that of humiliating the foreign deities in the sight of Assur whom they resisted.

"The wines, even the most delicate, are not drunk in their natural state; they are mixed with aromatics and various drugs, which give them a delicious flavor and add tenfold to their strength. This operation is performed in the hall, under the eyes of the revelers. An eunuch, standing before the table, pounds in a stone mortar the intoxicating essences, which he moistens from time to time with some substance. His comrades have poured the contents of the amphorae into immense bowls of chased silver, which reach to their chests. As soon as the perfumed paste is ready they put some of it into each bowl and carefully dissolve it. The cup-bearers bring the cups,

draw out the wine, and serve the guests. Even the
sentinels at the doors receive their share, and, standing
spear or club in hand, pledge each other as they mount
guard. The only persons who do not drink, or who drink
very little, through the necessity of retaining their
sobriety, are the eunuchs—who stand behind the guests
to fan them—the servants, and the musicians."

The ancient Hebrew conception of hospitality was
based upon tenets as pure as those of Menelaus, though in
later times the right was not binding upon them unless
the wayfarer was of their own people.

The place where Zipporah and her son stopped when
Moses returned to Egypt may well have been one of the
inns along the road between Egypt and the northeastern
countries. Owing to the fact that the Hebrews made no
distinction between a harlot and an hostess, we cannot be
certain that Rahab did not conduct an inn rather than a
house of ill fame. In any case, the spies of Joshua found
shelter under her roof and she received her reward. The
same may be said of the harlot at Gaza whose hospitality
Samson shared; but one episode there is which admits of
no double meaning; I refer to the return of the sons of
Jacob from Egypt. They stopped at an inn and opened
their sacks to give fodder to their sumpter mules. One is
also impressed with the fact that they carried supplies for
the return journey. Such places differed little from the
khans of present day Asia; establishments where there
was shelter for man and beast but where it was necessary
to provide supplies. On the second journey the brothers
received from the ruler of Egypt an abundance of supplies
and a train of mules and wagons as well. One well
furnished with necessities and perhaps a few comforts was
confronted, in these towns of Judaea, with some difficulty
if he had no friends or acquaintances, and often was compelled to go into camp in the public place, like a modern

Bedouin; proof positive that in the Hebrew villages there was often no shelter except that of the shrine of the oldest of professions.

When the angels arrived at Sodom they would have remained in the streets had not Lot pressed his kindly hospitality upon them, which probably meant that there was no inn to which they could apply.

The Levite of Ephraim, a stranger at Gaba, had gone into camp in the public place with his women, his servant, and his beasts of burden; the latter had received their fodder and he was even then getting ready to serve supper, when an old man, a fellow countryman, came to offer, in his own house, a hospitality which was accepted because of the common tie between them.

One can still see in the Jewish villages the open places where travelers pitch their tents, those spaces in the khans where the caravans still find shelter, and conditions today differ little from those of the days of Joseph. The khans are, generally speaking, built within the villages, whereas the enormous caravanserais are constructed along the roads and at distances of about eight miles from each other. Some described by O'Donovan are enormous and the discomfort which they offer is only exceeded by their size.

It is in the khans, however, that we find the nearest approach to the shelters which, in the times of Jacob, were to be found along the roads leading from Egypt; shelters which the Latin translators of the Holy Writ have probably rendered erroneously by the term deversorium, and the bleak desolation and utter lack of commissary are eloquent commentary upon the wisdom which prompted the sons of Jacob to prevent themselves from being placed at the mercy of those conducting such places, more especially where they were otherwise unknown and friendless.

The inn at Bethlehem where Joseph and Mary were forced to take such shelter as they could find in the face of the emergency which confronted the expectant mother was one of the khans such as are still the rule in those regions.   The crowd of travelers, caravan hucksters, which had already arrived, left not even a corner for the weary pair, and they were forced to find such comfort as they could in the stable.   There the mother gave birth to Him who was thereafter to be the Saviour of all humanity; she wrapped Him in swaddling clothes and laid Him in the manger because there was no room in the inn.

If the inns were by no means numerous in the Hebrew countries, the taverns were not more so, and an exhaustive analysis of the Holy Writ will produce no allusion to a cabaret, and this, notwithstanding the fact that much wine was consumed and that the Hebrews also knew how to brew beer.   In addition to the native vintages, and some of them were of the finest, wine was imported from Phoenicia and from Egypt, and, later on, from the Greek Archipelago and Ionia.

The promised land which lay at the end of the long exodus from Egypt was a land of milk and of honey, a land of wine and of plenty.   The grape and the pomegranate flourished, and the wines of Engeddi, Carmel, and Gelboa were famous, although not produced in sufficient quantities to meet the demand, and pomegranate wine and various artificial products were made.

Before quitting the subject of Levantine hospitality, we wish to introduce the readers to two pictures which, it is hoped, will enable the mind to visualize both sides of the subject, the sordid and the beautiful.   For this purpose we quote O'Donovan's description of the caravanserai at Kuchan, as he found it in the latter part of the nineteenth century.   The quotation is apt because the conditions he describes are in no way different from those which beset travelers in pre-classical ages, in the Levant, and could with equal propriety be attributed either to Persia or Palestine.

"After some experience of Kuchan, and especially of its caravanserai, I felt the strongest desire to get away from it. Of all the wretched localities of this wretched East, it is one of the worst I have been in. To people at a distance, the petty miseries one undergoes in such a place may seem more laughable than otherwise; there they do not at all tend to excite hilarity in the sufferer. For four days and nights at a stretch I did not enjoy ten minutes' unbroken rest. All day long one's hands were in perpetual motion, trying to defend one's face and neck against the pertinacious attacks of filthy blue-bottles, or brushing ants or various other insects off one's hands and paper. With all this extra movement, each word I wrote occupied me nearly a minute. Dinner involved a perpetual battle with creeping things, and was a misery that seldom tempted one's appetite. As for the time spent on the top of the house, lying on a mat, and which it would be a mockery to call bed-time, it would be difficult to say whether it or the daylight hours were the more fraught with torment. Every ten minutes it was necessary to follow the example of the people lying around, and to rise and shake the mat furiously, in order to get rid, for a brief space, of the crowds of gigantic black fleas which I could hear dancing around, and still more distinctly feel. The impossibilities of repose, and the continual irritation produced by insects, brought on a kind of hectic fever which deprived me of all desire to eat. All night long three or four scores of donkeys brayed in chorus; vicious horses screamed and quarrelled, and hundreds of jackals and dogs rivalled each other in making night hideous. After sunset the human inhabitants of the caravanserai mounted to the roof, and sat there in scanty garments, smoking their kaliouns, and talking or singing until long after midnight."

In contrast to this dreary picture we have O'Donovan's tribute to a comfortable hotel in Teheran. It is worthy of notice that there were and are certain establishments in Ispahan and other centers which have a charm scarcely to be found elsewhere except in some secluded garden in Seville or in the private grounds of one of the smaller potentates of the Asiatic tropics. The Café de Roses, the Café du Fleuve, the café de la Porte-du-Salut, with its sycamores, happy patrons and servants, lovely gardens and artificial waterfalls, has all the enchanting and haunting charm of a half remembered dream in which complete rest and relaxation fade slowly into oblivion only to awaken to a reality that becomes more haunting as it is better understood. Well did the philosopher remark that East is East and West is West and never the twain shall meet.

CHAPTER III.

The Lydians established the first inns and taverns (?)—The Greeks of the Heroic Age knew not taverns nor inns, but practised the highest standards of hospitality—Lesches, places of gossip, preceding inns— Pausanias's description of two casinos in Athens and Sparta.

Herodotus, who, as he is better understood, will be better appreciated, and who generally attempts to get to the root of a matter, would place the origin of inns among a people among whom he saw them and had experience with them for the first time, and he therefore attributes to the Lydians the establishment of the first inns and taverns. In those primitive times, however, the truth would be difficult to arrive at, if not utterly impossible, and we shall not contradict his statement; nevertheless, we doubt it, and we have many times asked ourselves why the Lydians and no other people should have conceived such an idea. It is true that they were jolly, light hearted, and passionately fond of amusement. Had that not been the case they would never have fallen so rapidly into a state of decadence after the conquest of Sardi by Cyrus, nor could they have taken so light a view of the captivity and humiliation of Croesus. And Polydore Virgil has defended his statement with a singular pleasantry and brilliance, on the ground that the thing is very natural. The Lydians, says he, invented games and they ought therefore to have been the first to conceive the idea of a tavern, and to open establishments, places, as he remarks, where games and gambling would always be held in great favor: "*quippe tale opus in cauponis maxime semper fervet.*" Larcher, the great French translator of Herodotus, is by no means agreeable to this. He does not accept in that sense the word *kapelos,* employed by Herodotus, and he is caustically critical of the translators of Herodotus who have rendered that expression by the Latin term *caupona.* According to him, the term of Herodotus should be taken in the sense of retailer, retail tradesman, and thus does he everywhere render it. He cites a great number of passages where *kapelos,* in effect, is used in the sense in which he maintains it should be taken, notably a phrase in Plato where it is said that "all commerce between towns other than bartering is called *kapelican,*" but with all the evidence he has cited, there is still room for disagreement and an opinion to the contrary may be maintained without any great difficulty. Scholarly candor, however, compels us to admit that, notwithstanding the various Latin versions of Herodotus, and even the evidence of Polydore Virgil, the word *kapelos* can be taken in a double sense, i.e., cabaret keeper and merchant. And this legend upon a sign could only have been embarrassing to a stranger in a Greek town, if he was searching for an inn and not for a retailing establishment. The habit of cheating, which from the earliest times has been inherent in the two callings, would be a complicating factor in the affair, and to do justice to such a situation one should give still a third meaning to the term *kapelos,*" i.e., that of pilfering or obtaining under false pretensions: and the verb *kapeleuein* is no less elastic in the meanings which it may convey, yet notwithstanding the various innuendoes which it conveys, in spite of the various shades of meaning which it takes on in different constructions, one well acquainted with the genius of the Greek tongue will unerringly arrive at the proper sense, and should the stranger seek a wine-shop he had but to ask where he could find an *oinopoles;* were he in search of lodgings, he asked the location of a *panddokos* or a *katagogos,* but notwithstanding all his care and precaution, he would find

himself in the presence of the *kapelos* whether he patronized the one or the other; and, in addition, he did well to
be on his guard against deception which often presented
itself in a guise as lovely as it was sweetly predacious.
The Greeks of the Heroic age were unacquainted with the
plagues which beset the ages in which inns and taverns
flourished. At that time there was literally no such thing
among them as professional hospitality, maintained for
profit. Each and every stranger had the right of sanctuary and asylum; every wayfarer, as though under the
protection of Zeus Xenios himself, was sure to find a host.
After the feast, a libation in honor of the god of hospitality
was poured upon the hospitable table, the protector of
strangers was honored, and the guest was then on even
terms with the host who entertained him. Pomp and
pageantry made not the slightest difference in the quality
of the welcome; a guest might arrive with a baggage train
of mules and slaves, or he might come as unostentatiously
as Orestes, in the Coephores, with a lean scrip, and leaning
upon a staff; he was a stranger, and sanctuary was his by
right. "At the voice of the stranger," eloquently remarks
Barthelemy, "all gates were opened, all his needs were
met, and, as a still more beautiful tribute to the homage
thus rendered to humanity, the host was not informed of
the state and birth of a guest until after the latter had
satisfied his necessities."

One phase of hospitality there was, in the Heroic Age,
which placed it far above the standards practiced by the
Hebrews, at least in the later ages of their history, and the
only examples which can be cited to compare with this
Greek standard are those of Abraham and Lot. To the
Greek, it made not the slightest difference whether his
guest was a Dorian or an Ionian, a Locrian, a Corcyrian,
or an Attican, it made no difference whether he was even
of Greek stock, he was entitled to food and shelter, and

also to protection while under his host's roof. The
Hebrew, in the later periods of his history, while always
hospitable, confined his charity and entertainment to
members of his own race, or to those closely allied to it.
The unlimited scope of Hellene hospitality will be better
understood after a thorough perusal of Homer. Let us
then attempt a description of the age in which he is said
to have lived, and perhaps we shall better understand the
entertainment of Telemachus by Menelaus, which is the
earliest and one of the finest examples of the hospitality
with which we are concerned. We need but cast a glance
at this cheerful, well contented, happy Homeric world to
be convinced that there was anything but a lack of social
amusement. At that time the cultus itself was a series of
light hearted entertainments, beautified by dances, singing, and joyous barbecues and banquets. In addition to
this, the council of the nobles, the court of the monarch,
and the assembly of the people, were, to all practical purposes, as much social as political or commercial, and their
debates, often acrimonious and generally entertaining,
with their cutting and thrusting, were entertaining to the
highest degree, and the innumerable special celebrations
and religious fetes in the houses of the king and the nobles
added still more to the variety and richness of contemporary life. After the banquet, virile youth hastened to
the palaestra to engage in athletic sports and match their
strength and skill against one another in a physical competition beneficial to both body and character alike.
From this custom the finest artistic sense of all time was
evolved. The elders looked on and decided the issues in
accordance with the merits of the contestants, and the
Homeric age produced few weaklings, or, rather, few
survived, which is not a left-handed compliment to later
and supposedly better times. Then followed a wonderful
old folk dance of lovely damsels and armed *epheboi*, such

BRINGING IN A COURSE

as are sometimes seen on the finer pottery of the time, a dance which was symbolical of life itself, and Dryden, in one little line, has caught the very spirit of that dance:

"None but the brave deserve the fair!"

Happy times, in that fairy-tale age of pure gold, when man at his best was "knee deep in June," when he led a healthy, vigorous life, uncontaminated at its source by a seething commercialism destined to devour itself and everything it touched; when Advertising, its crafty and specious spokesman, had not educated Appetite or tutored Desire. What Horace wrote as his conception of the ideal condition for man might be applied with equal propriety to that age:

Who covets much will ever want,
    But happy he on whom the gods bestow
With sparing hand, enough, and grant
    Him health, and industry to keep him so.

How do the majority of our social pleasures compare with these simple and healthy amusements? Are they as good, as constructive? Are they not too refined? Will not such a trend produce eventually a race of mollycoddles and cuddling moths if carried to its end? Let us note that in building the stadia at the various universities we are getting in tune with the ancient Greek ideal of robust health and the physical beauty which crowns it. And we shall have less of ennui, and of political indifference with which to reproach demagogues, as a result.

The first public institutions in Greece which can with any justice be compared with our inns and taverns, the so-called *leschai*, are, in all probability, a development arising at the close of the Heroic age. In the age which followed they were adapted to the needs of the Ionic cities, and larger towns, especially Athens. They were also known to Doric Greece, but to a much less degree.

The first mention of these *leschai* is found in Homer in that passage of the Odyssey in which an empty-headed maidservant attempts to scold Odysseus, disguised in beggar's rags, out of his own house:*

"Wretched guest" (Melantho, Penelope's adopted ward, is speaking), "surely thou art some brain-struck man, seeing that thou dost not choose to go and sleep at a smithy, or at some PLACE OF COMMON RESORT, but here thou pratest much and boldly among many lords and hast no fear at heart. Verily, wine has got about thy wits, or perchance thou art always of this mind, and so thou dost babble idly. Art thou beside thyself for joy, because thou hast beaten the beggar Irus? Take heed lest a better man than Irus rise up presently against thee, to lay his mighty hands about thy head and bedabble thee in blood, and send thee hence from the house."*

This is the only Homeric poem which contains such mention, and it is probably, as stated above, that the institution of public houses did not belong to the earlier Heroic age and the bard very likely carried an institution of his own time back into an earlier age. As regards the passage cited, Eustathius the scholiast informs us that *lesches* were buildings with open halls where people congregated for purposes of gossip and amusement.† Hesiod also admonishes against habits of idleness which these *lesches* fostered.

Gossip, however, was not the only conversation heard in these places; more serious subjects were also discussed, and as the gymnasiums later became the lecturing places and haunt of philosophers and their neophytes, so also these earlier substitutes served a like purpose. The passage from Homer quoted above shows also that these *lesches*, in addition to their social usage, served as shelter

*Book 18, 320 et sequitur;
†Butcher and Lang.

and sanctuary to the homeless and needy vagrants. As it
was unusual for the Greeks to foster a public custom or an
institution of a public nature without associating the same
with their religion and folklore, so they had also for these
institutions a patron: this was Apollo, who in this capacity was called Apollo Leschenarios. On this account
we need not be surprised at reading of these *lesches* as
being enumerated among the public buildings belonging
to the different cities.   The degree to which these gathering places were frequented, depended naturally upon
the varying social character of the native customs and
still more, upon their mode of living. Athens and Sparta
will serve as striking examples of what is meant. According to Pausanias, there were two such casinos, as we will
call them for want of a better word; one called the *Krot-
anon* or Club-room of the Crotonians, the other the
Painted Club-room, and in another passage, Book 10,
chap. 25, Frazer's translation, he speaks of another such
building at Delphi adorned with paintings by Polygnotus
and dedicated by the Cnidians.

Called by the Delphians the Club-room (*lesche*, place
of talk), because here they used of old to meet and talk
over both mythological and more serious subjects. That
there were many such places all over Greece is shown by
Homer in the passage where Melantho rails at Ulysses:

> And you will not go sleep in the smithy,
> Nor yet in the club-room, but here you prate.

Plutarch has laid the scene of one of his dialogues (De
Defectu Oraculorum) in this building. He says (chapter
6): "Advancing from the temple we reached the doors of
the Cnidian club-house. So we entered and saw the
friends of whom we were in search seated and awaiting
us." Pliny mentions the paintings of Polygnotus at
Delphi, but seems to suppose that they were in a temple.

(Hist. Nat. XXXV, 59.) Of the two series of paintings
in the club-house, the one which represented Troy after
its capture seems to have been especially famous; it is
mentioned by Philostratus (Vit. Apollon. VI, 11, 64) and
by a scholiast on Plato (Gorgias, p. 448 b.). Lucian
refers to the graceful eyebrows and rosy cheeks of Cas-
sandra in this picture (Imagines, 7). In the time of
Pausanias the pictures were already between four and five
hundred years old, and they seem to have survived for at
least two centuries more, for they are mentioned with
admiration by the rhetorician Themisteus, who lived in
the fourth century of our era (Or. XXXIV, 11).

The scanty remains of the club-house which contained
these famous paintings were excavated by the French in
recent years. The club-house is situated, in accordance
with the description of Pausanias, higher up the hill than
the spring Cassotis, a few steps to the east of the theatre.
It was built on a terrace, which is supported on the south
by a high retaining wall. A marble slab in this wall bears
this inscription:

KNIDIONODAMOS
TOANALAMMA
APOLLONI
"THE CNIDIAN PEOPLE (dedicated) THE SUPPORTING
WALL TO APOLLO"

Let it not be inferred that the other club-houses in
Greece were constructed and adorned upon standards so
beautiful as this, the most celebrated of them all, or that
the forerunners of Gil Blas and Casanova, when down on
their luck, lodged habitually in sumptuous quarters such
as these. The name *Leschai* must have undergone some
changes in meaning between the Homeric age and that in
which Pausanias wrote. The term was applied to any
place in which people gathered to gossip or to talk seriously. The agora and its colonnades, the gymnasia, the

shops of the various artisans and tradesmen, especially the smiths whose shops were frequented in winter because they were warm, all came under this heading. In Sparta these club-rooms were the scene of the deliberations of the elders on the welfare of the state and it was to them that new-born children were brought, there to pass physical examination for the purpose of determining whether the child should be reared or exposed to die, vide, Plutarch, Lycurgus, 16, 25.

In Athens, on the contrary, there were no less than three hundred and sixty such club-rooms. This difference had its cause in the inherent and national character of the Spartans, which was not so volatile, not so sprightly and talkative as that of the Athenians and Corinthians. Nor must one also overlook the other features of their public and private life—features of such a nature as to make such institutions almost superfluous. As is well known, the Spartans lived their life entirely in common. With them individual initiative, except in the field, was discouraged, and in some cases punished; such ambitions were always looked upon with suspicion. From boyhood to old age, the Spartan underwent the discipline of mass action. He was a cog in the wheel of a well oiled machine. He played, ate, fought, and slept in a common brotherly companionship. As a natural consequence, all classes, whatever their condition in life, and they were all relatively poor, felt no social urge for changed conditions and even discouraged the visits of Greeks from other parts of the country. The almost patriarchal state of society, with its military glamour, filled every need, social or physical. Sparta was never a commercial community nor was it adorned with magnificent edifices and temples. Nor were there any wonderful collections of art to attract outsiders. The stay of strangers in their city was rendered short and difficult by special legislation, and

the comparatively small number of aliens who succeeded
in evading their immigration laws found adequate shelter
and care in the homes of individual families, or, if they
chanced to be official representatives of other states, they
were cared for by royal arrangement, as the king always
placed matters of this sort in the hands of designated
individuals who were responsible to him and to the state.

CHAPTER IV.

Feast tendered Telemachus by Menelaus—Ardor of hospitality passes with the Trojan War—Tokens of hospitality, of copper, of brass, of ivory, issued in the Middle Ages—The origin of luggage checks—Tokens of credit—Vitruvius's description of apartments for guests and entertainment afforded—Origin of the proxy—The sumptuous inns of Persia.

After what we have just said of the Spartans we are impelled in justice to them to introduce Homer's description of the entertainment and hospitality tendered Telemachus by Menelaus. We shall find that in that age, the standards were the same.

"And they came to Lacedaemon lying low among the caverned hills, and drave to the dwelling of renowned Menelaus. Him they found giving a feast in his house to many friends of his kin, a feast for the wedding of his noble son and daughter . . . So they were feasting through the great vaulted hall, the neighbors and the kinsmen of renowned Menelaus, making merry; and among them a divine minstrel was singing to the lyre, and as he began the song two tumblers in the company whirled through the midst of them.

"Meanwhile those twain, the hero Telemachus and the splendid son of Nestor, made halt at the entry of the gate, they and their horses. And the lord Eteoneus came forth and saw them, the ready squire of renowned Menelaus; and he went through the palace to bear the tidings to the shepherd of the people, and standing near spake to him winged words:

" 'Menelaus, fosterling of Zeus, there are two strangers, whosoever they be, two men like to the lineage of great Zeus. Say, shall we loose their swift horses from under the yoke, or send them onward to some other host who shall receive them kindly?'

"Then in sore displeasure spake to him Menelaus of the fair hair: 'Eteoneus son of Boethous, truly thou wert not a fool aforetime, but now for this once, like a child thou talkest folly. Surely ourselves ate much hospitable cheer of other men, ere we twain came hither, even if in time to come Zeus haply gave us rest from affliction. Nay go, unyoke the horses of the strangers, and as for the men, lead them forward to the house to feast with us.'

"So they loosed the sweating horses from beneath the yoke, and fastened them at the stalls of the horses, and threw beside them spelt, and therewith mixed white barley, and tilted the chariot against the shining faces of the gateway, and led the men into the hall divine. . . .

"But after they had gazed their fill, they went to the polished baths and bathed them. Now when the maidens had bathed them and anointed them with olive oil, and cast about them thick coats and doublets, they sat on chairs by Menelaus, son of Atreus. And a handmaid bare water for the hands in a goodly golden ewer, and poured it forth over a silver basin to wash withal; and to their side she drew a polished table, and a grave dame bare food and set it by them, and laid upon the board many dainties, giving freely of such things as she had by her, and a carver lifted and placed by them platters of divers kind of flesh, and nigh them he set golden bowls. So Menelaus of the fair hair greeted the twain and spoke:

" 'Taste ye food and be glad, and thereafter when ye have supped, we shall ask what men ye are; for the blood of your parents is not lost in you, but ye are of the line of men that are sceptered kings the fosterlings of Zeus; for no churls could beget sons like you.'

"So spake he, and took and set before them the fat ox-chine roasted, which they had given him as his own mess by way of honor."

And in the first canto of the Odyssey we read of the welcome extended to the unknown goddess by Telemachus:

"But now I pray thee, abide here, though eager to be gone, to the end that after thou hast bathed and had thy heart's desire, thou mayest wend to the ship joyful in spirit, with a costly gift and very goodly, to be an heirloom of my giving, such as dear friends give to friends."

In the third canto of the same poem, when Telemachus and Pallas were entertained by Nestor, we find no inquiries until after food and drink have assuaged the weariness and hunger and thirst:

"But when they had put from them the desire of meat and drink, Nestor of Gerenia, lord of chariots, first spake among them:

" 'Now is the better time to inquire and ask of the strangers who they are, now that they have had their delight of food. Strangers, who are ye? Whence sail ye over the wet ways? On some trading enterprise, or at adventure do ye rove, even as sea-robbers over the brine?' "

Athenaeus comments very pleasantly on that usage so dignified and so in keeping with sturdy ideals:

"A guest was received," says he, "he was invited to drink, and lastly he was interrogated, and, his drunkenness aiding his sincerity, he sometimes told more than he wished." Thus speaks the spiritual disciple of Epicurus; but he did well; that liberal confidence, that hospitality open to all, the house of the father of the family was sanctuary and asylum, a shelter where the wayfarer knew a welcome awaited him, lodgings for parent or friend, it is certainly one of the most beautiful aspects of the Greek civilization of the heroic age and is entitled to the most sincere reverence which after ages can lavish upon it, if, as is said, imitation is the most sincere form of flattery.

Some men, more ardent in their humanity, sought to outdo even that pagan age with an élan more prompt to bestow the benefits of an evangelical charity and even went so far in their desire to confer hospitality upon all as to erect such places for this purpose. Among these was Axilos, son of Theutranus, native of Arisbe in Troad, who was slain by Diomedes.

"He had opened on the public road," says Homer, "a house in which he gave asylum to all who passed."

We should bear in mind that example of practical hospitality and its benefits as shown by the heroic age, also, as it has a vital bearing upon our subject and, as Pouqueville has very justly remarked, "It would be necessary to cite all antiquity to make known the importance which attached to hospitality in those times."

Still it should not be believed that this great ardor for hospitality was always general throughout and that sometimes it did not cease to function, for cause. When we reach the period of the Trojan War, the Golden Fleece, and the age of Theseus, that is to say, the end of the heroic age, this beautiful devotion begins to break down. That fraternal bond which had formerly seemed to unite all men even as though in one great family, that fraternal chain, let us call it, seemed little by little to break under the strain. All arms were no longer open to the wayfarer. We enter upon an epoch less primitive and more defiant wherein hospitality deserts the villages and seeks its shelter in the country, where Zeus and Hermes, driven away by an entire population hardened and haughty, could find no asylum except

in such a cottage as that of Philemon and Baucis. It
is nothing if not a complete break with the ancient tradition and no longer would it be as under the ancient
regime, that one saw the face of his host for the first
time when that host gave the wayfarer food and shelter;
hospitality came to have its preferences and to have also
its exceptions and reserves. In the cult of Zeus Xenios
one might place his faith, but he would be better served
were he to rely upon his friends and their near relations
and retainers, and the people who addressed them. Thereafter, hospitality flourished no longer as a general axiom,
nor was it actually accorded as a right except to such as
were deemed to have a just claim upon the host. It is
true that the question of defilement did not at that time
enter into the question as it had amongst the Egyptians
and Hebrews (it will be remembered that the Egyptians
could not eat with the Hebrews for such would have been
an abomination to the Egyptians, and the Jews were also
constrained by the same fetish, at least in the later periods
of their history. Daniel, for example, could not partake
of the wine and viands of the Babylonians for some dietary
reason, and many of the most savage riots between the
Roman legionaries and the Jews were probably caused by
the same considerations.

Thus, in course of time certain tokens came into circulation (tesserae hospitalitatis), which served to identify
the incoming stranger and enabled him to substantiate
his claim to the best the house afforded. These tokens
were issued as mandates of Zeus Xenios, although the general consideration to which he had been accustomed in an
earlier and happier age had long been atrophied. The
cabinets of Southern Europe have preserved several speci-
mens and as a general thing they were of gold or silver,
broken in an irregular way, each family keeping a part
which needed the other to complete it. Sometimes they

were of copper or brass, ivory or even of wood, so cut that
the line of cleavage by which they were joined was difficult to imitate and thus prevented fraud.

These tokens of hospitality, of which Tomassin has
transmitted to us certain likenesses, served still another
purpose during the Middle Ages, as tokens of recognition
for political purposes, and they played a sinister part in
the affair of St. Bartholomew, and earlier still in the Sicilian Vespers. From this system we derive hotel bills and
probably all checking systems, such as baggage checks,
and the like. When a guest parted from his host the
token was broken and each retained a piece. As no perfect result could be attained in matching up the whole
without the actual parts, the identification was sufficient
for all purposes. Nor did their usefulness pale with the
death of either major party to the contract: they could
be bequeathed to heirs on either side and were honored
as long as there was anyone left to honor them. In the
Poenulus of Plautus, the Young Carthaginian remarks to
Agoratocles, "Thy father Antidamus was my guest; this
token of hospitality was the bond between us," and
Agoratocles immediately made answer, "And thou shalt
receive hospitality from me."

When a stranger arrived, bearing the token, the apartments reserved solely for guests were prepared as expe-
ditiously as possible, even as the inhabitants of the French
provinces who are still the very soul of hospitality, to this
day maintain the guest chamber (chambres de reserve);
the household supplies were seen to, meals planned, and,
in a word, a feast was prepared which taxed the resources
of the house to the uttermost.

It is of interest to note in connection with these tokens
of hospitality, that there was an ancient Slavic custom
which was current in Russia, Poland, Servia, Bulgaria,
and other Slavic countries, down to a period of about a

hundred years ago, and by virtue of this custom, the peasants drank on credit. The token of credit was a stick, which the proprietor of the public house notched with as many notches as there were days in the calendar until their harvest of hops, barley, or wheat should be marketed. When the account was liquidated, the stick was broken in twain and debtor and creditor retained each his piece. Should it happen that the account was not liquidated as per contract, and there was no good reason for the failure to meet the obligation, the publican would threaten to break the stick and retain both pieces. This was tantamount to the ruin of the credit of the debtor throughout all the district, and furthermore, there was a quasi-religious significance to the ceremony which terrified the illiterate peasant to such a degree that he would even go on his knees to prevent such an untoward happening. The practice came to an end due to improved methods in accounting.

Vitruvius, in his treatise on Architecture has spoken of these special apartments, such as the owner of a house of the better class always kept in readiness for a guest whom Zeus Xenios might send him, and, curiously enough, he has described one of these receptions for us:

"The peristylium, and this part of the house, is called Andronitis, because the men employ themselves therein without interruption from the women. On the right and left, moreover, are small sets of apartments, each having its own door, triclinium, and bed-chamber, so that on the arrival of guests they need not enter the peristylium, but are received in rooms (hospitalia) appropriated to their occupation. For when the Greeks were more refined, and possessed greater wealth, they provided a separate table and triclinia and bed-chambers for their guests. On the day of their arrival they were invited to dinner, and were afterwards supplied with poultry, eggs, herbs, fruits, and other produce of the country. Hence the painters gave the name of Xenia to presents given to guests. Masters of families, therefore, living in these apartments, were quite, as it were, at home, being at liberty to do as they pleased therein."

It is readily seen that a host might have a certain amount of ostentatious vanity at stake in thus welcoming the arrival of strangers and giving them the run of his estates. Trimalchio had it in abundance, and Nasidienus had also his share. On this account Theophrastus has introduced a host entertaining his guests at open table to show their number and his own magnificence. Thus does the Greek caricature Ostentation.

"When he is living in a hired house, he will say (to anyone who does not know better) that it is the family mansion; but that he means to sell it, as he finds it too small for his entertainments."

Yet hospitable as the Greeks were, both in honest intention and deed, they nevertheless possessed types such as even a Trimalchio might have envied. Theophrastus has drawn one such to the life:

"Cool cistern-water has he at his house; and a garden with many fine vegetables, and a cook who understands dressed dishes. His house, he will say, is a perfect inn; always crammed; and his friends are like the pierced cask—he can never fill them with his benefits!"

Thus have the ancient customs atrophied when we reach the age of Theophrastus, who holds such pretentious masquerading up to the ridicule it merits.

Prudence counseled prospective guests to see that the house where they were to be entertained was not over-crowded lest the welcome wear thin, and what Molière said of esteem might easily have been thought by them:

Esteem is founded upon preference.

This is an ancient method surviving today.

In this connection let us listen to Aelian's recital of a little anecdote in which Stratonice, the flute girl, played a leading role, a guest disdainful of those houses too liberally opened to hospitality:

"Stratonice, the flute girl, having been accorded a welcome in a house which she had been invited to enter, would have been greatly flattered by such attention which she had found in a strange land in which she had no reason to expect hospitality and no ties to entitle her to that consideration.

"She presented her most graceful thanks to the host whose kindness had prompted such attention and received her with such good grace; but, arriving as an unexpected guest, and perceiving that the house was open to any and all who wished to stop and stay over; 'Let us go,' said she to her slave, 'we are like a pigeon that has taken to a tree, what you mistook for a house of hospitality is only an inn.' "

Again, it might happen that strangers would be excluded from hospitality through a certain disdain of ancient manners and customs, or because of certain preferences of citizens who refused to see a guest in a man who did not present the token of amity. It might happen that all the travellers recently arrived at some Greek village would be unable to evoke any tie of friendship, and therefore were placed under the necessity of finding a lodging. Nor could they, as in the Hebrew villages, go and camp in the public place. Some countries there were, as for instance the island of Crete, where a certain number of houses were perpetually kept in readiness for strangers, and where tables were always kept set and garnished.

"There were," says Athenaeus, "amongst all the habitations of the island of Crete two houses designated by the name of *syssities;* one was called the *andreion,*

the other the *koimeterion*, and these were the places in
which strangers were lodged.   In the house set aside for
the common repasts, two tables were set; they were called
hospitalieres, and the strangers were given the first place
at these tables, the others arranging themselves thereafter
in order."

In other parts of Greece they constructed near the
temples of the great gods vast shelters, veritable free
hostelries, where wayfarers found not only shelter but
also beds consecrated to the god adored in the nearest
temple.   The hostelry which the Lacedaemonians erected
in the precinct of Hera on the ruins of Plataea we may
suppose to have been an institution of the kind just spoken
of.   The passage of Thucydides in which he speaks of it
is very curious and we reproduce it here; moreover, it is
the only passage in the works of the historian in which
he speaks of the inns of that period, giving any details
as to their furnishings, style, and the like:

"They (the Lacedaemonians) afterwards razed the
whole place to the very foundations, and built near the
precinct of Hera an inn forming a square of two hundred
feet; it had two stories, and chambers all around.   They
used the roofs and the doors of the Plataeans; and of the
brass and iron articles of furniture found within the walls
they made couches, which they dedicated to Hera."

The religious usage which constructed for wayfarers
places of abode in the vicinity of the temples may probably have been derived from the devotional custom of
religious hospitality native to the Orient.

Lucian, in his Syrian Goddess, has a passage which
has a bearing on the question.   He is speaking of the
hospitality which was the due of those coming to worship
the goddess, if they be strangers:

"When he is arrived at Hierapolis, he lodges with a
host whom he does not know, as though he were lodged

with public hosts in each town, and he is received according to the country from which he comes. The Assyrians are called *tutors* as they are the ones who give wayfarers the necessary instructions."

The Athenian *proxenoi* of whom we shall presently speak were neither more nor less than the *tutors* of the Syrian countries. In bringing up the subject of the *proxenos* it may be well to discuss him and his function, as his descendant in our times, I mean the proxy of our boards of directors, scarcely measures up to the standard set by the archtype of the species. The ancient *proxenos* was not a "yes" man for any individual or state.

The office of *proxenos* grew out of public hospitality, that hospitality which subsisted between two cities or states, and the functions of the official closely approximate those of our consuls who love their duty and do it, in spite of political or tropical inertia. In the primitive times when the Greek tribes were under tyrants a quasi-public hospitality may have subsisted between the reigning families of the various tribes and this in turn may have produced similar relations between their subjects. With the abolition of the tyrants, the tradition was probably carried on as a heritage of the past. Then again, some prominent citizen of one state may have had great interests and influence in another and thus have been able to serve the interests of his fellow citizens in that state as well as their interests in his own. This he would do as a private citizen until his services were recognized and rewarded by one or both peoples. When public hospitality was established between two states and no private citizen presented himself as representative, it became necessary that persons be appointed in each state to look after the welfare of visiting citizens of the other, and show them hospitality, and the officials who were thus appointed were known as *proxenoi*. When a state appointed

a *proxenos* it could send one of its own citizens acceptable
to the authorities in the other or it could appoint a citizen
of the other state to represent its interests there.   The
Spartans, in early times, held to the former, but in later
times the custom of conferring the honor of *proxenos*
upon a citizen of the other state with whom *hospitium
publicum* had been concluded seems to have gained in
strength and usage.   With the exception of Sparta, the
common method of appointing a *proxenos* was by a show
of hands.   In Sparta, the king had the right.   The principal duties of the *proxenos* were to receive citizens coming from the state he represented, especially the ambassadors, to see that they gained admission to the assembly,
to see that they had seats in the theatre, to act as patron
to the strangers and to mediate between the two states
if any misunderstanding or dispute arose.

Should a stranger die in the state the *proxenos* of his
country took charge of his effects and property.

As regards the honors and privileges to which a *proxenos* was entitled from the state which he served, the
different Greek states followed different principles; some
honored their *proxenos* with the full civic franchise, and
other distinctions besides.   The right of acquiring property in the state of which he thus became a citizen does
not seem to have been general as when this was allowed
it was as the result of special legislation or authority.   A
foreigner appointed in his own country as *proxenos* of
Athens enjoyed in his own person the right of hospitality
at Athens whenever he visited that city, in addition to
all the other privileges that a foreigner could possess
without actually becoming a citizen.   Among these privileges, though they were not necessarily set forth in the
authority conferred upon him, were:

1. Epigamia . . . the right of additional marriage.
2. The right to acquire property at Athens.

3. Exemption from payment of taxes.
4. Inviolability in times of peace and war, on land and sea.

There were times when Athenian commerce was so heavy that almost every citizen might have been called *proxenos* (unofficially) because of the multitude of social and commercial ties which bound them to other cities. The *proxenos*, however, was a public character and acted as such officially. As an example, when the representatives of Megara and Corinth arrived the *proxenos* appointed by those cities lodged them in his own house, served them as guide, lent his credit to their negotiations, and in a word, as has been well remarked by Artaud in a note on the Birds of Aristophanes, "He met every demand which the strangers coming from allied cities could make upon him." The real distinction between our own consuls and the ancient *proxenos* was this: the primary and imperious duty of the *proxenos* was hospitality: everything else came in due order; whereas hospitality seems to be the last duty of our own officials who have inherited the chiton of authority under a foreign flag.

But even this institution which embraced so many of the needs of travelling inexperience failed to meet the requirements of that fine old humanitarian Xenophon, nor did it measure up to his generous ideal of what true Athenian hospitality should comprise. It was his desire that every foreign sailor who disembarked at Athens should find free and clean lodgings and that every stranger, from whatever country whatsoever, Greek or barbarian, would always be sure of finding shelter in a public inn. Therefore in his Treatise on the Causes of Revenue he demands the levy of a special impost with the proceeds of which he would construct such inns near the harbors for the accommodation of pilots and other watermen, "in addition to those already in operation," for those who should come to Athens.

All this Xenophon had seen in his residence in Persia, where a system of inns, posts, and everything necessary and convenient to people who travel was well organized. There is little doubt that what he had seen in that country had armed his criticism of the methods and crudities in his native land, and as for the Cyropaedia, it is worthy of credit. It was written at the request of a prince, but with the unmistakable intention of amusing and instructing the youth of Athens; it is not so much his desire to describe Asia and Asiatic culture, as it is to inform his countrymen of their own shortcomings and state of unpreparedness, that they may remedy them. His life among the Persians was an active one, and an observant; what he has written of, he has seen. Before the days of Xenophon's maturity, Herodotus had seen the Persian system in operation and had marveled at it.

"The first courier," says he, "turned his dispatches over to a second, the second to a third, and they passed them along from one to another just as among the Greeks the torch passes from hand to hand in the rites of Hephaestos. The distance traveled by a horse is called, in the Persian language, 'Angareion.'" There are several other passages in the writings of Herodotus in which he makes mention of the Persian posting system, and he devotes some space to one detail which Xenophon scarcely notices; the hostelry which the Great King maintained at each station. He rarely mentions one without touching upon the other.

Henricus Stephanus, in commenting upon this passage of Herodotus, emphasizes the immense distances in the empire of the Persians by saying that between the sea and Susa, the capital of the Great King, there were one hundred and eleven stations and caravanserai. The inns must have been exceedingly sumptuous, for we must remember that the king went so far in his luxurious and sanitary measures that he carried boiled drinking water with him in silver tanks, in an age that knew not Lister. Hence it must follow that when he stopped at an inn it must have been all that comfort could require and money could buy. Aelian also mentions these magnificent caravanserai that were in operation throughout the empire, from Asia Minor to Medea. Alexander stopped at one of these places when beginning his march against Darius: it was one of the *stathmoi basilikoi* on the frontiers of Phrygia, and Mithridates also stopped at the same caravanserai, deeming it a favorable omen as he was thus destined, as he believed, to follow in the footsteps of Alexander and overrun all Asia.

The Greeks, however, failed utterly to profit from the information conveyed by Herodotus and Xenophon. They detested the Persians so thoroughly that they scorned to learn from them and the rapid posts and luxurious inns of the Asiatic empire were never objects familiar to the sight and experience of the dwellers in the little peninsula. In many ways they were right, as the extent of their country was infinitely small compared to Persia, and their states were independent, whereas in the empire there was a powerful central authority.

In place of imitating the Persian system and deriving from it the things which might have aided their development, they gave a malignant turn to a term used by their former enemies in their posting service. We have spoken of the term *angareion*, as the distance a horse traversed; the Greeks adopted the word, made it into a verb and defined it as the sum of all tyrannical force well worthy of the King of Kings, who forced citizens to run with news at the peril of their lives. Strange destiny; that the labors of the father of history and the disciple of

Plato should avail their countrymen only in adding to
the scope of the dictionary, but should, in years to come,
aid the most powerful and deadliest enemy of Hellas in
keeping the country in subjection, and should finally
contribute the most to the overrunning of occidental
civilization with the hordes of Tourania! Alexander's
messages were carried as were those of his ancestors in
the days of Agamemnon, and the institution of the
hemeradromoi lasted until the Roman Empire instituted
a post road system modeled upon that of Persia; a system from which all that have come later were derived.
In the days of the lower empire the post system reached
its greatest excellence in Greece. The course of empire
had shifted from Rome to the city of Constantine and the
centralized authority was closer to the Balkan and Asiatic
provinces, a fact which sufficiently explains the improve-
ment.   Thus we shall arrive at the period when throughout all Greece as in the other provinces of the empire we
shall see magnificent military roads with relays of animals, and at every station a hostelry, where travelers
may lodge and where couriers may procure fresh horses.
The entire establishment shall be meant by the term
allage, which Eustathius has specifically informed us is
synonymous with *stathmos*, "by which," writes he, in-
formally, "we mean not only an inn and a stable but
also the places proper to make a halt, the stations where
travelers stay over to rest and recruit themselves." Thus
we have again the posting system of Persia, and rest
assured, that unless we have been deceived, the master
of posts will soon put in an appearance.

And as far as the term *angareion* is concerned, it has
not been lost; we still have it in the Latin *angariare* and
through low Latin in the French *hangar*, which conveys
accurately enough the impression of such shelters as the
stathmoi of Persia or the *allage* of the lower empire.

CHAPTER V.

Grecian inns of the fifth century before Christ—The inns of the pleasure-loving Athenians—The public houses, low dives, and public stews—Wine booths and dancing girls—The giving of names and signs to taverns the beginning of advertising—Keepers of taverns and cabarets held detestable and infamous—Drunkenness and harlotry prevail— Diogenes a frequenter.

Inasmuch as we have only found inns complete in needful details under the emperors, the question of whether the Greeks of former times actually possessed establishments where one could lodge and where his animals could be taken care of, may arise. The rapid decadence of hospitality, once it had set in, and the institution of the *proxenos* serve but to cloud the issue, and the unwary scholar might draw an erroneous inference from the facts. The shelters erected for pilgrims to religious festivals would also tend to bear out such an inference. There are several terms in the Greek language which denote inns, and many of these terms are classical, some few being even ante-classical, there are also numerous passages in the authors, sometimes obscure and ambiguous, but which, nevertheless, offer positive evidence that there were sumptuous establishments of the kind. A verse in the Inachus of Sophocles, cited and commented upon by Pollux, proves that as early as the fifth century before Christ, hostelries were already known in Greece. The *pandokos xenostasis* was an inn where guests only were lodged; but the *phatne* as well as the *stathmos* were used to denote a huge establishment where men and beasts found shelter. Athenaeus cites a passage in the Peltate of Ephippus as follows: "The place was furnished with stables for beasts of burden, stalls for the horses, and dining-rooms (*gleumata*)."

It was in places such as these that great and powerful individuals with carriages and baggage trains, such, for example, as envoys on their way to their posts of duty in foreign states, lodged. Such diplomats found the hospitality of the miserable little inns of Boeotia or Phocis little to their tastes, and dearly bought. We know this, thanks to a beautiful passage in the orations of Aeschines, in which the Greek orator tells us that the Athenian ambassadors lodged one of their companions, whom they suspected of treason, in an inn, and among other indications of their contempt, they refused to lodge or dine in the same inn. The *katagogion* was a very simple and very common hostelry, as was also the *katalusis*. According to Pollux there were many of that sort at Athens, and also throughout the whole of Greece, as is proved by many references in the Greek writers. It was in such an establishment as this that the famous case of murder and telepathy took place at Megara, as Cicero tells us. Secaldus, and the old man of Oree, found themselves in a like situation in Argolis and it is there that they recited to one another that mutual account of their misfortunes which Plutarch has transmitted to our times. People who went to consult the oracle, the devotees of Pythia and Apollo, who departed for Delphi or Tegyre, the place where the god was born, lodged there of their own free will in the hostelries, as is easily inferred from an anecdote related by Plutarch in his treatise On the Oracles Which Are No More, and the same may be said of certain Delians who had returned to Delphi. Had they not overheard the words of a certain innkeeper, they would all have been lost and would never have been able to return to their country. "During the Peloponesian War, the Delians having been driven from their island,

they were advised by an oracle of Delphi to search out
and possess themselves of the place where Apollo had
been born, and there to make sacrifices of a certain
nature: they marveled about this and demanded whether
Apollo might not have been born elsewhere than amongst
them, the prophetess Pythia advised them that a crow
would lead them aright. The representatives of the
Delians, on their return, passed by chance a village in
Chaeronia, and they saw a certain hostelry there with
some strangers frequented from the oracle of Tegyre to
which they wished to go, and as they were taking their
departure they heard the following conversation: 'Farewell, madame Crow,' and taking literally the response
of the prophetess, they made their sacrifice at Tegyre,
whereupon they were restored into favor and returned to
their country.''

But what were these hostelries, these Greek *pandokeia*, such as were to be found in these villages, scattered
along the great roads for those travelling through the
country? How were they distributed, what was their
extent, what were the conditions in them and what were
their charges? This we do not know. The fragments
of Menander tell us that wine was sold for a few obols
the pint and that for the price paid daily to a pandar a
whole family could live in comfort for a month. The
details concerning the institution at Plataea with which
Thucydides has furnished us are happy in their fullness,
we are not so fortunate, however, in material of the same
sort which will serve to illustrate the *pandokeia*, nor do
the writings of antiquity help us, in this respect. They
may have been simple caravanserai as Pouqueville imagines, and might be compared with the khans of modern
Greece, in his estimation; those vast and miserable sheds
where beasts of burden and men were herded indiscrim-
inately into a hurly-burly, and of which Buchon gives so

piteous a description.   We are of the belief that a passage
of Plutarch will prove that in those hostelries of Greece,
even as in the khans of Modern Greece, the life of the
wayfarer was identical in every respect, and, using the
expression of Buchon, "everything is done in the presence
and before the eyes of all."

But in Athens these conditions were entirely different.
Putting aside the fact that from their very character,
pleasure-loving, witty, sprightly, and volatile, they would
naturally form a larger number and a greater variety
of social relations, they also possessed a civic life infinitely more cosmopolitan and sparkling.   They harbored
a constant influx of strangers from the ends of the earth,
traders, merchants, brokers, all in search of business and
profit; travellers and art lovers, seeking to learn and to
enjoy, sages come to pay respect to the shrine of philosophy and literature.   It was only natural that with
them the need for hotels and inns soon brought them into
being.   In the life at Athens such institutions are often
mentioned, and the difference between conditions at
Athens and Sparta is very neatly and caustically summed
up in a witticism delivered by the philosopher Diogenes,
which Aristotle has preserved for us.   This cynic once
said: "The public houses are the *Phyditerien* (a bagnio
where flute girls entertained and ministered to the desires
in any way requested [see Aristophanes for extended
note]) of the Athenians."   If from this witticism one
were to argue a greater frequenting of the public houses
this must be understood only of the lower and lowest
dregs of society, and therein lies the basic difference between the public house of the ancient Greco-Roman
civilization and our own.   There were exceptions, however.   When the Athenian ambassadors were sent to
negotiate with Philip of Macedon, they lodge everywhere
in inns.   Dionysus (Aristoph. Ranae, 114), makes inquiry

as to the quality of the inns on the road to Hell, and what shall we say of those special provisions made by the public to provide shelter for wayfarers coming to Athens and Corinth to participate in the great religious festivals and games? In Athens, however, the better classes of the people had nobler and finer occasions for social entertainment, though this was often very costly at Corinth. Horace has remarked that not every man could afford to pleasure there, and we have no less an authority than Demosthenes to bear him out. The public houses had little influence on the greater number of the upper classes of society though these same upper classes were unanimous in holding publicans and all their ways in contempt not only because of the natural contempt of the aristocrat for the underling, but also because these rogues and scoundrels, fracturing by their very calling one of those beautiful and sacred tenets of a semi-primitive culture which carried out the rites of hospitality even to remote generations and nourished the guest-friend even in the face of war, could only be such and shelter the stranger within their gates for gain. Then, too, the adulteration of wine and devious methods in merchandising were only too well known in classical times. According to Petronius, Socrates used to boast that he never had looked into a tavern, but it is more probable that what he meant to say was that he never looked around in one. But the almost universal disrepute in which the aubergists were held may be inferred from a multitude of passages in classical literature. Among the most striking is that passage in the Characters of Theophrastus in which he describes an individual so lost to shame and so lacking in intelligence that he would even be capable of conducting a public house. Isaac Casaubon, in commenting upon the passage of Theophrastus cited above, hints at the facility with which publicans lent their services in

the matter of pimping; and decries that zeal in the public
service which would procure service for the paying guest
who wants what he wants when he wants it.   In fact,
the austere post-renaissance scholar goes so far as to sum
up the attributes of hosts who did better than serve their
patrons with a savory dish or a rare vintage, calling them
pimps and their establishments public stews.   The
moralizing Socrates says somewhere that not even a slave
with a shred of respectability would risk eating in a public house.   This seems somewhat exaggerated, however,
for from various passages in Aristophanes one learns
that the more common class of citizens and their wives
as well did not hesitate to enjoy themselves in such
houses.   But that persons of position and dignity, on
the contrary, did not visit such places and that they
were partly constrained by law from visiting them can be
inferred from Hyperides as cited by Athenaeus, who
states that if a member of the Areopagitus had ever
entered a public house, even on a single occasion, his
colleagues would no longer have tolerated him as a
member of that assembly.   As to the establishments
themselves, the Greek language defines them and places
them in different classes.   First then we shall mention the
wine booths.   Here wine was sold only on the street.
Then there were ale or beer houses or taprooms, at least
the lexicographer Suidas expressly differentiates the mere
wine seller from the publican.   Such were the places
where Demos amused himself with flutists and lyrists
and dancing girls who were agreeable in other ways.
Whether all these wine shops also sheltered strangers, or
whether the rights and limitations of these houses were
so exactly defined and established and regulated by the
authorities is not known.   This definite division does not
seem to have taken place.   There is still another class of
public houses mentioned which seems to have provided

At the Door of a Tavern

especially for the shelter of strangers.   These were known
by a characteristic name, *pandokian*, All Receiving, open
to all.   Booths also, it seems, were sometimes connected
with these inns.   Some establishments doubtless stood
somewhat higher in the scale than those mentioned, for
even if a large part or even if the greater part of strangers
stopping in Athens found shelter with hospitable friends,
there must have been a considerable number who had
no such connections and were therefore compelled by
necessity to avail themselves of a public house.   However, it is not at all to be expected that with the carelessness and indifference which even yet prevails in the
Levant and Orient and even in the Latin countries, the
comfort of travelers was looked after to the same degree
as in our inns and hotels of today, especially in those of
the larger cities.   That the Greeks, like ourselves, had
painted signs on such establishments may be ascertained
from a passage in Aristotle.   Nevertheless, the fact that
in Aristophanes and other writers no further trace of the
use of such signs is to be met appears to weigh against
the universality of the custom, and as this usage would
have furnished many an opportunity for sarcastic comment, its absence is indicative of the fact that the custom
was not widespread.   That the omission is accidental is
too much to suppose.   The custom of giving names and
signs to inns and the like is perhaps the very beginning
of advertising as we understand it today.   For instance,
we have the familiar sign of the two triangles laid one
over the other, and also the bush set up in front, both of
which go back to Graeco-Roman times, as will be shown.
The Greek innkeepers had a special patron saint just as
our publicans have theirs, in Pandolphus and Julianus.
They placed themselves under the patronage of Mercury,
who, by the way, was also the very prince of purloiners,
of whom Horace wrote:

Choused of his cattle, Apollo in a rage
Demanded restitution, with a frown;
Threatening thee gamin, impish and sage
Who laughed, and, his impotence to crown
Didst filch his quiver with thy guile
And he could only swear—and smile.

Such, then, was the manner in which the public houses
of Athens were instituted in general, and, as will be seen
from the foregoing, they were bound to differ immeasur-
ably from ours in importance and in the esteem in which
they were held. Yet the writer well remembers more
than one wayside forest inn along the former bound-
aries of western Russia and eastern Germany and Aus-
tria which were strongly reminiscent of the standards to
which the ancients took such universal exception and he
is here tempted to enlarge upon the statement of Sir
Samuel Dill, in his Roman Society from Nero to Aurelius:
"The Roman inns, from the time of Horace to Sidonius
Apollinaris were in bad standing and even dangerous."
Had Sir Samuel journeyed through the forests of eastern
Russia he would have commented upon these inns and
harpies at some length. The inns of Greece and Asia
Minor then belonged in general to a very low place in
the social order and the need they filled was limited,
while our public houses, in their large number and
variety, our ale and beer houses (O shades of Gambrinus
and the golden age), inns, wine rooms, coffee houses,
casinos, clubs and restaurants, are patronized in the
evening by the greatest number of all those who have
become weary during the day by application to business
or even by sheer lack of all employment. The reason
for this contrast is not difficult to adduce or to understand, for why should a free Athenian have wished to
seek entertainment and social intercourse in such a place?
Was not all life a series of gay festivities and activities

which stimulated his mind? There were the numerous religious fiestas, venerable and national, and, almost coaeval with his traditions, built on the very foundation of his character and its needs, beautiful in their simplicity and symbolism; and in addition there were the games, the philosophical schools, folk dances, and the ever present spectre of war among themselves which kept alive the glamour of military tradition and service.

In the theatre he saw his gods on the stage, in the majesty and grandeur of Aeschylus and Sophocles he heard their utterances, and the memory lingered until the next occasion and lingers still. The greater part of his time, however, was occupied with political duties and activities. He presided in the popular assembly as a magistrate or attended as a citizen, he spoke, or listened to the speeches of others, which sometimes tended to benefit him but often injured him, and which always entertained him. He elected officers and he was elected to office, or he sat in open court as judge or as spectator. Everywhere subjects were discussed which touched his interests closely, and the debates were such that by their wit and energy of expression, their brilliant rhetoric and the exquisite artistry in the manner of their presentation, they were then supreme and have never been surpassed or even equalled to the present time. Aristophanes has flayed the designing Cleon, and he was not alone in demoralizing Demos, sycophants and subserviency often had such plausibility that they were able to overthrow honor and lead even the most scrupulous citizen into a dangerous and expensive lawsuit, but when that age came Greece was on the decline even as has always been the case with other nations. "Men," said Aristophanes, and after him Petronius, "men are lions at home and foxes abroad."

Only the results of all this were tragic, however; in

the daily and ordinary activity of these institutions there
unfolded itself on the other hand, a certain strength of
mind and activity of thought, a stimulating of the faculties and an energy of action compared with which our
public life forms a contrast almost as marked as the difference between life and death.   We must be cautious in
condemning lest we condemn ourselves and our own
institutions.

One should do whatever will benefit his health, sing,
declaim, or if he so desires, walk up and down in the great
room of a hostelry, whether strangers be present or no,
"it makes no difference whether one is a passenger aboard
ship or whether he is lodged in an inn with many others,
if the attendants are inclined to laugh and make sport
it makes no difference, it is no less dishonest to eat than
it is to take one's exercise."   From this passage it would
appear that no separate room was allotted to each individual traveler, and the pandokeion was a common
refectory and dormitory.   Would it then follow that the
same disorder of men and beasts would have been found
there as in a modern Greek kahn?   We do not think
otherwise.

We base our belief on the passage of Epphippus cited
by Athenaeus, and upon another not less curious found
in Pollux.   In his precious chapter upon the settings of
a play and the decorations of Greek theatres, he informs
us that ordinarily they opened through the proscenium,
three doors; that in the middle might open upon a palace,
a cavern or grotto, or the house of a nobleman, but that
the second, on the left, invariably opened upon an
inn, whilst the one on the right led to a temple in
ruins or remained vacant.   In tragedies, on the contrary,
the inn or "door of strangers," according to his diction,
was on the right, and one discovered a prison on the left.
These details, while of interest, go far to prove that inn

life was well known and was a familiar part of daily living in ancient Greece, otherwise they would never have had a part in the drama of the times, and have been always introduced in the scenic scheme of the theatre; but let us give the passage in the words of Pollux: "In the comedies, an awning was stretched over a carpet, it was always stretched near a tavern doubtless so that those passing might cool themselves in the hot hours of the day, and nearby one saw the stables for the beasts of burden, and the great gates which the Greeks called *klisiades*, and they passed through these to enter their carriages." Here, then we see one of those edifices of the Greeks, great halls for the guests, near by stables for the horses and sumpter mules, and great doors for the carriages. But at that point our information comes to an abrupt end.

As to the masters of these establishments, we cannot think ourselves better informed, in fact, our information is, if anything, even more scanty and sketchy. We only know that, as in the case of the keeper of a tavern or cabaret, the calling of him who conducted a pandokeion was held detestable and infamous. Pollux has transmitted to our admiring curiosity the entire index expurgatorius of infamous callings and damaged goods and we have good reason to suppose that the legislator was very wisely occupied with such subjects in placing the ban of a public scarcely less moral, all those who lodged for the night, all the tavern keepers in the villages and towns, or along the great routes of Hellas.

Their women were for the most part strumpets from the lowest stratum. In absolute proof of this we need only cite a very curious passage from the Theodosian code, as later on we shall, that such women were absolved from the penalties carried by the law against adultery, so true was it thought that their hideous calling was but

one facet of the profession still older; a few phrases from
Theophrastus's chapter on Slander shall suffice for the
present.   He tells us that the daughters of Thrace, so
numerous at Athens, many being of the nobility of their
own country, but for the most part slaves, sellers of rib-
bons, tavern girls, all combining the calling of sweet
predaciousness with their other métier; our evil speaker
launches an epigram at the sons of such abandoned
women, imputing the same qualities to her son—like
mother like son, as it were: "His mother, I may add, is
a noble damsel of Thrace, at least, in the language of
Corinth she is called 'my life, my soul,' and such ladies
are esteemed noble in their own country, they say.   Our
friend himself, as might be expected from his parentage,
is a rascally scoundrel.   Such women snatch the passers-
by out of the very street.   That house has not the best
of characters.   Really there is something in that proverb
about the women.   In short, they have a trick of gossiping with men . . . and they answer the hall-door themselves."   In other words, such hostesses conducted hostelries along the great roads, but the pleasure of their
guests was the most serious and profitable concern of
their lives.   Nor should we be astonished at this information when we remember the nature of the company
thus brought together in the stalls called, by way of
compliment among the Greeks, inns, and we find the
high minded Plutarch greatly insensed and defending
well born men from tavern friendships and familiarities.
He says to them: "That they should not do as many do
and imagine they have the substance of a good time
when they have but the shadow, gaming with dice, playing
mora, lodging with innkeepers and picking up gambling
friendships with tavernkeepers in the villages to the
glittering spell of games."   And a saying of Plato in his
Laws wherein he sets forth his ideas upon a Utopian

government is as much to the point in some favored countries today as it was when he enunciated it.   I refer to the passage in Lib. XI, sec. 918 of the Laws.

There is, of course, little doubt that the unpopularity of innkeepers in Greece arose in part from the feeling against receiving pelf for hospitality, but their tendencies toward adulteration and substitution, extortion, espionage, and the like, also contributed to their ill repute.

"On this account (eagerness for gain) all the lines of life connected with retail trade, commerce, inn-keeping, have fallen under suspicion and become utterly disreputable.   For if what I trust may never be and will not be, we were to compel, if I may say a ridiculous thing, the best men everywhere to keep taverns for a time; or carry on retail trade, or do anything of that sort; or if, in consequence of some fate or necessity, the best women were compelled to follow similar callings, then we should know how agreeable and pleasant all these things are; and if all such occupations were managed on incorrupt principles, they would be honored as we honor a mother or a nurse.   For the sake of trade, a man opens lodgings in a lonely place, a long way from anywhere.   He receives bewildered travelers in barely tolerable quarters, or affords warmth, quiet, and rest in his close rooms to people driven in by angry storms. And then, after receiving them as friends, he does not provide them with hospitable entertainment according to that reception but holds them to ransom like captive enemies whom he has got into his clutches, on the most exorbitant, unjust, rascally terms.   It is these offenses and others like them, shamefully common in all such callings, which have brought discredit upon all ministration to men's need."

Is it any wonder that Dionysus in the Frogs inquires what are the best inns on the road to Hell?

No, Theophrastus, you were wrong; the reckless man would not become a tavern keeper with such profits in sight.

The impudent predaciousness and harlotry of the women of the inns and taverns were able foils for the unprincipled thievery and general rascality practised habitually by the men of the house; hungry for profits, they cared not a fig what the source might be. They had taking ways, but their charity was hypo-microscopic and could only be awakened by some wily impostor with a supposititious legacy to leave or some other motive of paramount interest; arrogant where they did not fear personal chastisement, they bore admirably the tradition of Aristophanes, that "men are lions at home and foxes abroad."

They held the stranger in contempt who was careful of his expenditures and did not hesitate to manifest it when they dared. All these, and other characteristics are meant by the term *kapelos*.

Any man possessing a tavern where entertainment was to be had passes, if that were possible, for even a greater knave than the innkeeper. It was always a disgrace to frequent his establishment, and any man making such a place his headquarters would have been held to be without shame and utterly lost to all sense of honor, and would have blushed to have been seen sitting at table there. A certain Demosthenes, not the orator, as he was a drinker of water, was seen one day by Diogenes the Cynic, getting drunk in a tavern, and was greatly put out, according to Plutarch, and wished for nothing so much as to get away from the place undiscovered. "The more you pull back," said the Cynic, "the further you get into the tavern," meaning of course infamy. Although Diogenes spoke to that purpose, he was none the less a frequenter of such abandoned places, in true

cynic form. Before he took his perpetual headquarters
in the patched tub in which he crouched, he had spent
practically his whole life in taverns. He took his meals
in them, too. Once when he was dining amongst a
crowd in a tavern he saw through the open door Demosthenes the orator passing by in the street. He called
to him, and as the other heeded not the invitation, but
continued his walk and turned his head, "And why,"
yelled the Cynic after him, "are you too proud to approach a place where your master does not disdain to dine
and spend his time?" "It was his desire," remarks
Aelian, who has transmitted the anecdote to posterity, "to
speak to people in general, and to citizens in particular,
intimately, individually; such he deemed the office of
the orator; and such as harangued the public for reasons
of state are but the slaves of the multitude."

CHAPTER VI.

Realistic night in a Greek inn, from Marcel Schwob—Adventure of the poet and the slave—Beggars' guild, their methods—Theophrastus on ostentation—Night life in Athens—Arts of Athenian innkeepers— How they avenged the dupes—Their finesse in substitution—Plutarch on capacity—Price of wines—Gentle art of obtaining something for nothing—Wine inspectors.

Let us now cite a pleasanter picture, conventional, it is true, but not lacking in beauty. The gem is from the works of Marcel Schwob, Mime IV, The Hostelry. (Edition of Mosher, 1901.):

"Hostelry, o'errun with vermin, the poet, bitten till deplete of blood, salutes thee. Not to thank thee for having sheltered him one night on the borders of a dark highway; the route is miry as that which leads to Hades —but thy cots are broken down, the lamps smoky; thine oil is rancid, galettes mouldy, and, since last autumn there are white worms in thine emptied nut-shells.

"But the poet is grateful to the venders of swine who came from Megara to Athenae (thy partitions are thin, O hostelry), and renders thanks also to thy vermin, which kept him awake by preying upon his whole body, swarming in hurrying masses upon the beds.

"For, since thus he might not sleep, he sought to breathe the white moonlight through an opening in the wall; and from thence he saw a vender of women who came knocking at the door very late at night. The merchant called: 'Child, child!'—but the slave was snoring, face downward, and with upstretched arms muffled his ears with the coverings. Then the poet wrapped himself in a yellow robe, of the same shade as nuptial veils: this crocus tinted robe had been left in his possession

one morning when a young love-maiden deserted him
clad in a new lover's robe. So the poet, with the out-
ward seeming of a servant, opened the door; and the
vender of women ushered in a numerous band. The
breasts of the young girl who entered last were firm as
the quince fruit; she was worth, at least, twenty minae.

" 'O servant,' said she, 'I am weary; where is my bed?'

" 'O my dear lady,' said the poet, 'thy friends already
occupy every bed in the inn; only the servant's cot is
left; if you wish to lie thereon you are welcome.'

"The miserable wretch who cared for all these fair
young girls flared the light of the great charred lamp-
wick in the face of the poet; perceiving a maid-servant,
neither too beautiful nor well arrayed, he uttered no
word of dissent.

"Hostelry, the poet, bitten till deplete of blood, thanks
thee. The woman who rested with the maid-servant
this night was softer than eiderdown, and her fragrant
throat was like to a perfected fruit. But all this had
remained untold, O hostelry, but for the noisy prating
of thy cot. The poet fears that the little pigs of Megara
may have thus learned of his adventure.* O ye who
listen to these words, if the 'coi, coi' of these little pigs
from Agora to Athenae falsely relates that our poet
indulges in low amours come to the hostelry and see his
little friend whose love he knew—she whose breasts are
as firm as the quince fruit,—this poet bitten by the
blessed vermin on a moonlit night."

The principal frequenters of the taverns of Athens,
then, would have been the lower classes, the sailors and
watermen (*pronneikoi*) of the Piraeus; and the rascally
scapegraces which Suidas and Harpocration include
under the name *peristatoi*, idlers and vagrants, turbulent
rioters of the Agora; their especial haunt the tavern

*From Aristophanes, the idea at least, but the basket is missing.

which harbored abandoned women; obstreperous hecklers
of the demagogues of the Pnyx, where Demosthenes himself, though affecting to despise their good or evil opinion,
labored, nevertheless, for their favor, never ceased in-
triguing for their backing, and was always attempting
to win their applause and support.

The more hardy of the beggars' gild forgathered in
the vicinity of the cabarets, the mob of impudent brag-
garts such as the one of whom Theophrastus speaks in
the skit called Aponoia (The Reckless Man):

"In character a coarse fellow, defiant of decency,
ready to do anything; just the person to dance the
cordax, sober and without a mask, in a comic chorus.
At a conjurer's performance, too, he will collect the
pence, going along from man to man, and wrangling
with those who have the free-pass and claim to see the
show for nothing. He is apt, also, to become an innkeeper or a tax-farmer. . . . And he would seem, too,
to be one of these persons who collect and call crowds
about them, ranting in a loud cracked voice and haranguing them."

Beggars' gilds are not new under the sun, and the
leader of the clan, a ruffian hardier and more brazen
and enduring than any of his cohorts, furnished, through
his lieutenants, the pittances of silver necessary to
effectuate the carrying out of any predatory campaign
contemplated against the peace and pocketbooks of
the community, or to bait the traps and snares set for the
feet or appetites of Inexperience or Lusty Age, or to
buy the wine for some poor devil who had been picked
to the bones while drunk and irresponsible. And from
each enterprise he took the lion's share, holding his
slaves and serfs to a daily accounting. It is for this
reason that Theophrastus has depicted the hero of the
episode quoted above as: "Great in lawsuits, now as

defendant, now as prosecutor, sometimes excusing himself
on oath, sometimes attending the court with a box of
papers in the breast of his cloak and satchels of note-
books in his hands. He will not disdain either to be a
captain of market-place hucksters, but will readily lend
them money, exacting, as interest upon a dollar, twenty-
five per cent per diem; and will make the round of the
cook-shops, the fishmongers, the fish-picklers, thrusting
into his cheek the interest which he levies on their gains."

But night was the greatest friend of designing idleness. The cabarets were always open, and the pick-
pockets dancing attendance upon their dupes were as
alert as bird-catchers watching their snares. The courtesan of the Ceramicus glided noiselessly into the light
from the somber darkness of the side-street, a wavering
light from a dim lamp that lit up the sign over the door,
she took her place in this Athenian medley along with
the thieves and smugglers, she boldly demands drink
in her hoarse voice, "*Crasi, crasi*," she calls to the host,
she drinks deeply in a manner worthy of an Athenian,
and although her head may be hot, her reasoning para-
sitism is cool enough to take instant advantage of the
slightest opportunity of gain and to make the best of
such meager advantages as nature has endowed her
with. The design carried out, she takes her share and
vanishes, but alas, not into oblivion, for day will dawn
and with it will come the overlord who must be paid
and whom there is no avoiding.

The poor dupe did not remain to seek revenge; the
police of Athens were not more numerous than active,
they were not equipped like our own with eyes that
outnumbered those of Argus, there it was the tavern-
keeper himself who avenged the wrong, a sort of lex
talionis, a gentle and insinuating blackmail that knew
the value of well paid silence as well as the best method

of communicating the fact that he possessed knowledge and probably a dangerous gift of eloquence. Little by little the spoils would find their way into his till and all was well. Mine host knew so well the whole band of robbers, he served them with adulterated vitriols (kykeon) in delightfully small cups, veritable nectar as he would call it, and the cistern water with which he tempered his munificence was the most valuable portion of the drink. To put it bluntly, our tavern-keeper was not only a blackmailer and a thief, but he was also a poisoner, and we are guilty of no euphemism when we charge him with having undertaken to avenge the dupe, and settle his losses in full.

The tavern-keeper of old Greece was not lacking in expedients for doing business in a dishonest way with a bold front and behind a mask of injured innocence. If he had been very long in the business he knew every resource of his calling; he was a good mixer and an adept adulterator. He knew his wines. Unfortunately, we know nothing definitely of the methods or perfidious ingredients which took the place of the grape, and which gave the synthetic mixture its taste and color. The Greek vintner may have made it as a substitute for the wine of Crete or Cyprus, just as a Parisian vintner of the sixteenth century made a substitute for malvoisie, producing a wine of the same native growth, as Beaujeu informs us, or again, as the merchants of the eighteenth century with no less effrontery made an imitation of muscat. At any rate, according to a recipe left by Olivier de Serres, they mixed together water, honey, orval juice, and the dregs of beer, to attain the horrible mash. But supposition has no place here. Thanks to the indiscretion of Plutarch, there is one manoeuvre of the Greek tavern-keepers that has not escaped us. They would serve their customers with potable vintage until the wine had made itself felt in their finger tips and then substitute a vile vintage (*oxos*). Our host also had the benefit of false measures, the eternal expedient which those who sell anything seem to inherit by instinct. "Is it the tavern-keeper of our neighborhood, who is always cheating me grossly with her half pints?" asks Blepsidemus, in the Plutus of Aristophanes. In the Thesmophoriazusai, we have another passage: "If any male or female publican falsifies the legal measure of the gallon or the half pint, pray that he may perish miserably." The fraud against which the dramatist is contending is the alteration more or less bold of the public measure which the government of Athens had established by law, and all sellers of liquids were bound by it not to use utensils of capacity less than the legal standard. "It is true," says Plutarch, in a curious passage in his Symposium, where he attempts to prove that one should drink according to the measure of his own stomach, a standard highly specialized and never the same in two individuals, sometimes increasing or diminishing even in the same individual, "it is true that we go to the tavern to purchase our wine according to the same measure and uniform, which is public, but at our tables, each stomach is the standard by which one is governed, which does not fill itself with an amount uniform and universal, but according to the capacity which each has at the time."

With the measures themselves, we are little concerned in a work of this scope, but with wine as cheap as it was in the days of Menander, and later of Polybius, it is difficult to understand how false measures or adulteration could have contributed enough in profits to make it worth the while. With the rare and costly vintages it would of course have been different, but these were not often to be had of the tavern-keeper. Menander, in a fragment of his Treasure cited by Stobaeus, speaks of an Athenian vintner named Kantharos who was unusually expert in adulterating wines, so much so that his skill passed into a proverb "Cunning as Kantharos."

Very frequently, thanks to the quality of the customers who came in along with the frequenters of the drinking place, the Athenian tavern-keepers, who were generally gifted with many of the less admirable attributes of the fox, found much to engage their conversation. They were generally abusive, and always on the lookout to cheat. The tavern-keeper had to serve his product before receiving his money, and often the guest drank to his health and departed hastily without having paid for his wine.

These tricks of Greek villainy renewed their venom in the warm baths of the Cynosarges, the retreat outside the city for those not of pure Athenian blood, such as vagrant philosophers, pretty ladies, parasites who were fasting for the time being; places which were warmed for the proletariat in the winter. In Theophrastus we read of an episode which parallels the experience of the Athenian tavern keeper:

"He is apt, also, to go up to the coppers in the baths, —to plunge the ladle in, amid the cries of the bath-man— and to souse himself; saying that he has had his bath, and then, as he departs,—no thanks to you!" In explanation of the above passage it should be stated that a shower bath was sometimes taken by having water dashed over the head. It was the bath attendant's duty to do this service which our Pyrgopolynices does for himself, saving his money, and depriving the attendant of his fee. In all disputes the voice of the tavern-keeper was likely to be heard in the land, first of all, loudest of all. "Whom do you take me to be?" asks Poverty, in the Plutus of Aristophanes, after having threatened the

admirable Blepsidemus and Chremylus, who are intent
upon expelling her from the hearths of all the just people
in Hellas: "Some hostess (bar harlot), or pulse-porridge
seller," responds Chremylus promptly, "otherwise you
would not have screeched at us, having wronged you
in no way."   It was held shameful to enter into a con-
troversy with a courtesan, a bath attendant, a tavern-
keeper, a fish monger, or an itinerant peddler of any kind.
Aristophanes is almost positive evidence on this point,
and Theophrastus is almost equally outspoken.

Furthermore, as we have said above, it would have
dishonored any man of good morals to even have been
seen in a tavern no matter what the circumstances, aside
from taking part in the revelries and brawls which so delighted the idle Athenian proletariat, where not even a
respectable servant could have passed his spare time and
saved his moiety of reputation.

Athenaeus quotes Cynulcus on the frequentation of
taverns and cook-shops as follows:

"And do you dare talk in this way, you who are not
'rosy fingered,' as Cratinus says . . . and do you bring
up again the recollection of that poet your namesake,
who spends all his time in cook-shops and inns? Although
Isocrates the orator has said, in his Areopagitic Oration,
'But not one of your servants ever would have ventured
to eat or drink in a cook-shop; for they studied to keep
up the dignity of their appearance, and not to behave
like buffoons.'   And Hyperides, in his oration against
Patrocles (if, at least, the speech is a genuine one), says
that they forbade a man who had dined in a cook-shop
from going up to the Areopagus. But you, you sophist,
spend your time in cook-shops, not with your friends
(hetairon), but with pretty ladies (hetairon), having a
lot of cadets, male and female about you, and always
carrying about these books of Aristophanes, and Apollo-

dorus, and Ammonius, and Antiphanes, and also of
Georgias the Athenian, who have all written about the
pretty ladies at Athens. O, what a learned man you
are!"

Public morality, such as it was, decreed that the
frequentation of these places was infamous, and the ban
extended even to the man who went there but once.
The public of Athens seems to have had a well developed
sense of the proprieties, and reserved for gluttons, members of the oldest profession, brawling roisterers, and cynics,
spoken of above the privilege of immune frequentation.
The law left such inhibitions to the discretion of the
populace, and the opinion of disadvantage which was the
companion of such infractions of the moral code lay also
in their hands; we have no proof that the law ever occupied itself seriously with the taverns and their keepers,
save only in cases where false measures had been used or
in cases of murder or treason, nor have we been able to
adduce evidence of law in the matter of taverns and inns
except such as is conventional or hypothetical, as in
Plato.

There was, on the other hand a peculiar edict of
Xerxes levelled against the Babylonians after their revolt
and appeal to arms. He promulgated a decree which
carried with it the severest penalties; a ukase which
prescribed that the Babylonians from then on were to
pass their lives in taverns and other places where revelry
ran rife, in order that such character and manly vigor
as remained to them should be disintegrated and leave
them a supine assemblage of slaves ripe for tribute and
utterly unfitted for self government or the effort necessary to secure independence.

One institution, however, proves that the police of
Athens were not entirely indifferent to the orgies of
drunkenness common in Athens, and the brawls and

breaches of the peace which followed in their wake: I mean the *oenoptae*, or inspectors of wine. Athenaeus says of them: "The ancients affected so much of luxury and grandeur that they had cup-bearers for their tables, and in addition, inspectors of their wines." The Athenians made a public charge of that inspection. Eupolis speaks of the same institution: "O city of Athens, you are happier than wise. You who are commanded by those whom you have condescended to name inspectors of your wines."

The oenoptae, however, had no right of inspection over the taverns. Like the gynoeconomos, whose care was the public weal, and who took precautions that the number of guests did not exceed thirty, and that no seditious gatherings should take place under pretext of political banquets or excursions into the country, the oenoptae did not concern themselves with particulars of a dinner, they merely saw to it that such as drank did so according to law.

"Now," remarks Athenaeus, "their function is unimportant. The oenoptae number three, and they furnish guests with necessary information during a dinner. Therefore they have come to be known as 'eyes.'" There might have been an official over the inspectors, an official whose powers were more far reaching; he might, for instance have had control of the enforcement of all laws concerning drink, the imposts, and especially the sale to the public, and therefore to the taverns. A passage from Plato, unfortunately incomplete, but cited by Pollux, is of interest in this connection. It seems that Plato desired to praise a man named Strabo for his excellent management of the duties incumbent upon the administration of the wine trade, and for that reason calls him a taverner. A most peculiar tribute, and one which might be tortured into a tolerable epigram.

The Athenian innkeeper had not only to contend with the officials of the wine business, he was also subject to the visitations of the opsonomos, the official who had authority over food stuffs; and whose chief aim in life seems to have been the prosecution of retailers of commodities who had recourse to misrepresentation and lying in carrying on the affairs of business at a profit. The Athenian inns dealt in food and drink, and were frequented for both purposes even as those of Europe today. These places served meals in proportion to the excellence of the cook, the difficulty experienced in carrying the carved pieces of the sacrificial victims from the altars, and the complaisance of the landlord, and Hermes regretted bitterly the effect Plutus has had upon hospitality in the Athenian taverns:

HERMES: I used to enjoy all the good things in the female innkeepers' shops as soon as it was morning, wine-cake, honey, dried figs, as many as was fitting for Hermes to eat: but now I go to bed hungry and sleep in a garret.

CARIO: Is it not then with justice, who sometimes caused their loss, although you enjoyed such good things?

HERMES: Ah me, for the cheese-cake that was baked on the fourth day!

CARIO: You long for the absent, and call in vain.

HERMES: Ah me, for the ham which I used to devour!

CARIO: Leap upon the bottle, there in the open air.

HERMES: And for the warm entrails which I used to devour!

CARIO: A pain about your entrails seems to torture you.

HERMES: Ah me, for the cup that was mixed half and half!

THE VEGETABLE COOK

CARIO: You cannot be too quick in drinking this besides and running away.

HERMES: Would you assist your own friend in any way?

CARIO: Yes, if you want any of those things in which I am able to assist you.

HERMES: If you were to procure me a well baked loaf and give it me to eat, and a huge piece of meat from the sacrifices you are offering within.

CARIO: But there is no carrying out!

The Greek restaurants had one door on the street, always open, and the most delicious aromas and odors streamed out to assail the senses and stomachs of the passers-by, where custom hesitated and was lost. Often these odors would awaken a sluggard who would send a slave out to find the morsel so much to his taste; this usually completed the conquest and was sound advertising. Such was the experience of Philoxenos, glutton and poet, one day. He was always keen upon the delights of the table as soon as he was awake. He chanced to pass by the door of a famous innkeeper and his nostrils were assailed by the delicious emanations from a goulash or ragout which seems just to have attained the very acme of culinary perfection. "Run out and get that dish for me," he commanded in a voice vibrant with ravenous desire.

"But," replied the slave, who tested prices by the poignancy of the aroma, "it will be very dear."

"Very well," replied Philoxenos, "so much the better!" Surely an exclamation worthy of Brillat-Savarin!

All inn-kitchens, however, were not equally good, and unless the fastidious customer paid his compliments to the best known establishments, as for instance one whom Athenaeus has cited under the head of cook and vintner, he was likely to meet with a rogue, a bad dinner, and a malodorous experience, all at the same time, and might find no one in and the ovens cold. There was a certain Lacedaemonian wholly uninformed as to anything which concerned inns and taverns, and, being a Lacedaemonian, he would know nothing of such things, and he addressed himself to one of those kitchen keepers who was out of everything. The former happened to be a man of some rude wit and spirit. "The Laconian," says Plutarch, from whom we have taken the anecdote, "gave the traditionally soft and brief answer; having purchased a fish in a tavern he delivered it to the taverner whom he had accosted. When the taverner demanded of him vinegar, cheese, and oil, he made answer as follows: "If I had had what you demand of me, I would not have bought the fish."

There were itinerant retailers of foodstuffs who had portable ovens which burned charcoal. They were numerous in the streets of Athens, but their favorite haunt seems to have been the Agora and its vicinity. They sold all sorts of underdone foods from their little ovens, and, almost without exception, they had the makings of excellent rascals in them. They were more guileful than even those oakum dealers and horse traders of whom Aristophanes speaks so pointedly as being worthy to succeed Cleon in conducting the governmental affairs of the city. Nevertheless, customers often were able to procure from these peripatetic retailers such delicacies as were not served in the kitchens of the inns. Hot sausages highly seasoned with pepper, let the venders of hot dogs take notice, hash, omelettes wrapped in fig leaves (probably the remote ancestor of the hot tamale), and a sort of fruit pudding such as the English know today as plum pudding: the Athenian commoner was exceedingly fond of these last two delicacies. It is true that such dishes were grossly prepared, but they tickled to admiration the tastes of the sailors and other plebeian sojourners in the city. They also dealt in sweets such as honey cakes and preserved fruits, blanc-mange, disposed handily in rows in their shallow baskets woven from fragrant rushes, very convenient and appropriate for the purpose. Carrying their stocks in trade they trotted up and down the streets of the city and also sold their wares at the games and other spectacles. Aristotle, who would never have been suspected of having been interested in such things, has said much of their hawking methods and their cries as they glided through the crowds of the amphitheatre and worked their way by degrees to the topmost benches, to offer some customer their wares. According to the grave philosopher, who has been suspected of having a sense of humor, the success of a play, whether tragedy or comedy, was always in inverse ratio to that of the hawkers with their merchandise. If the play was uninteresting, the audience appeased its appetite with cakes in recompense for the disappointment to its curiosity, but if the play was gripping, as for instance, the Oedipus of Sophocles, or if the sublimity of Aeschylus had found an instrument worthy to interpret it, the hawkers met with the short shrift which should overtake all vociferous votaries of Lucrum when they punctuate a Chopin nocturne or a Beethoven sonata with their appeal to the flesh. It would be highly interesting as well as entertaining to try some such comparison in our own theatres; I mean in such of them as still permit an ox-like public to be annoyed and harassed by the demands of such gentry. The article vended might, for convenience, be packages of salted peanuts, or other tidbit with a volatile base. The greater the sales, the more the audience would enjoy the play.

These petty peddlers of dainties were always pros-

perous and numerous at Athens, but only in Athens.
In every other Greek city, even in those in which it might
have been thought that conditions were favorable for
their trade, they found it unprofitable or utterly impossible. We do not include Sparta in our survey, because
gormandising was always regarded there as a crime, and
cooks, caterers, and the like were classed as poisoners
and driven from the country, like any Sicilian mal-
content.   Corinth, the luxurious harbor of pleasure and
new sensations, is the city we have in mind; Corinth,
which placed such extravagant values upon hidden assets
and virgin territory. "Not everyone," laments Horace,
"can go to Corinth."   Yet with all its love of luxury,
Corinth was far behind Athens in matters of eating and
taste in choosing, and one of the characters in the Merchant of Diphilus is advised to hold in check his gas-
tronomic preferences and comply with the law. "If,"
says he indignantly, "one sets a splendid table, the magistrates promptly inquire into his manner of living and
the manner in which he employs his time; they ascertain
whether his revenues are sufficient to meet the outlays
demanded by such luxury. If his expenses are greater
than his income they will not permit it, if he persists in
his course, he must make amends. Should the day arrive
when he has no more property and he still persists in his
manner of life he is turned over to the executor of justice who inflicts an infamous punishment upon him."
See how they dealt with luxury in one of the most luxury
loving republics of Greece!

Alciphron speaks in the same manner of Corinth, but
what Diphilus imputes to the severity of the laws,
Alciphron lays at the door of avarice. "One need only
approach that city to become aware of the miserly selfish-
ness of the rich and the misery of the poor. It is noon,
I sally out to the bath, I see a great many young people,

handsome, with faces gay and spirituel; none take the road leading to the houses of the wealthy, all direct their steps toward the Kranion, where the wine merchants and fruit sellers have their booths. I see that they keep their eyes bent upon the ground; some rake together the pods of peas, others the shells of nuts, examining the heaps with attention to see whether there is anything there upon which to grind their teeth. They scrape with their nails the peeling of the pomegranate; the tiniest morsels of bread which have been trampled under foot do not escape their search and are eaten."

Taverns and inns would not prosper in a city in which the wealthy were restrained from extravagance by rigid sumptuary laws, and the poor were forever constrained by their melancholy condition to a diet of air sparingly tempered with bread. The city was scarcely visited by lighters except for the purpose of supplying their daily allowance of wine, so that a single tavern-keeper could have supplied all the custom to be found there. Plutarch relates of Dionysius the Tyrant, that when he was living in exile at Syracuse, his condition was no better than that of a porter, and that he was compelled to purchase his wine of the tavern-keeper, and that this was only the stronger proof of the ignominious level to which he had fallen.

But how different were things in happy and light hearted Athens! The taverns were always open there, day and night; you could always get a joint from some succulent sacrifice in the inn and in good company; always, somewhere in Athens these fraternities which we shall later see again in Rome, were holding a banquet with the delicate cuts which the gods with as much wisdom as good taste refused. At Athens it was not regarded as shameful to go daily to the tavern to buy wine, and the wealthy did not blush to sell the same. According to an ancient usage in France, the abbots of monasteries, the high magistrates, even the kings sold in detail the products of their vineyards; a custom common also in Italy, and especially in Florence and Naples. The wealthy Greek vineyard owners left such wines as they wished to dispose of in their houses in the city, under charge of their slaves. The disgrace lay not in selling the wine but in selling what purported to be wine, and adulteration was deemed a disgrace which only a vintner or tavern-keeper could be guilty of.

Yet in that lovely city so redolent of the soul of gayety one could find no place in which to eat and drink in good company, without some disagreeable individuals to spoil the evening. The taverns, as we have said, were impossible; therefore the wealthy men-about-town, who had time on their hands, dropped into the booths of the perfumers and the barbershops to exchange the news and discuss matters of interest.

The women were forbidden to enter places where they might mix with men or find themselves in male company, and this was especially true of the taverns; they therefore betook themselves to the gristmills to gossip, just as the rural English woman frequents the ship chandlery. Here they sang their songs of hero and spindle, and love and life, while the men assembled in these shops of good repute, principally those of the barbers, predestined, according to Theophrastus and Aristophanes, to be the centers of all the chit-chat, the headquarters of writers and playwrights who decreed peace and war and made or unmade the destinies of the State, according to the visionary plans which they wrote in charcoal on the walls. Aristophanes would have us understand that all Athens was agog with the sudden good which had befallen some dandy, and the barbers were entirely responsible for the spread of the news. In many places Aristophanes mentions a certain Cosmos, a perfumer, in whose shop the critics of Cleon met to discuss him and his policies, and of the crowd of demagogues who raised such an uproar in front of the tribune of the leather currier. Nor was there danger in thus taking part in the political criticism of the time in these shops, the haunt of the well-to-do idlers and literary critics, the radicals of the times. Radicalism is not often in conflict with the police unless it is clad in rags. It was a contention of Demosthenes that Aristogiton, the better to convince the people of his loving devotion to their interests, made it a point never to be seen in the shop of perfumer or barber; and the only instance I have been able to find of a man of evil reputation slipping in and intruding himself into such company is the arrogant upstart whom Theophrastus satirizes in his Characters.

In addition to the taverns where wine was sold, and the shops of the perfumers and barbers, there was another institution where gossip ran rife, I refer to the thermopolia. These establishments were very popular in Greece and especially so at Athens, and we shall find them well established at Rome in due course. The thermopolia were places where hot drinks were sold. The word is of purely Greek origin as is seen from the roots, and in addition there is a passage in Pollux which confirms the statement.

It is well known that in antiquity hot water was esteemed as a delectable beverage and, in addition, it was thought to possess certain hygienic virtues. Plutarch in his Treatise on the Preservation of Health remarks that it may be drunk without thirst, that it relaxes and refreshes the body, and that it fortifies the bodily forces. The eulogies of Dr. Sangrado must be taken as the sum and total of all the opinions of antiquity, setting aside, of course, that of Antonius Musa:

"In fact the wine had made me very thirsty. The suspicion of anyone else but Sangrado would have been awakened by the thirst that consumed me, and the great draughts of water I tossed off; but he, fancying seriously that I was beginning to acquire a taste for watery potions, said to me with a smile: 'I can see, Gil Blas, that you no longer have such an aversion for water. Od's life, you drink it like nectar. That does not astonish me, my friend; I knew that you would get used to this liquid.' 'Sir,' I replied, 'there is a time for everything; I would give just now a hogshead of wine for a pint of water.' This answer delighted the doctor, who did not lose so good an opportunity of extolling the excellence of water. He began a new panegyric upon it, not as a calm orator, but as an enthusiast.

" 'A thousand times,' he exclaimed, 'a thousand times more estimable and more innocent than the taverns of our days, were those water-establishments of former ages, whither men did not go shamefully to prostitute their wealth and their life in glutting themselves with wine, but where they met to amuse themselves, decently, and without risk, by drinking warm water! We cannot too much admire the wise foresight of those worthies of the State, who established places of public resort, where water was given to all comers, and who confined wine to the shops of the apothecaries, permitting its use only by prescriptions of the physicians. What a stroke of wisdom! Doubtless,' he added, 'it is by some happy remains of this ancient frugality, worthy of the golden age, that persons are found to this day who, like you and me, drink nothing but water, and who as a preventive against, or as a cure for all ailments, believe in drinking warm water that has never boiled; for I have observed that when water has been boiled it is heavier and sets less easily on the stomach.'

"Whilst holding forth thus eloquently, I more than once thought I should burst out laughing. Yet I maintained my gravity. I did more; I entered into the doctor's views. I blamed the use of wine, and pitied mankind for having acquired a taste for so pernicious a beverage. Then, as my thirst was not yet quenched, I filled a large goblet with water, and after taking a deep draught, said to my master, 'Come, sir, let us quaff this beneficent liquor! Let us revive in your house the ancient water-taverns which you regret so much!' He applauded these words, and exhorted me for a whole hour never to drink anything but water. I promised him, in order to accustom myself to this beverage, to imbibe a large quantity every night; and, the better to keep my promise, I went to bed resolved to go to the tavern every day."

Had the good doctor prescribed his aqueous specific at the same low price at which hot water was served in the thermopolia in Greece, and had he used as an excipient infusions made from rare plants, charging, for example three half obols, which the comic poet Philemon has declared was the price of a cupful, he might have transformed that sovereign remedy into a popular beverage, and have gone down into history as the inventive genius whose ingenuity produced the soda fountain and all its products.

Success was in his grasp had he but taken the trouble to follow the precepts of the authors from whom he must have amassed his information. Had he, for example, stimulated the tastes and appealed at the same time to the vanity of his patients by following the classical procedure, and mixing equal volumes of very hot water and very cold excipients in the form of decoctions, his practise would have been enormous, and had his excipient been wine, there is no saying where it would have ended.

And it is true that this method had much to recommend it. Fluids could not be taken boiling hot, and it
was long deemed dangerous to drink ice cold beverages
in a hot climate. The temperature of the potion after
the mixture of the two was pleasant and salubrious, and
the trouble it necessitated made it only the more to be
desired. There is a passage in the letters of Aristaenetus
which bears directly upon the practice of mixing cold
water and hot wine. It is as follows:

"The cup bearer, skilled in his calling, has heated
the wine, which he will mix with cold water, in just such
proportion that the coldness of the water will lower the
temperature of the wine, excessive heat being moderated
by extreme cold, and the resulting beverage will be gra-
cious to the palate in taste and in temperature."

Patients in raging fevers were not so scrupulous and
drank their wine ice cold. A courtesan was once entertaining the comic poet Diphilus at supper and presented
him with a cupful of wine cooled with snow: "By all the
gods," exclaimed the poet, "you have an ice-house in
your well." "Yes," answered the Athenian courtesan
with all the sprightly spirit of her class, "I throw the
prologues of your comedies into it when necessary. It
need not astonish you, Diphilus."

Finally, let us say, in praise of the uniform sobriety
of Greece, and to give the lie to the slander philosophical
reprobates later made current in Italy, that the term
pergraecari (to drink like a Greek), to get beastly drunk,
that in the times of which we speak, they mixed their
wine with water in Hellas. If it was taken pure, it was
the exception and not the rule.

And also, in the Heroic Age, when tradition assumes
that the whole nation was plunged into drunkenness,
which was continual and habitual, and was said to be
insatiable for the finer vintages of the soil in the Heroic

Age, let us repeat, it was even as it was in the times of which we treat, with, perhaps, the factor of moderation still more preponderant. One who knew the secret of procuring the most subtle mixture of wine and water was deemed worthy of a statue; a lesson which seems to have been lost upon a later but more inwardly degenerate age. In the Homeric age, these mixtures of wine and water were mixed before anything else was considered. Large amphorae were employed for the purpose, and the cups of the guests were filled from these, just as we have seen that at Assyrian and Babylonian feasts, the cups of the revellers were replenished from the huge silver urns which stood almost as high as the eunuch slave's breast. Drunkenness at these entertainments in pre-classical Greece was not the rule; on the contrary, the aim was to secure the maximum of effect with the minimum of evil results, and, like Friar Tuck, they loved to feel the grape at their very finger tips without invading their intelligence or cheapening the reputation for good repute which was one of the most precious attributes of primitive strength. Because of that continual sobriety, that detestation of pure wine, that continual dilution with water, which must have been particularly grateful when they opened the acrid pipes from Arcady or Here, which rendered those who drank them dull and torpid, and the ceramia which caused women to miscarry, or even in the case of the vintages of Laconia which were thick and heavy, or those of Boeotia and Phocis, which were a mixture of grape and pine cone extract, water made them all more pleasant to the taste and less liable to overpower the head, as it helped to dilute whatever poison they contained. The use of water, however, might be questioned by a fine taste where the rare vintages of wines of Smyrna, decanted as they were in the shadow of the temple of the

mother of the gods, were concerned, or the white polios
wine of Syracuse, the wines of Lesbos or Thasos, gleaming
like gold in the pale yellow depths of their shimmering
volume, so exquisite to the taste with their sweet and
generous flavor, and which as they aged more and more
came by degrees to have much of the odor of the finest
apples. And one might well demand why they deemed
it necessary to debase the wonderful vintage of Chios
by incorporating it into any mixture? Or why adulterate
the delicate wine of the Aegean Islands with impure
water, as the Latins say? a wine so rare and costly that
when it was used even at Rome it was at only the most
sumptuous entertainments. It was regarded as the glory
of the island from which it came, and the Chian vintage
was celebrated with medals on which were engraved a
sphinx crowned with clusters of grapes on the one side
and on the other an amphora. Rare and costly indeed
was this wine, probably the rarest of all antiquity, and
was so precious that those who sold it sometimes drank
it from the amphora as such an ambrosia could give them
more pleasure than the profit they would take later on
from its sale. Goguet remarks that the preference of
the Greeks for mixtures of wine and water were founded
upon long established custom and on the headiness and
high alcoholic content of the native vintages. "All
Greek wines were luscious," says he, "and if one drank
but a small quantity it flew to the head and rendered one
tipsy. In order to combat these tendencies they evolved
the method of exact dilution best suited to each vintage,
and when this was once worked out, they followed the
rules. Some wines were diluted more, some less, each
according to its quality. Homer proves this in many
passages."

One should not suppose that the professional drunkards took kindly to the usage, however, as there were

many cynics whose dispositions were scarcely less acid
than their countenances, who would have thought their
cups and their persons profaned if a single drop of water
had come in contact with either, and our encomium on
the general sobriety of Greece would not ring true were
we to omit stating that there were many such tipplers
and bottle-nosed sages in Athens and Sparta, in Thebes
and in the Greek settlements of Asia Minor, and, in fact,
throughout all Greece.

Aelian has preserved a list of the more celebrated
devotees of the flowing bowl, and we confess to some
little confusion at finding it so long. The tyrants of
Hellas were all given to alcoholic excesses, Dionysius
(The Younger), of Syracuse, of whose exile in Corinth
we have spoken above, Charidemus, against whom
Demosthenes exercised his talents in vain, it was said
of him that wine acted as a spur to his cruelty but it
certainly detracted little from his subtlety. There are
many others in Aelian's list, but it seems unfair to chron-
icle a leader's evil deeds without saying something of the
good he did as well, and unless the evidence is well authen-
ticated, we shall not record such matters.

After the tyrants, the philosophers are given a place
of preference on Aelian's list. With them we shall not
be moved to leniency, as they did but dampen the dry-
ness brought on by their arid doctrines. "Lacydes and
Timon," remarks Aelian, "were not so well known as
philosophers as they were as drunkards."

Anacharsis, also, who was not enough of a Scythian
to take keenly to water, has a place in the middle of the
list, and our narrator of anecdotes states that while at
the court of Periander, his philosophical escutcheon was
besmirched by his drunken pranks. Diotomus was also
a great tippler. On him was bestowed the surname
"Funnel," because he took the largest funnels he could

lay hands on, put the end in his mouth, and "swallowed all the wine they could pour into it." He was certainly a high priest of Dionysus, and the only guzzler that can even be compared with him is that son of Syracuse who, as Aristotle says, placed fresh eggs upon a carpet and set a hen upon them, meanwhile, that no time might be lost, retiring to a tavern to drink at his ease and wait for them to hatch out. Cleomenes of Sparta also loved his wine, but he lived amongst a populace which detested alcoholic excesses, and would not tolerate them in individual or king, and Aelian's malignity can bring forward but one charge against his sobriety: "he drank his wine pure, in the Scythian fashion."

The Scythes, as is well known, were greatly given to drunkenness, and among them a warrior's courage and resource were reckoned and evaluated according to his capacity to outlast the rest of the company in a drinking bout. While there is no absolute evidence as to this, other barbarians who had come from Scythia to Athens had been known to drink almost to frenzy in the low dives of the Piraeus or the Agora, on the days of solemn festivals, and then stertorously sleep themselves sober on the steps of the Parthenon or on the massive stairs of the deserted Phyx. This seems to have been rather common amongst such barbarians as were in the guard of the archon, or the porters of the Areopagus or temples.

The Thracians, who were especially numerous in Athens, where they formed almost the whole of the domestic population, were by nature very like the Scythians, and as drinkers they held their own with all comers. Aelian has not included them in his index, but what he has said of a barbarian race to the north may well be applied to the Thracians. "It would be safe to affirm that they live in wine; as other peoples use oil to anoint their bodies, so do the Tapyrians soak themselves in wine."

Byzantium, whose sailors went in great numbers to the port of Athens, its metropolis, was, among all the cities of Thrace, the one in which there was the most debauchery and drunkenness. Athenian depravity, reacting upon the native coarseness and addiction to such entertainment, gave such impulses free swing. Vice flourished there, vice rude and robust, always brutal, and insatiable. "It is said," writes Aelian, "that the Byzantines loved wine so passionately, they quitted their houses and rented them to the strangers who came to live in their city, in order that they might establish themselves in taverns. They also left their women to the foreigners and thus committed two crimes at the same time, drunkenness and prostitution. When they had become inebriated, they took the greatest pleasure in playing the flute; the sound of that instrument being in closest accord with gayety: they were not titillated by the thrill of a trumpet, a thing which will enable one to sum up their skill in arms and their fitness for war. . . . During the siege of Byzantium, Leonidas, their general, seeing they had abandoned their posts on the walls, which were then being heavily attacked by the enemy, and that they passed their entire days in their accustomed haunts, ordered taverns to be established upon the ramparts. That ingenious artifice held them, although a little late, and they did not again abandon their posts. There was no longer a reason for doing so."

"Byzantium," writes Menander, in a fragment of an unidentified play, "Byzantium makes all the traders tipsy. The whole night through for your sake we are drinking, and, methinks, 'twas very strong wine too. At any rate I get up with a head on for four."

Everything in Byzantium announced it to be a city in which brazen-faced debauchery and drunkenness were normal and universal. Even the coin of the realm bore on its faces the mark which characterized the national morality: and, circulating throughout the ports of Hellas, confessed through the Bacchic emblems stamped on their faces the genuineness of the Byzantine orgiastic rites. The images thus represented, we must suppose to have been copied from the signs of certain Greek inns and taverns, though it would startle Reform to see a cabaret with a sign flaunting such advertising as this. These were no grapes clustered on their slender stems, nor were they pot-bellied amphorae, with huge handles, nor, finally, were they heads of Bacchus crowned with ivy wreaths.

The detestable addiction of the Byzantines for drunkenness was later on to be the cause of their downfall and end. We have already spoken of the defense of the city by Leonidas, and the ruse by which he prevented them from falling victim to their enemies. Their fate was reserved for a later time, and it was the destiny of the Spartan Clearchus, who had resolved to conquer them, to base his strategy upon their dissolute habits, succeed in his military ambition, and ensnare the Byzantines by using their own vices against them.

Let us then cite Polyaenos, who, in his work in Strategy, has furnished us with a full account of this curious affair, probably the most interesting episode in the entire history of Greek inns and taverns.

"When the Byzantines revolted, Clearchus was fined by the ephors, and fled to Lampsacus with four ships. He dwelt there in such a manner and made such an appearance that it would be thought that he drank and lived merrily and sumptuously. Meanwhile, Byzantium was besieged by the Thracians, and they sent the commanders of their forces to demand assistance of Clearchus. He affected to give the impression that he was steeped in drunkenness, and it was not until the third day that they were able to gain an audience with him. Having heard their prayers, he told them he pitied them, and promised them aid.

"In addition to his four vessels, he armed two others, and made sail to Byzantium; there he convoked the assembly, and advised that they embark on his ships all the troops, foot or horse, for the purpose of attacking the Thracians in the rear. That plan was executed, and the pilots were already under orders from him to proceed immediately to sea and lie to under arms, as soon as they saw the signal of battle raised on high.

"When this had been carried out, Clearchus, staying ashore with the two commanders, said: 'I am thirsty.' And, finding himself near a tavern, he entered with them, then, with the guards which he had posted in this ambuscade, he murdered the two leaders. The tavern was closed immediately afterwards, and the keeper ordered to hold his tongue; thus, having removed their commanders, and having succeeded in getting their forces out of the city, he was able to march his own guards in, and remained master of the place." (Polyaenus, Lib. II, 2, 7.)

Let us then bring this curious history of Greek inns and taverns to a close with this no less curious episode, as when a tun is broached, the wise do not remove the bung and faucet, after having drawn off a huge bumper, and taken a long pull at it. But having thus finished with these hostelries of ancient Greece, with the taverns of Athens and Byzantium, which none of the scholars, not even Barthelemy, or Scaliger or Casaubon have known, or at least, have not discussed at any length, disdaining the subject, Athens was noted for many things, and not the least lovely among them were the violets which crowned the city's beauty; Hymettus was famous for its honey, and the murmurous humming of the myriads of bees which gathered it, yet the penetrating and haunting fragrance of the wild thyme with which the slopes of the eminence abounded and with which they still abound is a memory that time itself cannot destroy; an ethereal haze of perfume, the very spirit of Hellas, the Hellas of Theocritus, and Bion, and Moschus. It charms even the wild and picturesque loveliness of a scene hallowed by the associations of centuries, and the tributes of great poets, and seen, alas, through the mists of antiquity. Still, let me hope that I have been able to diffuse a little of the freshness and spirit which permeates the traditions of Greece, to distill for moderns a little of the perfume which almost intoxicated me when writing of this subject, and finally, without infraction of the law, to perfume, alas, but faintly, our own dry atmosphere with the fragrance of those fine old tuns from Biblos in Phoenicia, or with the exquisite bouquet of the vintages of Lesbos, Rhodes, or Herachia.

The need to be complete and exact has, perhaps, forced me to introduce many dry details, some dissertations of critical dullness, some philological curiosities, but I have striven to blend them with other details more absorbing and so retain the interest of my readers. Let him accept this work as the Greeks did their wines: the acrid pitch was necessary, and when a tun was found full of sea water, they merely tossed it back into its natural element.

CHAPTER VII.

Rome—Wealth brings its attendant ills—Tavern keepers still held in contempt—Not admitted to military service—Hospitality tokens held in high respect—Amusements and festivals wild and brutal—The circus and its bloody games—Heliogabalus—Nero—Claudius, Vitellius and Otho, frequenters of vile inns—Nero the author of the worst enormities.

We come at last to Italy, and the western civilization, for by that, and all it implies, we mean Rome.   In Italy, we shall find that publicans and their establishments were held in as great and abiding contempt as in Greece.   If anything, the Italians detested such innovations even worse, and the reasons are not hard to discover.   First of all, as among the Greeks, was pride of race, the outstanding characteristic of the Roman from the days of Romulus to those of Ammianus Marcellinus.   One may, without difficulty, imagine the attitude of Appius Claudius toward hospitality which was bought and paid for; and the rude and virile enemies of Pyrrhus, who scorned to remove a foe that had proved his superiority to valor of the highest type, would have also scorned anything savoring of commercialism in the matter of a tired traveller's necessities.   In a short time, however, we find an increasing internal trade making demands upon conditions unfavorable to increasing travel, and when we reach the age of the most polished of the Latin dramatists, we find Terence, at twenty-seven, unknown, poorly clad, a manumitted slave, in the house of Caecilius, at that time the popular dramatist of Rome, whither he had been sent by the Curile Aedile, that the author of reputation might pass upon the Andrian.   So excellent was the work that the poor foreigner was invited at once to share the dinner of his host and to lodge in his house.   In the interval

between Plautus and Terence the great Roman houses had
by degrees assumed more and more of the tone of princely
character.   The conquests had begun, and the inhabitants of the peninsula were brought more and more into
contact with the outside world and with manners and
usages foreign to their culture and their way of thinking.
Wealth flowed in incalculable profusion, and it brought
all the attendant ills in its train.   Syrian and Greek,
Egyptian, Jew and barbarian migrated to the center of
things and each found a fertile field for the exercise of his
own particular calling.   Although the ancient rigid
standards had weakened materially at the beginning of
the first century before our era, the tavern keeper and
the petty tradesman were held in no less contempt than
had been the case in earlier times, and we shall find this
true almost without exception for a period of over a
thousand years in the history of the greatest of the ancient
seats of culture and power.   Numerous forceful passages
from the works of Roman writers could be cited in proof,
but it will suffice to show the position held by such trades
in the eyes of the law, and from that evaluation, we can
easily estimate their position in the social life of the time.
In the eyes of the law, the innkeeper, the pander, and
others of like standing were on the same footing, and the
wife or concubine of a tavern keeper was so lightly
esteemed that she was exempt from the provisions of
legislation against adultery and other problems of domestic triangulation: her position was so lowly that the
law might have been offended if she failed to break it,
or even if she heeded it at all.   Innkeepers were not
admitted to military service, nor so far as I have been able
to ascertain, did they form a gild, as did other tradesmen.
This may have been accidental, but I am inclined to
doubt it from one or two fugitive passages in Petronius
and the Theodosian code.   It need not seem strange to

us when we find the consensus of classical opinion almost unanimous upon the evil repute and the dastardly character of the publicans generally. Furthermore, most of them were probably of foreign extraction; the kind we in the Pacific littoral designate as the "kind that can't go back"; and down until the very end of the Republic no man having due regard for decency and honor would frequent such a place or even enter it. On the other hand, under the empire, the finest gentlemen could enter with impunity the various schools maintained for the purpose of instructing budding genius gladiatorial, and accumulating a competence sufficient to purchase a cosy little tavern not too far from the arena, even as the sailor's fondest hope lies in getting a pay-day large enough to enable him to purchase a public house in Wapping, or Limehouse, Paradise Street, or George Street, and live at his ease the rest of his days. As among the Greeks, shelter and nourishment were provided for among the Romans as a right rather than a necessity from which to wring a profit, and as a general thing a stranger or traveller of importance had hospitable or friendly connections in the city which made him independent of inns and lodging houses. There were also current among the Romans those tokens of hospitality such as we have seen amongst the Greeks, and they were as scrupulously honored until the time of Marcellinus. Nor did their virtue expire with the death of the original holders of the parts; they could be bequeathed as a valued inheritance from generation to generation. The circulation of such tokens was of course greatly increased after Rome had begun her march of conquest; the conditions governing hospitality were then transferred more and more to foreigners; and sometimes to entire cities and even states, and almost without exception, the powerful patrician families at Rome belonged to the municipal council or was in some manner associated with governmental affairs, and had in their clientele whole provinces which had the right to look to them for necessities. Naturally, when such individuals came to Rome they were never thrown upon the tender mercies of an innkeeper, and it is probable that such travellers formed a large percentage of the number of transients visiting the city. Foreign ambassadors, unless the intention was to neglect them, were never dependent upon inns and taverns; it was customary to welcome and entertain them either in the house of some prominent Roman, or to lodge them in some mansion which was the property of the state itself. The reception and entertainment of the Rhodian ambassadors were examples of the former, that accorded the Carthaginian envoys, of the latter. We shall have occasion to speak of both a little later.

The free Roman citizen was under no such necessity to go to a tavern for recreation, festive enjoyment or even variety, as was, until a short time ago, the case with us. His everyday life was not so largely occupied as ours with the struggle for a living, and he consequently had more leisure on his hands. The authorities met such a dangerous condition as this in the same manner that their preceptors the Greeks did: by festivities, entertainments, and military service. The more prominent among the Roman citizenry, if they were not in camp, and as a rule practically everyone spent many of his younger years there, were continually active in their political interests, as magistrates, senators, consuls, aediles, and the like. The demands made upon such officials were frequently crucial, but, unlike the exactions of modern business, wearied but at the same time stimulated; it rarely caused the individual to "break," as we today understand the term. Neurasthenia was not common at Rome. The sum and total of the philosophy of political activity was the oral treatment of problems, public participation and discussion; and a play of the emotions, perhaps sometimes too free, but more frequently restrained and constructive, and, by their very nature, they did not dull the mind because they compelled the individual to exert all his faculties, while the demands of the military service compelled him to keep in excellent physical trim. Whenever a Roman of the class described above had time to get away from his political fence building, he generally lavished it upon agriculture, at least during the republican period and the early empire, but as culture became more general, he divided his spare time between agriculture and literature. Such was the noble *otium* of the Roman statesman. I regret that I know of no word in our language which can define the term I have been compelled to use, but John Morley's life is the best example among the moderns.

Great patricians and men of wealth who had more predilection to sensuality than to agriculture or literature had in their villas and country places every means for the gratification of their inclinations whatever they might be and, until a very late age, there is little to be said in such circles of inns and taverns.

The public life and civic interests of the masses were in their way almost as rich as that which fell to the lot of the patricians, and the amusements and pleasures lavished upon them were on a scale not to be found in any capital in the modern world, with the possible exception of Spain. The Roman commoner annually elected his magistrate, often amid scenes of factional warfare; he could listen to the pleaders such as Hortensius or Cicero or Papinian; his tribunes, who were well versed in mob psychology, played upon the emotions and passions of the proletariat, by biting sarcasms and stinging repartee. He was an interested witness to all that passed before his eyes, and

Rome was the maelstrom of the civilized world; infinite
variety; an ever changing panorama for its citizens to
examine, criticize or praise: he was nothing if not hyper-
critical, cynically so, and captious. This magnificent
city that ruled the world held many beautiful things in
its powerful grasp; the varied throngs from every province, barbarian or semi-barbarous, furnished an unending
pageant of living and gorgeous color as inexhaustible as
the combinations of a kaleidoscope; and no matter where
her nationals might be, it was sufficient for them to pro-
claim their nationality and fealty; these were their protection and their refuge. "I am a Roman citizen," said
Paul, in the hands of his enemies; "I appeal unto Caesar."
Many of the spectacles were at times too wild and brutal
for modern standards, but they were probably never dull,
and they were always full of life and movement.

An elastic religion, a cycle of festivities and holidays
that extended through the entire year, processions and
festivals of every sort, some for all the populace, some for
special sects and cults organized for liturgical purposes—
there were many of these latter in ancient Rome. The
circus offered its pageants and games for their amusement; the chariot races, so much a part of the national
character that the various political factions came to take
their names from the colors of the drivers: riots and street
battles often had their origin in the differences in course
of settlement between the various factions and their ad-
herents: well might the Roman commoner cry "Bread and
Games" as the sum of the blessings to be extracted from
life itself. In the theatre he could enjoy the attempts of his
dramatists and poets to confine the fluid ease and airy
elegance of Greek fantasy in a Roman setting; an attempt
doomed at the very beginning to failure; even as French
and Italian opera will always fail in English because of
the impossibility of reproducing the psychology of the

Italian and the Gaul along with their meaning. Among
the Romans, however, the theatre was never so highly
esteemed as was the circus and its bloody games. Huge
carnivora fighting to the death, the net thrower pitted
against the heavily armed gladiator, duels à outrance
between heavily armed antagonists of equal skill; such
spectacles served to amuse the leisure and cultivate the
lusts of a populace cruel by nature; a populace that in
later ages was better qualified to view such spectacles
than to take an active part in them; a truism graphically
illustrated in the bull fights of Spanish speaking countries, and among our own captious baseball writers and
fans, who boo at the so-called age for hitting a homer,
but who, alas do not write like one.

The games of the circus were of frequent occurrence
but they were not held daily, and the Roman sought the
Campus Martius to while away a little of each day's
leisure. On this wide plain on the bank of the Tiber
the young engaged in athletic games while the elders
talked of affairs which ruled the destinies of all the world
between Britain and Parthia. As with the Greeks, so
also were the Romans favored in the matter of public
baths, which served the people as places of assembly and
amusement.

Some of these institutions, called *thermae*, were splendid establishments, erected by the wealthy to prevent the
consequences of serious thought and concerted action on
the part of a populace no longer capable of either. Booths,
shaded arcades, promenades, even libraries were found
here; and the miserable ministers to appetite were
specialists in their callings. They had need to be; then
as now it was survival of the fittest, and a Commodus
would not have hesitated for an instant to order a bath
attendant to be thrown into the furnace if the water was
not hot enough, nor would a Heliogabalus have refrained

from ordering an unfortunate caterer, whose new fangled sauce was not piquant enough to titillate the jaded taste buds of the parvenu, to eat nothing but that sauce until he had compounded another which met the requirements of the imperial taste. Under conditions such as these one may assume that the standards were at least as lofty as the capacity for enjoyment. Why, then, should the Roman have desired to confine himself within the four walls of a pot-house or a cabaret?

The everyday life of Republican Rome was characterized, until the last century of its existence, by an austere and provident simplicity which regarded extreme wealth with contempt and suspicion, and which relieved poverty in just moderation. There are many inns and taverns mentioned in Plautus and there were probably many such places in Rome and Magna Graeca, but after all, Plautus was writing from Greek originals and may have overstated the facts slightly.

It is worthy of note that in the reigns of the succeeding emperors public activities gradually ceased, and the populace, having no longer important and more worthy occupations to fill their days, began to frequent inns and taverns; and, as the city declines and public character decays, we shall find that these places will become more and more the haunts of the quasi-respectable, and even of the patricians, and no longer, as was formerly the case, be patronized largely by the slaves and vagabonds. Notwithstanding the degradation of national character, the standing of the publicans was not improved; on the contrary, it was even rendered more contemptible by direct legislation and by action of the courts. Claudius and Nero were frequent visitors in the taverns, Vitellius and Otho were also guilty of the same indiscretions. Let us cite for our purposes the favorite author of Mark Twain; I mean Suetonius: "Often," says mine author, in speaking of Claudius, "often he showed such heedlessness in word and deed that one would suppose that he did not know or care to whom, with whom, or when or where he was speaking. When a debate was going on about the butchers and vintners, he cried out in the House: 'who can live without a snack, I ask you,' and then went on to describe the abundance of the old taverns to which he used to go for wine in earlier days." (Chap. XL.)

Both Claudius and Nero were wild, and Nero was more dissolute and abandoned than his father-in-law, but as both were base at heart, Nero, being the younger, had better opportunities. Claudius was a dullard and his welcome would be in proportion to his ability to spend, and in direct ratio to the terror with which his name inspired those in the tavern. Nero had a personality which could be very pleasing, and his character has been something of an enigma to writers of history. In him was combined an artistic sense of some discrimination, an ability to appreciate good literature, and latent tendencies toward ferocity that had, in some cases, the added stigma of refinement. A character which had been restrained and guided by Seneca and Burrhus, suddenly threw off all restraint and went the limit in gratifying the ferocious appetites that drove it on until, as was the case with other and better tyrants such as Aurelian, and still more dissolute despots, such as Commodus and Phocas, the unknown designs of the emperor became a menace to his familiars, and led them to take such measures as should prevent the consequences of satiety, or of that morning after feeling which has so often led to the downfall of the most trusted ministers and officers. Tacitus has left us an admirable sketch of the times of that odious tyrant Nero:

"The consulship of Quintus Volusius and Publius Scipio was remarkable for the tranquillity that prevailed in all parts of the empire, and the corruption of manners that disgraced the city of Rome. Nero was the author of all the worst enormities. In the garb of a slave, he roved through the streets, visited the brothels, and rambled through all by-places, attended by a band of rioters, who seized the wares and merchandise exposed to sale, and offered violence to all that fell in their way. In these frolics, Nero was so little suspected to be a party, that he was roughly handled in several frays. He received wounds on some occasions, and his face was disfigured with a scar. It was not long, however, before it transpired that the emperor was become a nightbrawler."

Yet, dissolute as Nero was, such as he would scarcely have frequented such places in earlier times, and we base this contention upon a passage in Cicero in which he denounces another Roman no less dissolute than Nero, but much more courageous, and abler. I refer to Marcus Antonius.

"Judge then of the nature of this fellow," says the orator, in speaking of Antony's arrival in Italy. "When he arrived at Red Rocks at about the tenth hour of the day, he skulked into a petty little wine-shop, hid there, and kept on drinking until evening. From thence, getting into a gig, he was driven rapidly into the city and came to his own house with his head veiled."

In another passage the great orator speaks of the humiliation which he suffered at the hands of Piso, and excoriates the latter for his love for such places.

"Infamous fellow," says the sage of Arpinum, "do you remember that when I came to you with Caius Piso, about the fifth hour of the day, you came out of some hovel or other with your head wrapped up? And you were wearing slippers, too, were you not? and when you had suffocated us with the vile stench of that cookshop, with which your foetid breath was loaded, you made the excuse of your health because you said that you were compelled to have recourse to some vinous remedies? and when we had admitted the pretense, (for what else could we do?), we stood a little while amid the fumes and stench of your gluttony till you drove us away by filthy language and still more filthy behaviour?"

In concluding this introduction to everyday life in Rome I wish to state that it was disgraceful for a family of even moderate means to be without its own cellar, bakery, and elaborate cuisine. In support of this I quote again from Cicero's speech against Piso:

"In his house there were no dishes of silver, only very large cups, and these are in fact all from Placentia, due to his desire to avoid the appearance of scorning his countrymen. On his table one sees no oysters, no fish, only large chunks of meat which is almost tainted. Dirty slaves wait on the table, and among them even old men. With him the cook and serving man are combined into one person; he has not his own baker, and no cellar. Bread and wine he buys from the dealer and from the inn."

Thus we see the attitude of the upper class citizen toward petty dealers and especially towards inns and taverns. And there is also a lesson to be learned; not that we have ever shown much ability to learn from the past and thus forecast the future; the lesson is this: in ancient times it was not necessary for the citizenry of character and ability to frequent roof-gardens or taverns in order to exchange social obligations and discuss questions of the day. On this account, the Greeks and Romans could leave such dens to their proper denizens, the slaves, the rabble, and that general class which neither toils nor spins but which, like the lily and the green bay-tree, flourished then, but fared never so sumptuously as now.

CHAPTER VIII.

The era of the Roman emperors—The great highways—The growth of the Persian Post Service—The menace of the imperial public houses— The Roman Diploma (diplomata tractarium) necessary for travellers— Landlords in Italy in the times of Polybius—Petronius and Trimalchio —Cicero and Macula, the inn-keeper—Horace and taverns—Inns dangerous places of refuge.

Let us, then, reverse the hour-glass of eternity, that the sands of time may filter backward until we have reached the era of the emperors of Rome: Augustus, or the timid and inhuman Domitian, Marcus Aurelius, or that stern disciplinarian Aurelian, who lived two centuries too late. Rome was then the sovereign city of the known world, bound to every province by those wide and solid roads, the number and ruins of which astonish us to the present day, and which, after the ascendency of barbarism, were still the arteries of such transportation as existed through the dark ages. It made no difference in what country the traveller found himself, if he was bent upon leaving Gaul, or Germany, or Greece, or Iberia, the highway he followed led him towards the Eternal City, and all roads lead to Rome.

The stages of travel were so admirably calculated that the end of each day's journey found the traveller at a station where fresh horses and pack animals could be obtained, and where food and lodging were procurable. The post-houses were, in reality, great imperial inns which served as ration depots and halting places for military details, as well as the putting up of travellers, when otherwise unoccupied by imperial missions or other official guests. The entire system was an outgrowth of the Persian Post Service, but in many ways the Roman aggressiveness improved upon the model.

Officials, known under the collective term *frumentarii*, were assigned to the administration and inspection of these great public houses: in addition to which they also maintained a system of espionage which was useful in keeping the authorities informed as to everything going on in the neighborhood. Some of these official delators were by nature so meddlesome that they placed this duty even above their actual official calling, using every means in their power to overhear the conversation and plans of those lodging with them. If these plans appeared to them treasonable, no time was lost in denouncing the culprits to the emperor or to the praetorian prefect. It is to be regretted that mere suspicion was too often equivalent to condemnation, and Gibbon's strictures were justified. Taking this interpretation, these great inns were not so much a place of sanctuary, a shelter from the storms of winter in dreary climes; they were the lairs of espionage; in place of pleasant lodgings offered free of charge, they were rather snares perfidiously set and cunningly baited.

By virtue of such a system, the police, operating as a huge organization could arrest and detain a far greater number of criminals and malcontents than would have been the case had these great hostelries been maintained for official use alone. Gibbon has pointed out the utter impossibility of escape under the emperors and has cited one attempt under Tiberius, in which the fugitive was apprehended and brought back. So perfect was the organization, however, that even Tiberius saw nothing to fear from the example and the matter was dropped. In later times, however, this was not the case, as Aetius probably owed his life to his escape from inimical authority, and Attila would probably have won the battle of Chalons had Aetius been apprehended before he could sue for pardon at the head of sixty thousand veterans devoted to his interests.

As the institutions of which we are speaking were imperial, it need not astonish us to learn that some credentials were necessary in order to gain admittance and procure the services of the master of posts and his organization. The document in question was called the *diploma tractatorium* under the earlier empire, but under Constantine it came to be known as *epistola evictionis*, a more specific term according to Bergier. The writ, for such it was, consisted of two leaves, hence its name; and the imperial couriers, who corresponded to what the British call king's messengers, were of course always provided with the diploma. Travelling emperors lodged at these *mansiones* and held there a sort of local court to receive the homage of local authorities and their suites, and from this we may suppose that at times these inns were accessible to all the world; they witnessed a ceaseless coming and going of nobles and high officials, tourists of position, and even mere tradesmen. On this account an official lodged there was always exposed to danger no matter how carefully precautions for his protection had been taken, and the emperors therefore reserved for themselves the entire establishment when putting up there. The *epistola evictionis* was the instrument used to clear the way for them and their suites. All such documents bore the imperial seal and were either issued by imperial authority direct, or by some high official to whom that power had been delegated.

In spite of all the care taken to shield him, Titus fell a victim to the dangerous and criminal enterprise of his brother Domitian, in a *mansio* (post-house) in the Sabine country, almost at the very gates of Rome. He was taken with that raging fever which caused his death, and tradition has it that the fever was the result of a poison which set his blood on fire. The assassination of Aurelian by his trusted general Mucapor in the post-house at

Coenophrurium, between Heracleia and Byzantium, proved yet again that notwithstanding the most painstaking precautions, the gravest danger could still attend and menace even princes in these imperial public houses. Therefore we stress the fact that the *diploma tractatorium* was a most difficult document to procure, and the reasons for requesting it must have been vital and unavoidable. Pliny the Younger, a powerful minister high in the favor of Trajan, begged the emperor's indulgence for having granted Calphurnia post-horses without first having obtained imperial authorization, and this, notwithstanding the fact that her business was so pressing as to admit of no delay. The bearer of an imperial diploma was literally able to command such service and attention as not even Lady de Winter, in Dumas's Three Musketeers could have procured with Richelieu's famous letter of absolution: "It is by my order and for the good of the state that the bearer of this has done what has been done." On the other hand, should an individual or official present himself at a *mansio* and either seek or force service from the imperial establishment, he was liable to the most drastic punishment, no matter what his station or influence. An episode in the life of Helvius Pertinax, who later became emperor, will serve to illustrate the severity of the regulations governing the posthouses and service. Julius Capitolinus relates that when Pertinax was *praefectus cohortis*, serving in Syria, he was punished by the governor of that province for having levied post-horses without the diploma, being ordered as a consequence to proceed on foot from Antioch to the place to which he had been ordered as legate. Under the later empire it became very fashionable to apply for this all powerful diploma, which was good for a certain time and which became void automatically upon the death or removal from office of the emperor or official granting it. When such a request was honored, the

lucky recipient had great cause to congratulate himself
because of the prestige which the possession of such a
document conferred upon the bearer, whose importance
was at once augmented. He was empowered to take
any route that might suit his fancy. In special cases the
emperor granted a sort of perpetual diploma which was
good during the life of the possessor or during that of
the emperor whose seal it bore. In fact, due allowance
being made for the times, a *diploma tractatorium* was
equivalent to a pass good on any railroad or steamship
line, and in addition it granted the bearer carte blanche
in the diner and buffet car, as well as in the Pullman
stateroom, or for that matter, a special train, unlimited
service, and prompt and respectful obedience. The nearest approach which we know of is the *haticherif*, until
recently furnished to Turkish officials; a document which
carried with it most of the powers conferred by the old
Roman diploma, both as to hospitality and to horses,
supplies, and so on. King's messengers are also believed
to possess credentials almost as powerful. Upon the mere
presentation of the diploma, the bearer thereof did the
post-master the honor of receiving from him horses,
beasts of burden, and all the food and supplies of which
he and his suite might have need. Should the station
be short of supplies, a condition which did not often
occur, the stables empty of fresh beasts, the cellars dry,
the *mansionarius* or *stationarius* would levy upon the
local inhabitants to supply his needs, and a requisition
such as this had all the weight of imperial sanction.
The rustics were ordered to furnish such animals and
stores as were enumerated in the diploma, and in numbers, quantities, and quality, as specified therein. The
term used to denote such requisitioning was *angariare*, in
allusion to a usage prevalent amongst the Persians and a
saying current among the Greeks, of which we have

spoken before. Marculphus, a Gallic monk, wrote a work entitled Formulae, in which he compiled and preserved the actual texts of many legal forms. To his industry we are indebted for the text of one of these *diplomata tractatorium*, or, as they were known in his time, circa 660 A. D., *epistolae evictionis*. The reader need not be surprised at the munificence of the emperor in thus providing for the needs of his legates, as they sometimes travelled with an innumerable train of officials, secretaries, slaves, and the like; and in some regions supplies were scarce and had to be transported with the traveller. (*Name of Emperor*), *Emperor:*—

To ALL OUR OFFICIALS AT THEIR POSTS OF DUTY. *Greeting:*—

Know ye that we have delegated....................., an illustrious gentleman, to be our legate or ambassador to .... We therefore command you by these presents to aid his excellency, to provide and furnish his excellency with......horses, to collect such quantity of supplies as to him shall seem good and reasonable, in places proper and convenient; furnish......ordinary sumpter horses and ......in addition; ......bread; ......hogsheads of wine; ......barrels of beer; ......sides of bacon; ......cattle; ......hogs; ......suckling pigs; ...... sheep; ......lambs; ......geese; ......pheasants; ...... chickens; ......pounds of oil; ......pounds of pickle; ......pounds of honey; ......of vinegar;......of cummin; ......of pepper; ......of coste; ......of cloves; ......of aspic; ......of cinnamon; ......grains of mastic; ...... dates; ......pistache· ......almonds; ......pounds of wax; ......of salt; ......of oils; ......ricks of hay; ......of oats; and......of straw.

Look ye that all these things are furnished him in full and entirely, in a place convenient, and let everything be accomplished without delay.

From the foregoing, it is easily evident that life under the emperors was full and abundant in all that concerned their agents and legates, and we have reason to believe that they acted with equal liberality toward foreign ambassadors and august prisoners of war. Witness the treatment of Zenobia by Aurelian and that of Gelimer by Justinian, and neither of these princes was noted for his liberality. Such profusion did not greatly antedate the empire, however, and the complaints voiced by the deputies from Rhodes, and of those from Macedonia, inform the reader that Rome, during the period of the Punic Wars, sumptuously entertained foreign ambassadors of friendly states and lodged them in a house owned by the government; but that representatives whose home governments were of doubtful allegiance, might possibly be subjected to some indignity. Legates of the enemy were adequately cared for.

"Quintus Fulvius Gillo, a lieutenant-general of Scipio, conducted the Carthaginians to Rome; and as they were forbidden to enter the city, they were lodged in a country house belonging to the state, and admitted to an audience of the senate at the temple of Bellona." (Livy, XXX, 21.)

In the case of the envoys from Rhodes, we find these ambassadors expressing their displeasure at what they considered a breach of diplomatic usage, as follows:

"In former times, when we visited Rome, after the conquest of Carthage, after the defeat of Philip, and after that of Antiochus, we *were escorted* from a mansion furnished us by the public into the senate house, to present our congratulations to you, conscript fathers, and, from the senate house to the capitol, carrying offerings to your gods. But now, from a vile and filthy inn, scarcely gaining a reception for our money, treated as enemies, and forbidden to lodge within the city, we come, in this squalid dress, to the Roman senate house; we, Rhodians, upon whom, a short time ago, you bestowed the provinces of Lycia and Caria." (Livy, XLV, 22.)

A little later on, however, when the republic had become more conscious of its strength, it absolved itself from courtesies other than those of wood and salt, which were the least that even a *parochus* or an innkeeper could have done; and we find envoys lodged very simply, friend or enemy, in an inn of the street.

Wayfarers, however, unless provided with the diploma, that magical charm that opened more doors than sesame, would perforce be driven by necessity to apply to such establishments as the inns for food and shelter when travelling, but, as Marculphus would have us see, the mere presentation of the diploma bearing the seal of the reigning prince, (those of Augustus bore a sphynx), at once procured the bearer a hearty welcome, excellent fare, a comfortable lodging, and all the heart could desire. The remains of the Roman *mansio* in the Great St. Bernard have been excavated and examined, and I take great pleasure in quoting from Lanciani's Roman Campagna, pp. 32 and 33, to fill in the details of the picture:

"The Roman hospice (*mansio in summo Paenino*) stood a quarter of a mile to the south of the present one, and comprised a temple to the god of the mountain, a hospice for travellers, stables, and watering troughs, and store-houses for fuel and provisions. The *mansio* or hospice was built of stone, with an elaborate system of hypocausts and flues for the distribution of heat through the guest rooms. The roof, made of tiles from the lime-kilns of the Val d' Aosta, had projecting eaves in the old Swiss style."

In the times of Polybius, almost contemporary with the Rhodian envoys of whom we have spoken above,

inns were numerous along the great roads of Italy.
This is proved by an interesting passage in the works of
the great historian of the Punic War. He was a cultured Greek of good social position. His travels took
him well over Italy, and he commented upon what he
saw. After having stated that in his time the price of
wheat was four obols per Sicilian *medimnus* (about ten
gallons), and that of barley two obols, a *metretes* of wine
costing the same as a *medimnus* of barley, he goes on to
say "that the cheapness and abundance of all articles
of food will be most clearly understood from the following
fact. Travellers in this country, who put up in inns, do
not bargain for each separate article they require, but
ask what is the charge per diem for one person. The
innkeepers, as a rule, agree to receive guests, providing
them with enough of all they require for half an *as* per
diem, i. e., the fourth part of an obol, the charge being
very seldom higher." (Lib. II, 15.)

Unless human nature has undergone a very decided
change, we are forced to the conclusion that the table
set in such places must have been meagre and plain in
the extreme, and the landlord of classical Italy must
have been a blood brother to him of whom Gibbon said,
in his Autobiography:

"Under an air of profusion, he concealed a strict
attention to his interest," yet the master of sarcasm does
not complain of the table. The only difficulty in the
situation lies in the continual carping and clamoring of
the travellers who, if they paid no more than half an *as*
for a day's lodging *en pension*, could not be said to have
paid anything, and for that reason could not be accorded
the right to damn their dinner, as Fielding says.

In early times, the inns of this class were no better
than hovels, badly roofed and insecurely fastened. In
Petronius, the revellers return to their miserable sanc-

tuary at night and cannot get in because the old beldame, their landlady, had been swilling so long with her customers that you could have set her afire without her knowing it. Trimalchio's courier rescued them from a night in the street by smashing in the door. Many of these establishments were mere sheds such as used to be seen along the Appian Way, and which were called, according to Festus, *ceditae*, because a certain Ceditius had been the proprietor of a great number of them. As the rental of such huts to an innkeeper assured the owner a good profit, and, according to Varro, played no unimportant part in supporting the cultivation of a piece of land on which the house had been built, nearly every landowner followed so common-sense an example and built such a shed at the boundary of his property.

Wealthy landowners sometimes refused to lease to innkeepers, reserving to themselves such rights, and erecting little booths along the road which bordered their property. Here they could break the tedium of a long and tiresome journey, have a comfortable place in which to rest, and avoid placing their persons and educated palates at the mercy of innkeepers and their scullions. The great patricians had many estates in the various parts of the peninsula; these they visited, as their moods dictated, and, as a general thing, they maintained small establishments such as are described above for their personal comfort and convenience. To institutions such as these, the name *diversorium*, or the diminutive *diversoriolum*, were given. Cicero wanted a lodge of this kind on the road to Terracina, in order that he might not always inflict himself upon Fabius Gallus when he visited in the neighborhood, but he either lacked the means or the amount necessary was always spent in advance on books and statues, and when he no longer travelled as a governor, and no longer possessed that

title and the right to avail himself of free lodging such
as the *parochi* supervised and kept in readiness along the
great roads, he was always forced to fall back upon the
hospitality of his friends; accepting shelter with Gallus
whenever he returned from Sicily, or with Lepta if he
came from the other direction; but in the absence of his
friends he had no other choice than that of lodging in an
inn.   In his case he was fortunate, for Macula seems
to have been a much finer type of innkeeper than was
commonly to be encountered.   This innkeeper knew his
duties and appears to have confined his activities strictly
to them and to proprieties far above his own station in
life.   The wine he served was good, he himself esteemed
it and drank it, though Cicero seems to have preferred a
mixture of this wine and a little Falernian; he had only
a few rooms in his inn, and they were so small that the
great orator, on his way to meet Caesar who was returning from Spain, feared there would not be room for the
equipages and attendants.

The inns along the great roads, then, were mere ordinaries and such dining-rooms as they maintained were
small and few in number, in fact, a majority of such public
houses must have been huts where the individual could
obtain food and shelter, but often they were equipped
with neither stables for the animals nor sheds for the
vehicles.   Others there were, however, in which conditions such as these did not obtain: they were stables out
and out, and travellers were obliged to bed themselves
down upon a "donkey's breakfast," among the horses
and mules.   Places of such rustic simplicity were necessarily poorly constructed and probably lacked bolts and
bars to fasten their doors.   There is a legendary episode
in the life of Severus which is said to have occurred in
such an inn.   The future emperor at the time of this
adventure was serving as a centurion, and necessity

bedded him down on the straw of a stable. As he was making the most of his situation a serpent glided in and coiled itself close to his head. It did not strike him, however, and, at the first startled outcries, it disappeared and an adventure which for the moment threatened him with grave danger was turned into an omen favorable to his future. It was construed as a divine portent which announced to Severus the lofty destiny in store for him.

The collective term used to denote an inn was *deversorium;* this applied to an establishment with or without stables, but when reference was made to the keeper the term used was *stabularius:* should the institution be one of those dingy, moth eaten, vermin ridden pot-houses, the term used to describe it was *caupona.*

The *taberna deversoria* were slightly more pretentious; here one could lodge and eat and drink; it is probably one of these establishments which was conducted by the hostess in the Isernian inscription.

The *taberna meritoria* were a sort of rooming house and tavern combined. Their custom seems to have been less transient than that of the *taberna deversoria.*

It is of the *deversorium* that Horace speaks when he scolds his nag for turning in at every inn and tavern along the road; poor habit-ridden beast, had your owner had you long in his possession?

> Baiae, Musa protests, will not do for my case,
> And has caused me no little ill-will in the place,
>
> .   .   .   .
>
> Needs must, then, to change my old quarters, and spur
> My mare past the inns so familiar to her.
> "Woa, ho! I'm not going to Baiae's bay,
> Nor to Cumae!" her choleric rider will say,
> Appealing to her through the left rein, because
> Saddle-horses, you know, have their ears in their jaws.
>
> —Epist. Lib. I, 15, Martin's Translation.

There is no rancor in this passage, and Horace's experiences along the Baiae road must on the whole have been pleasant. It is otherwise, however, in regard to the inns on the road between Capua and Rome, and the term employed by Horace to characterize them expresses the contempt in which he holds them, a term not to be literally translated here, though the passage reads thus:

> But surely, friend, the man who gains an inn,
> Besplashed with mud, and soaking to the skin,
> When on his way from Capua to Rome
> Will not desire to make that inn his home.
>
> —Epist. Lib. I, 11.   Martin's Translation.

And with what care the refined taste of the poet evaded the pot-houses on the road to Brindisium, whenever possible. How cheerfully he said farewell to such asylums; how easily he contented himself with the slim and precarious hospitality of the little cottage near the Campanian bridge and the meager rations issued by the *parochus*. How worn out with boredom he was when he paid his compliments to the swarming inns and taverns of Caudium, *Caudi cauponas*, on his well provisioned way to the villa of Cocceius, so magnificent, so well stored with luxuries of every description, and so well found in necessities, *plenissima villa!* Then continuing his route, he tarried with the innkeeper at Beneventum. Here the fiery ardor of the landlord had nearly set the place on fire, for while that worthy was turning some thrushes which were roasting over a hot fire of grape vines, a blazing brand flew out of the brazier and set the kitchen on fire. The scullions and guests were greatly excited, the latter chiefly because their supper was thus menaced; with one accord they rushed to the rescue of their food and then put out the fire raging in the kitchen:

A Tavern Bedroom

Hence without halting, on we post
To Beneventum, where our host
Escaped most narrowly from burning;
For while he was intent on turning
Some starveling thrushes on the coals,
Out from the crazy brazier rolls
A blazing brand, which caught and spread
To roof and rafter overhead.
The hungry guests, oh how they ran!
And frightened servants, to a man,
The supper from the flames to snatch,
And then to quench the blazing thatch.

The beds in such inns were not softer than sleep, and
the mattresses, as we learn from Pliny, were stuffed with
the largest tufts of a certain species of reeds, in place of
goose feathers.   Horace knew by experience that upon
these narrow couches one was visited more frequently by
insomnia than by dreams.

For this reason, that he might charm away a little of
the dreary emptiness of a "white night," which lay ahead
of him, he made certain advances to one of the strapping
slaveys attached to the establishment for the purpose of
rendering all manner of service to a none too discriminating public.   There were always several of these rustic
Hebes about the premises, and, in the eyes of the Roman
law, none shirked this double duty.   This lass, it seems,
not looking forward with any degree of pleasure to a night
spent in such distinguished company as that of the poet,
preferred to rendezvous more pleasantly, and perhaps
more energetically, with that distinguished individual
who served Horace in the capacity of master of horse.
His night, therefore, came to naught.   To naught, did I
say?   Nay, let us read what the poet himself says, in
this, the only passage in all his works in which he can be
accused of absolute sincerity in speaking of the fair sex;
the sex, which, alas, he often found magnificently false:

'Twas there, O fool, O dolt supreme,
I waited for a lying jade
Till Sleep on me his finger laid,
And I, still panting with desire,
My pulse athrob, my blood afire,
Sank into slumber; and it seems
That I possessed her in my dreams.

Those whose associations had accustomed them to a finer environment would have always missed something in these inns: the kitchen was very likely to be carelessly kept and was often ill provided. The wine was often vile but in some parts of the country the lack of good water was even more keenly felt; especially in Northern Italy: and even in Rome, notwithstanding the marvelous system of aqueducts, there were continual brushes between the water porters and the publicans, who waged a never-ending warfare over a matter of a pint. The *aediles* were being constantly involved in such brawls, which always spread to the rabble and roistering vagabonds whose ends were best served by fomenting disorder to serve as a screen for their designs upon the money and goods of those in the neighborhood. The officials, on their part, were always on the alert to prevent fraud in measures or by adulteration; to prevent trespass upon the aqueduct system and damage to the same, with the consequent waste, which might have interfered with the supply which kept the fountains going. At Ravenna, conditions were much worse; there it was sometimes difficult to find even a single cistern which was not dry to the deepest part. All publicans were reduced to the dreary lot of him of whom Martial makes sarcastic mention: Epigrams, Lib. III, 57.

In an inn at Ravenna, the other day
    I was bilked by the wiles of a cheat;
When I ordered my wine mixed with water, the gay
    Deceiver retailed me wine neat.

and again mine author says in another pungent epigram:

> I'd rather own a cistern at Ravenna
> Than a vineyard in a clime more favored still,
> For I could then sell water
> At a price that soon had oughter
> Make me richer than the dreams wine could fulfill.

Their only hope of relief lay in the showers of rain that filled the cisterns in succession: for them it was better than a heavy crop of grapes and a plentiful vintage.

"My Dear Ovid," writes Martial, "you report that the rains have made havoc with the vintage. What of it? The rain is far more beneficial for wine than you would think. Coranus, the innkeeper, was able to refill a hundred amphorae or so."

Wealthy travellers, who knew beforehand what the penury common to inns had in store for them, took their precautions far in advance whenever the chance of the road obliged them to apply there for lodgings; in the manner of the Epicurean Philoxenes of Cytheria, who only travelled when preceded by a train of slaves loaded with wines and everything proper and necessary for even the most educated and delicate of tastes; it was probably his example which prompted Sir Walter Scott to emulate him in Peveril of the Peak: and Regnard the subtle harp of malignant indirection remarks:

> Who are not always burdened by books of the law
> Bear their pepper ground fine and their food in their maw.

When wealthy and powerful transients arrived at such establishments, it was with an entire train of slaves and sumpter mules, minions, lapdogs, carriages and all the panoply of ostentation. They also carried with them a complete culinary apparatus, and on some occasions, when the highest caste was involved, portable garden plots with growing melons and early vegetables were transported, as was done by Tiberius.

Ordinarily, however, the wealthy classes, though holding in extreme contempt the chipped and dirty cups and
the lame dishes of the inns and taverns, contented themselves with merely carrying their own dishes and paraphernalia along with them.   In this latter class we may
place Martial's Calpetianus (Lib. VI, 94):

"Calpetianus is always served from golden vessels;
whether he dines in the city or at home; whether he goes
on a picnic or not.   Thus also is he served at a tavern,
and thus in the country.   Has he no other service?   He
has none of his own."

Those who adventured with such spoils as these into
the clutches of the innkeepers frequently did so at considerable risk.   The inns were generally isolated, sometimes at some little distance from other habitations along
the great roads which themselves were but little frequented except by those engaged in repairs: they were
commonly under the eagle eye of an accomplished scoundrel, the receiver and fence for all the robbers and night-
pads in the district: such hostelries were nothing if not
out and out Snug Harbors for the predatory classes whose
methods lacked the sanction of law if not that of common usage.   There were many such inns to be found
along the more deserted roads in Italy; the proprietors
doubtless chose their locations with due regard to custom, immunity, and rapacity, and all the art of a specious
landlord could not detract from their aspect of sinister
purpose, at best it could be softened down: as an example
we have in mind the *malalbergo* on the long road between
Bologna and Ferrara, the only inn in the whole district,
or, yet again, the post house at Monteroni on the Roman
Campagna (Torre di mezza via), of which William Savage
speaks so eloquently and with such spirit:

"One abandoned enough to have ventured himself in
such a place ought to have gone to the gallows; a sentence merited ten times over."

Every dangerous refuge such as this was almost certainly the sanctuary of vagabonds and criminals, and the *caupona* of ancient Italy, and, I regret to say, the *deversoria*, as well, were closely allied in creed to the establishment of which Savage speaks.

Savage also speaks of the mal aria (malaria) which aided the cause of the cutpurses, and which still infests the Roman Campagna. It was a case of danger succeeding danger, and, as is easily seen, from the remarks of Didier on the post-house at Monteroni, the ancient Roman station (ad turres), the robbers which caused such terror of old have yielded before the fever which today has everywhere established itself:

"A great house of stone, in these reaches a rare thing, rears itself from the edge of the road; it is Monteroni, the only posting house between Rome and Civita Vecchia. I enter, solitude reigns throughout; not a soul comes forward to receive me. I call, and a silence as icy and impersonal as death responds to my voice. At last I discover two postillions lying on the floor on a filthy and ragged mattress; two others are lying wrapped in their cloaks, not before the fire, however, but in the center of the hearth itself. Every one of them had the fever and they were so weak that it would have been impossible for any of them to have mounted a horse. Of them I was unable to obtain bread, and it was the same with water."

CHAPTER IX.

The fate of the Arcadian merchant—Dangers lurking in inns—
Petronius and Giton—Drunken flute girls and Gaditaman dances—
Scenes of debauchery—Edicts grant absolution—Liquor situation under
Domitian—The Syrians and Levantines—Looseness of their women—
Courtesans and their arts of pleasing.

There would be little difficulty in citing a thousand
instances of thefts and murders perpetrated in the
cauponae of the ancient world, but we shall content ourselves with two, Cicero and Valerius Maximus shall supply the narrative, and we shall reserve for ourselves the
easier task of the commentator.   First, let us begin with
the tragic fate of the Arcadian merchant; a study in
telepathy and crude psychology.   It is true that the thing
took place in Greece, but it might as easily have happened in Italy.   It is one of the selections from the works
of the great orator which in the past were used by the
instructors to give their pupils a thrill and to show them,
perhaps, that not all Latin classics were as dry as a too
thorough going knowledge of grammar and prosody would
have them seem.

"Two Arcadians who were intimate friends, were
travelling together; and, arriving at Megara, one of them
took up his quarters at an inn, but the other went to
lodge at the house of a friend.   After supper, when both
had retired, the Arcadian who was staying at his friend's
house received a visitation from the apparition of his
fellow traveller at the inn, the specter besought him to
come immediately to the assistance of his friend, as the
innkeeper was bent upon murdering him.   Alarmed at
this intimation, he started from his sleep, but, on reflection, thinking it nothing but an idle dream, he lay down

again. Presently the apparition reappeared to him in his sleep, and entreated him, that though he would not come to his assistance while yet alive, that he would not leave his murder unavenged, at least. The spectre told him further, that the innkeeper, after having murdered him, had cast his body into a dung-cart, where it lay covered with filth; and begged him to go early to the gate of the town, before any cart could leave the town. Much wrought up by this second visitation, he went early next morning to the gate of the town, and met with the driver of the cart, and asked him what he had in his wagon. The driver, upon this question, ran away in a fright. The cadaver was then discovered, and the inn-keeper, the evidence being clear against him, was brought to punishment."   (Cicero De Divinatione, Lib. I, 27.)

In commenting upon this passage it is my belief that here is related one of those sombre and sordid chapters in Criminal Law, used as an illustration common to human experience: in other words, history of inns and taverns was, in ancient times, an integral part of the history of brigandage and thuggery; and many of the hospices in Western Russia and the provinces bordering that great frontier are strikingly akin to this little inn at Megara.

In another work Cicero relates an affair of the same sort as an example of conjecture, or question of fact in a criminal matter, and for that very reason it lends weight to the case itself as a corollary thereof. The passage occurs in the treatise on Invention, Lib. II, chap. 4:

"At present, let us begin with the conjectural statement of a case of which this example may be sufficient to be given.

"A man overtook another on his journey, as he was going on some commercial expedition or other, and carrying a sum of money with him. As men often do, he entered into conversation with his new acquaintance on the way, the result of which was, that both proceeded together, with some degree of friendship, and, when they had arrived at the same inn, they proposed to have dinner together and to occupy the same apartment. Having dined, they retired to rest in the same room. But when the proprietor (for that is what is said to have been discovered since, after the man had been detected in another crime), after the proprietor had scrutinized one of them closely, that is to say, the one who had the money, he came in the night, after having assured himself that both were sound asleep as men usually are when worn out, drew from its sheath the sword of the one who had not the money (he had the sword lying by his side), murdered the other man with it, took away his money, replaced the bloody weapon in its sheath, and returned to his bed.

But the man with whose sword the murder had been committed, arose long before dawn and called his companion over and over again; he thought that because he did not answer he was overcome with sleep, so he took his sword and the rest of the things he had with him, and departed alone on his journey. Not long afterwards, the innkeeper raised a hue and cry that the man was murdered, and in company with some of his lodgers, set off in pursuit of the man who had gone away. They arrest him on his journey, draw his sword out of its sheath, and find it bloody. The man is brought back to the city by them, and is put on trial. On this comes the allegation of the crime: "*You murdered him*," and the denial: "*I did not murder him*," and from this must be gathered the statement of the case. The question in the conjectural examination is the same as that submitted to the judges: "*Did he murder him or not?*"

This conjectural statement serves but to instruct us in the dangers that lurked in ancient inns, more sinister, for all their covering screen of creeper roses, than those gaunt and ill reputed hospices of Calabria and the Roman Campagna.

Although nocturnal gullet slashers practiced their calling until it became a crime of habit, the thief and the fence were even more frequently guilty of derelictions which savoured of habitude, and a rascally steward or some slave trusted with the keys to cellar and storehouse was the surest and best purveyor of supplies. Rarely did the good host neglect an opportunity so opportune to get such useful tools completely into his power; a custom that still thrives in certain parts of Italy. His larder was stocked with wines and supplies from the estates of wealthy patricians who knew not the extent of their holdings, but who would have unhesitatingly punished robbery with flaying, if not with actual crucifixion. In connection with expert methods in buying, let us again cite William Savage.

"The innkeeper at Tavolato," says he, "serves no vintage other than that which the waggoners smuggle, or frequently steal from their masters and carry to the town; this is well known to every Roman. In exchange, the landlord gives them food. The innkeeper at Porta San Pancrazio furnished his cuisine in that way with fish brought by the fishermen who stole them and smuggled them into the town."

Should we then wonder that the tavern-keepers of the ancient world gave such commodities a welcome none the less cordial because of the sources from which they came? And then, they were very cheap! Did not the Romans have a market for stolen goods, and did not Ascyltos and Encolpius determine to sell there the mantle which they had come by in the same devious manner in order to redeem the ragged tunic with the gold pieces sewn into its hem, and thus at a small sacrifice, procure for themselves a handsome profit? What difference if they knew

themselves forced to buy back their own property.
Ascyltos plumbed the situation when he manifested so
little stomach for the law, and the night prowling shyster
lawyer who would sequester the spoil in hopes that the
owners would not dare claim it for fear of being charged
with crime, is a final touch as eloquent as it is penetrating.   Let us not hesitate to speak the truth of these lowly
financiers, in any case they cannot invoke the law of libel.

As their profits were never equal to their avarice,
they invoked other expedients to eke out their gains,
expedients not more elevated than the natures and individuals whose needs they were to satisfy; thus a lucrative
sideline was added to their vile calling and served to
accentuate it, as they were always ready, for a price, to
lend their assistance and establishments for purposes of
entertainment.   It is at the door of an inn at the corner
of a deserted cross-road that Petronius has Encolpius
discover Giton, that classical prototype of all the fairy
god-children who have come after him, it is in an inn
that most of their relationships are consummated, it is
in an inn that Giton confesses to Encolpius his suspicions
of Ascyltos, and his reasons for them, pressing the tears
from his eyes with the balls of his thumbs; and that narrative furnishes us with proof positive that the *deversorium*
was an excellent counterpart to the *lupanar* of Sotades.
The boys attached to the inns were ordinarily accomplices,
though sometimes the victims of these frightful debauches.
On this account we find in Plautus that the *puer caupon-
arius* has all the attributes of Hylas and Giton, and out
of the fullness of experience one might have spoken for
the other.

Much is to be said of the different kinds of hospices
and inns, their arrangements, and the life which went
on in them, but the best source of information lies in the
names they bore.   Of the *deversorium* we have already

spoken; it was a stopping place. There is little doubt that these institutions catered to demands other than mere lodgings and food (which was generally bought by the guests themselves), but their principal custom was probably derived from transients and strangers, rather than from the natives. The *caupona* and the *taberna meritoria*, in addition to sheltering transients and strangers maintained bar-rooms and restaurants as well; it is therefore probable that the bulk of their patronage came from the natives who forgathered here to drink and gossip, amuse themselves with singing girls or flower girls, and drive away dull care generally. The *caupona* were at least partly furnished, and this was certainly true of the *stabulum*, in proof of which we quote Petronius, chapter 97:

"Eumolpus was speaking privately with Bargates, when a crier attended by a public slave entered the inn (*stabulum*), accompanied by a medium sized crowd of outsiders. Waving a torch that gave off more smoke than light, he announced: 'Strayed from the baths, a short time ago, a boy, about sixteen years of age, curly headed, a minion, handsome, answers to the name of Giton. One thousand *sesterces* reward will be paid to anyone bringing him back or giving information as to his whereabouts.' Ascyltos, dressed in a tunic of many colors, stood not far from the crier, holding out a silver tray upon which was piled the reward, as evidence of good faith. I ordered Giton to get under the bed immediately, telling him to stick his hands and feet through the rope netting which supported the mattress, and, just as Ulysses of old had clung to the ram, so he, stretched out beneath the mattress, would evade the hands of the hunters."

A traveller of the better class would have found only a mediocre standard of comfort here, however, as we shall see from a further scrutiny of Petronius and Horace.

to say nothing of Hadrian's biting criticism of such places, and the numerous tenantry who lived at public expense but paid no rent.

"The public servant, however," again the Arbiter is speaking, "was not derelict in the performance of his duty, for, snatching a cane from the innkeeper, he poked underneath the bed, ransacking every corner, even to the cracks in the wall. Twisting his body out of reach, and cautiously drawing a full breath, Giton pressed his mouth against the very bugs themselves."

Innkeepers were necessarily privy to all the disorders originating in their neighborhood. If they happened to be old, as was the case with the hostess in Apuleius, they were go-betweens as subtle as they were shameless. An excellent example of such a character is seen in that mime of Herondas in which the old woman whose guile has long since taken the place of beauty and charm, is brought to bear in favor of the rich young suppliant who desires certain little favors at the hands of the young wife of a soldier away in the wars.

The younger members of the sorority of *coparum* did not place insuperable difficulties in the path of a mutual understanding, and money or other valuable considerations rarely failed in making easier the path of conquest. The *deversorium* and the *caupona* were sometimes denoted by another term, *ganea*, a word which old Calepin renders in his archaic manner—*taverne bourdeliere*—a pimp's pothouse.

If, on the other hand, we adopt the etymology pointed out by Festus, the term *ganea* should mean a subterranean tavern, hidden away in the rocks and woods, such as bordered the banks of the Tiber almost to Ostia, and the coastline of the Gulf of Baiae. The Roman women, who, in obedience to Nero's orders, changed the austere stola for the vestments of tavern singing girls, were compelled to establish themselves in these grottos of revelry, and comport themselves in a manner natural to their new calling. Suetonius has pictured them, standing at the thresholds, hailing all the passing boats with their cries, and inviting sailors and passengers alike to land and partake of their hospitality.

It was guttlers (*helluones*) such as these that Cicero flayed so savagely because of their social habits, their everlasting readiness for an orgy; and when one of them answered an appeal such as this, and entered the low and narrow door of the *ganeum*, the *comessatio* began, and, after having been prolonged for days on end, resulted in a horrible mess of broken cups, upturned tables, sodden serving-boys sleeping off the effects of their wine, drunken flute girls, and Gaditanian dancers exhausted with drunkenness and with the voluptuous contortions of their native dances.

The *ganea*, then, were generally the abodes of clandestine debauchery where License veiled itself in impenetrable mystery and shadow. Sometimes they were known as *lustra* (a den of some animal, sometimes a stew) because of the secrecy in entering them, even as an animal will not betray its den; and those forgathering in such places took the greatest precautions against being seen and recognized. Swaggering roisterers pursuing new sensations entered the *ganea* with covered heads, as did Antonius the tavern at Red Rocks, and their exit was as well screened as their entrance. The law required that women of the town be registered on the rolls of the *aedile*, but the number of clandestine evaders probably equalled, if it did not exceed, the number actually registered, and a large percentage of these evaders were in some way associated with the *ganea*.

The extreme caution which was exercised in regard to these establishments was due then to two causes: the

desire of the frequenters to escape the obloquy which
would certainly have followed detection and publicity,
and the necessity which drove the entertainers to avoid
the *aedile's* register and the exile which would have
resulted from discovery of their actual profession.   No
noisy arguments or drunken laughter were loud enough
to be heard on the outside and attract unwelcome attention and curiosity, nor were brawls permitted to menace
the sanctuaries frequented by the wealthy and influential
classes.   The Roman police were not the dupes of these
deceptions, they kept a tolerant watch more for effect
than anything else, although it is highly probable that
the question of refined blackmail often came up for
settlement.   The real difficulty lay in the fact that the
classes frequenting the more sumptuous of the *ganea*
were beyond the reach of police regulations by reason of
their wealth and influence.

In the taverns and inns, however, no such caution
was necessary, as the very calling which tavern girls
followed absolved them from the penalties imposed by
laws against adultery and prostitution.   When edicts
were issued the authorities generally granted absolution to
such entertainers of this class as had come into their net.

"Such persons," it is the formal language of the code
of Theodosius, "such persons shall be held as being immune against the judicial proceedings of the law against
adultery and prostitution, as the very indignity of their
life is an insult to the laws they should observe."

Nor were the innkeepers dealt with severely by the
law makers.   It is true that they were responsible to
guests for belongings and property stolen or misappro-
priated, unless they could prove that due care and dili-
gence had been exercised to preserve the property and
protect the owner.   But in those cases which we, with a
well developed genius for evading responsibility, lay at

the door of the Almighty, no ancient landlord was responsible. He had no such blanket alibi. It was due to the calling they followed, their penchant for prostitution, their professional hospitality, their substitution and adulteration of wines, that they were denied the free enjoyment of their goods. They could not act as guardians for children, they were deprived of the right of taking oath, and, except in special cases, they were not permitted the right of accusation in justice. Let us contrast the situation of these Roman innkeepers and procurers with that marvelous Pornodidascalos in Herondas. Here indeed is hardihood untrammeled by the slightest scruple.

Unfortunately, laws had their loop-holes then as now, and were generally ineffective in restraining rascally innkeepers because the latter, by their very birth and calling, were below the law and, as Gibbon says, "beneath contempt." The only punishment which could legally have been inflicted upon gentry such as these was to expel them from Rome and its environs, and thus striking at the very root of their calling. Such a proceeding was, of course, entirely out of the question because of the great inconvenience, not to say actual hardship, which would have beset a multitude of innocent bystanders in a center of population as great as Rome.

Under Domitian, another method of dealing with the liquor situation was briefly tried out. It is interesting as constituting what is probably the earliest chapter in the history of what the late B. L. Taylor loved to call "The League For Making Virtue Odious," and is related by that amiable old pagan Suetonius, in his life of that odious tyrant. Imperial Caesar dropped his fly swatter long enough to sign an edict forbidding the planting of any more vines in Italy, and decreeing that half the vineyards in the provinces must be uprooted (Chap. 7).

In chapter 14, we learn the sequel, we are informed that, due to the subtle propaganda contained in a clever Greek verse which was scattered broadcast, Domitian was led to moderate his aquanacreontic ardor and set aside his decree. We append a translation of this little verse: a translation freely made which is still as literal as it is exact:

> Though you devour me to the root
> Sufficient wine I'll still produce
> For every sacrificial use
> When Regal Caesar is the goat!

What shall we say of the citizenship of these inn-keepers, these pestilential pot-house peelers? Ordinarily, they were freedmen who had emancipated themselves by one method or another and refused thenceforth to place themselves under communal law, but more frequently still, they were strangers, of a servile race which had been conquered by the Romans in the Levant. They had emigrated to the city and came, at last, to infest the whole of Italy. These are the wages of conquest: the women of a more sophisticated but less virile race will play no unimportant part in avenging the infamies of their country upon its conquerors by expert instruction in new and more demoralizing lessons in social manners and morals, and new sensations. So it was with the Vandals in Africa. In like manner the men of the subject races play into the hands of their female allies, and the final result is a civilization literally bled white financially and physically. Horace had much of this in mind when he wrote his Hymn to the Romans: that grand and stately lamentation which, viewed in the light of what later came to pass, seems to have been of the very stuff of which true prophecy is made—prophecy indeed, requiring centuries for its fulfilment:

How Time doth in its flight debase
Whate'er it finds! Our fathers' race
  More deeply versed in ill
Than were their sires, hath borne us yet
More wicked, duly to beget
  A race more vicious still.

—Martin's translation.

The Syrians and other Levantines, "nations born for slavery," as Cicero cuttingly says of them, were especially numerous at Rome, and preyed upon her vitals by the exercise of the vilest professions. They bound themselves to the service of the overseers of the games, sprinkled the sand of the arena, watered the horses, had the care of the great awning which shielded the spectators from the rays of the summer sun. They competed with the untutored labor of the city and introduced problems which California understands better than the Eastern portions of our own country. They even entered the service of rich patricians and matrons; they delivered notes and letters, in a word, they supplied the needs of the most infamous callings, and frequently at some little peril to their own skins. In the fragments of Menander (The Arbitrants) we have a Syriscus (Syrian), a charcoal burner and tenant slave; and, strange to relate, he is one of the finest characters in the play; he is good through and through. In the Adelphoi and the Self Tormentor of Terentius, we have a Syrus.

Levantine women likewise entered service, even as did the designing Syrian in the Mercator of Plautus; but when circumstances permitted them to follow their inclinations and choose freely, they reverted to that condition to which their oriental surroundings and habits of life had accustomed them, debauched adventuresses, worshipping their figures, lascivious dancers like the Gaditanian gypsies of the present day, players of lyres,

singers of obscene odes and Fescennine verses at the
cross-roads and taverns; in a word, *ambuniae*, as Horace
calls them, in one of his Satires which is never translated;
flute players whose lack of morals and restrained decency
were compensated for by physical beauty and an insatiable desire to please in any way that might yield a
handsome profit.

Even at Rome the name they bore had a popular
significance closely allied to that which is the heritage
of the gypsy of the present time, and the *ambuniae* came
to be associated with that class of sinuous and supple
Syrians, adepts, *doctae puellae*, if you will, in every phase
of the finer and more sensuous varieties of such entertainments.

The greater part of them, and they had a gild, or, as
Horace calls it, a college, the greater part of them to
lend an air of refinement worthy of their calling (call it
an artistic background if you will), had opened, either
in Rome itself, or in the immediate limits and suburbs,
inns and taverns in which music and dancing were usual
and a part of the entertainment; the ancestor of the
nautch girl of Algeciras or Cairo or Bassora. Her exquisite discernment prompts her naturally to choose the
raiment which will add most to the advantages with
which a benevolent nature has endowed her: if she be
of exceeding loveliness, her *strophium* will be Grecian in
simplicity; if her beauty has reached its acme and begun
to wane she will adorn herself with colors of Syrian
gorgeousness, a confession that she can no longer afford
the simplicity that scorns adornment and relies solely
upon its own excellence. In her are combined all the
attributes of all the courtesans, all their arts of pleasing
and entertainment, yet the *strophium* is always there
because it is an integral part of Syrian cultus, an emblem
sacred to Dionysus. On the occasion of orgies and dances

they are unwound by the expert fortune tellers, imported along with other superstitions from the Levant. If, at times, they drop their clacking castanets, whose sexy clucking punctuates their dancing and makes their audience more pliant to their demands, it is but to take up the sceptre of the seeress, to roll the threads of a thousand colors around the magic rhombus, or, better yet, with herbs of secret virtues, to compound philtres to restore lost love and virility, philtres such as have cost many a husband or flagging lover sick of an old passion, his life. One of the herbs of which they made continuous use took its name from their cult: *ambujea;* and, if Horace, in his second satire has classed them with the *pharmacopoliae* or poisoners, it is surely because he was well informed as to their empiric practices. *Lysistrata* was not a name common among them.

The atmosphere of mysticism which surrounded them, their fortune telling, the utter lack of knowledge prevalent in those times, caused the common people to regard them as witches, and popular imagination endowed them with strange and horrible attributes. Fingers were placed softly upon lips when they were passing by; their dances were regarded with secret terror, and the more timid and superstitious dared not go near the places where they lived, or take a guest and dine in an inn conducted by one of them. It was said and believed that they served travellers with a kind of cheese which immediately changed those who had eaten it into beasts of burden. St. Augustine has an interesting passage in which he satirizes popular ignorance on such a subject, and the terror with which the ignorant regarded the witches of the inns.

The sensible man, however, saw in such gossip a sure protection, and permitted it to go unchallenged; although he would never have permitted himself to be caught in

such company, any more than he would have dreamed
of associating with the common lot. Such patricians as
Piso and Antonius furnish illustrations as to what is
meant; then, too, there was a fraternity, if such I may
venture to call the unsexed of Cybele, who were fully
alive to the possibilities of advantage and profit which
were to be extracted from miracles and sorcery; they
stood in no awe of the *ambuniae*. The poets also frequented the rustic taverns kept by such charming hostesses; the strange charm of these women, so subtle, so
beautiful, and finally, so mentally able, attracted the
bards, and drunkenness forged the chains that held them
captive.

Lucilius made a famous journey from Rome to Capua,
and from Capua through the Straits of Messina, a long
and charming voyage. Horace, in his trip to Brindisium,
followed as closely as possible in the footsteps of his
predecessor, and his account of his own trip was probably
based upon that of Lucilius.

Lucilius made one of his happier halts at an inn kept
by one of these Syrian hostesses: who or what she may
have been, we do not know. Was she the counterpart
of the toothless old crone whom Apuleius describes, or
was she a lithe and lissome *ambunia?* The unique
hemistich which preserves that little episode in the poet's
excursion tells us nothing of this except by inference.

"However, she was a Syrian tavern-keeper." That
is all the fragment tells us, a mutilated remnant of what
was the third book of the Satires of Lucilius. If only
he had informed us of the place and manner in which
he met that Syrian! But no; the word "she," cannot
explain or amplify what followed the meeting, and one
may only infer, from the place which the fragment occu-
pies, that Lucilius was almost at the end of his journey
when he met her. The word "however," might cause

the reader to believe that inns were not numerous at the place, and, though the inn may have been sadly lacking in comforts, he saw possibilities in the nationality and person of his hostess which might, in a measure, annul the other disadvantages, although he had for some time sought for a resting place to his tastes, and that his arrival was in the nature of that of a providential guest. Was he well entertained? Did he find there a crackling fire and a cosy hearth? Some authors would have the reader see, in that Syrian's tavern, a wretched establishment like that of which another fragment makes mention, and which, on a par with the inn in which Horace was so well smoked at Beneventum, could supply Lucilius neither faggots, oil, nor asparagus, "nothing which he wanted," but, as far as we are concerned, knowing what we do of the inns kept by the *ambuniae*, we will give the preference to that exquisite little pastel of the ancient poet which delineates a Syrian; a pretty house with a well filled larder of which he speaks in yet another fragment of the same book. She it is whom we prefer to see at the head of a table loaded with food well cooked and tastefully served: "an exclamation of starvation," as Labitte remarks, "we will open our jaws and devour the profit." And, if, on that trip, more famous for fasting than feasting, he might well make the most of such an opportunity for an orgy as is indicated in still another fragment, and write, in its honor, that verse of lively jubilation, "the jugs are standing on their heads, and our sober senses with them," which surely ought to be the case during that same dalliance at the shrine of the Syrian hostess.

Such an hypothesis would be utterly without meaning in a tavern which was sordid, a dirty and smoky lodging, and I find myself in full accord with what the poets have told us of these oriental inns.

CHAPTER X.

The cabaret dancer—Banquets of the Patricians—Voluptuous dances—Gallus describes the charms of a siren—Dice throwing and gambling—The murder of Claudius—The Appian Way—The first Christians.

Happy and fortunate in finding a little gem of antiquity less mutilated than the remains of Lucilius, we will attempt a translation or paraphrase of Virgil's Copa: the most charming and the most authentic of all the fugitive poems attributed to him under the collective title Catalecta. A famous French savant has described this bit of realism as a beautifully cut cameo. The charm and grace of this figure have left their impression, and the deftness of the hand that chiselled her is unquestioned.

THE CABARET DANCER

"Copa Syrisca, caput Graeca redimita mitella,"
A Grecian head-band binding her hair,
The wine-flushed Syrian siren sways
To the titillating clack of her castanets,
In the spell of the dance that Passion begets
Of smouldering Desire that seethes to flare
In the smoke of her tavern: sinuously fair
She sings her appealing lay:
"Ah, why wilt thou broil in the dust and heat,
When wine awaits in a cool retreat,
And a couch of grass, or a garden nook
Trellised with roses? A shepherd's flute
Murmurously twitters, a brawling brook
Writhes on its way to the strum of a lute:
Pitch-covered puncheons of beaded wine,
Chaplets of crocus and violets blended,
Garlands of buttercups studded with roses,
Wicker-work baskets of fresh lilies, tended
By water-sprites: yon osier hamper discloses

A Cabaret Girl

Cheeses and chestnuts and plums . . . all are thine:
Apples that blush with the vigor of Fall,
Mulberries blood-red, grapes in great clusters,
Bice-colored melons that hang from their stems,
Ceres her daintiest gifts for thee musters,
Handmaids of Venus to fly at thy call,
Bromius waits, and all kill-joys condemns.
Priapus guards with his sickle this spot,
Heavy his attribute, but maids fear him not.
Enter, Sir Falstaff,* spare thy jaded ass,
Vesta's delight . . . nay, nay, thou shalt not pass;
The thickets resound with the katydid's song,
The lizard has lurked in her cool retreat long,
Come! Lie on a couch and recline at thy ease,
Slake thy thirst with new wine, in surroundings that please;
Come! Weary One, rest in the shade of the vine
And thy heavy head quickly with roses we'll twine;
Aye, kiss while ye may yon tender young mouth,
While the tide of thy life sets strong from the South;
Away with those grim puritanical ways,
Mere dregs of those ruder and earlier days;
Wilt save these fragrant wreaths to mourn thy dust?
Or crown thy tombstone? Nay, that were not just!"
"Bring wine and dice! Tomorrow's cares for them that are so dumb,
Death tweaks mine ear and whispers low, Live while ye may, I come."

Not a detail is lacking in this picture, nor is there the slightest forcing to render it cheerful and true to life. We can see ourselves in a dining-room, a shady arbor of creeper-roses festooned with leafy vines; from such a sanctuary, simple in its elegance and taste, we can look out into the glaring sunlight and see the heat waves tremulous in the air while we quaff our cool wine or acidulous beverage in the fragrant shadows of the arbor, and lazily watch the dancing and listen to the

*Exception may be taken to an anachronism in rendering Caly-bita by the Shakespearean Falstaff, but those who are gifted with penetration may applaud. The others matter nothing to the translator.

music: the midwatch lookout on a sailing vessel in the
tropics offers no finer opportunity for philosophical intro-
spection than we have here, where everything attracts
to rest and repose. Rare indeed is the intellect that has
the power of divorcing itself from its immediate surroundings, or the memory of those which have oppressed
it, and thinking deeply and constructively, following the
course of a thought from its birth to the effectuation
of the plans it has germinated. Propertius has written
delightfully of "tables set under an arbor of vines," and
in another pointed passage he makes allusion to the
suspicions with which the mind of his mistress was
charged: if the text be in order, Propertius was a frequenter of taverns:

"Learn what this night struck panic through the
watery Esquiline; when all the neighbors ran headlong
through the New Fields, when a noisy brawl broke out
in a secret tavern, and brought shame on my fair name,
though I was not there." (Eleg. Lib. IV, 2 and 3.)

Cups of every size, amphorae, chalices, flutes, stringed
instruments, all were tossed in a heap upon the violets
and roses with which the floor and tables were strewn,
but alas, the wine which spouted from these vessels was
not generally of the finer vintages, it was probably *vappa*,
a product which the discriminating Spaniard or Frenchman would contemptuously term "corked." Such a
product as this stood in need of all the fortification which
pitch could give it.

The hostess of Virgil is the prototype of her to whom
the Abbé de Bernis paid troubadour compliment many
centuries later, nor were her wines more potent than her
eyes:

> The mistress of the cabaret,
> A sweet enchantress sans her comb:
> The god of Love designed this fay,
> A lissome Hebe, in her home.

> And Bacchus, seated on his cask,
> Mistakes her for a water-sprite;
> Were water all her world could ask,
> 'Twere still the same: her eyes are bright.

Here will never be found the luxury and the succulence that characterized the banquets of the patricians, the infinite number of dishes and delicacies, and the rarity and age of the vintages. The charm that enchanted genius and enthralled the limpid soul of a Virgil or a Theocritus, given naturally to a gentle melancholy induced, perhaps by frail health and an extraordinary insight into causes and effects, lay in the utter and poetic simplicity of nature. Here such a rare personality could dream, his brain could teem with harmonies and nocturnes too beautiful for expression: melodies unheard are sweetest, says Keats, who, perhaps of all moderns, had most in common with the Mantuan, whose sombre spirit, which imbued whatever it touched with exquisite delicacy, found at last in the shade and soft atmosphere of Parthenope a peace and a requiem such as Stevenson must have dreamed of when he wrote his greatest poem: "Under the wide and starry sky."

Little remains to be said, except that the tables were always set, the latch-string was always out, and the larder was always full. It is almost as though one were present at the repast with which Philemon and Baucis regaled Zeus and Hermes, or in the rustic cottage of Hecale when Theseus partook of her hospitality; flowers, dairy products, fruits: here we have the soul of all that is hospitable: the gifts of Flora and of Ceres:

> The linen, decked with flowers, with dainties piled high,
> A little milk, fruit, garden stuff, that Ceres don't deny.

Whether it be Ovid, or Rutilius, it is still a commentary upon Virgil or Theocritus!

As with Baucis, so with the Syrian hostess, the little cheeses, so fresh that they smear the wicker work osiers in which they are to dry, the plums, the late fruits of autumn, the chestnuts, the sweetly blushing apples, the melon with its coloring of the tropic seas, where soundings are not too great, and when clouds and sun are right, the blood red mulberries, the choice grapes on their vine cuttings: it is a repast true in every way to the standards of the Georgics, to those of the elder Cato, or to those of Columella; and the writer remembers well many such repasts served in the *patios* of Spanish *hachendado's* houses in happier climes under a canopy of *cadena de amor*, and to the music of harps! Mantua, your son has done you greater service than even Shakespeare! The only factor that jars is that he also wrote the Moretum, which could not have been served in such surroundings as these.

As we have invoked the genius of things as they ought to be, let us also strengthen the illusion by imagining, in the distance, that we can hear the twittering of the rustic pipes, in the hands of a master worthy to compete with Marsyas, swelling from the dim and cool aloofness of a Menaelian grotto, and mingling its dulcet complainings with those of the clear, cold, twisted stream as it foams and chatters through its rocky bed, leaping in cascades that caress the verdure with their vapor, and that enchant the ear with the witchery of nature: pebbles roll along and the water foams deliciously around them, the very source of the water of life and certainly one of the finest opportunities to enjoy its most ethereal moments, "Whose limpid sweetness seems to speak of love," as only a Frenchman could have said.

Now the guests are coming, they laugh in merriment as they cross the threshold of the little Roman roadhouse; some of the gayer address some pointed pleasantry to the worm-eaten wood god, serving the cabaret as guardian genius and sign: formidable still because of the huge attribute with which he is endowed and which was often used to club trespassers and thieves, or otherwise to coerce them. Truly a most picturesque mirror in which to see ourselves and the place into which we have come!

Then, too, our hostess has greeted an arrival in a manner which outdoes the finesse of the Widow Wadman: "Welcome, Calybita (Falstaff)," the guest has much of the rogue about him, but alas, nothing of that hardihood which appeals most subtly to women: "It is easier," says Quartilla, "it is easier nowadays to meet a god than it is to meet a real man!" Falstaff, you are older than one could have imagined, but no, I seem to recall the melancholy destiny of Abishag, a doubtful comfort in so dark an age!

Yes, that fat rascal who has just arrived, and is even now dismounting from his puffing mule, is one of the priests of Cybele, one of that curious fraternity immune to half the ills that human flesh is heir to, a peripatetic evangelist who trains the fat of laziness with drunken sprees in every tavern in country or village. The worn-out mule is tied to a tree near the gate of Rome, along with the relics sacred to the ritual, relics which sometimes include a simulacrum of the goddess. Apuleius has described such a pilgrimage and the palmers who took part in it, their slow progress through the country districts, punctuated by the clash of cymbals and the clucking of castanets, the lying prophecies that distilled alms without in the least instructing the superstition of the inhabitants. They danced their way into a scanty and doubtful competence, but their real goals were the drinks and larder of the tavern where their style would be less cramped. Here such a bonze could dance himself into the stupor of exhaustion, recuperate himself, and, if necessary, hypothecate his tambourine or cymbals to pay his score and obtain the means of returning to the city.

We shall follow the fat satyr into the interior of the establishment. The odors of the kitchen will appeal more to his senses than the fragrance of the garden, and the smoky atmosphere of the little inn will furnish a setting more in keeping with the proprieties to which he is accustomed than the clear and clean air of the country. He has come to this place to get away from himself; he would never admit this, he is probably unconscious that it is true; he wants to dance, to drink, to sing, and perhaps it is not too much to say that he even has a flair to experiment at close range with the few active sensual possibilities which still remain to him after an outraged nature has exacted her inexorable dues. Through half closed eyes he watches the lithe and harmonious play of the muscles of the *ambunia*, in her bacchantic posturings. She is a past mistress in the art of the cordax, and at last, as a tremulous shiver, an erotic tic, runs through the length of that slim lithe figure, as the yellowish eyes open slowly, voluptuously, the lambent flame in their depths scorches the onlookers, as the nostrils twitch, and a crooning sigh comes throbbing from a bosom charged with all the passions of all the ages, as this descendant of Semiramis, this cousin of Artemisia and Rhodope, this Roxena with vigor and skill enough to exhaust a dozen Alexanders, this human leopardess as impersonal as a sphinx stands mute before her audience, her little hands grasping convulsively the firm little breasts whose nipples protrude through the apple green silk netting which confines them—ah, the charm, the subtle appeal that lies in their artificially colored tips, so deeply ruby if under twenty, so golden after twenty, her head thrown back until every cord

and muscle of her symmetrical neck stand out, and give
a tonus to her entire being; verily, in the words of Fielding, the favored among her audience must have had very
much or very little of the hero about them if her appeal
proves unavailing! Now she has rested, and wearily,
automatically she dances the dance of the Maenad; a
little wine, a little ripple of applause, her color heightens,
her eyes grow brighter; her movements become more
and more spirited, the thyrsus has been tossed aside,
and the cluck cluck of the crotals in her hands stimulates
her audience as though they were being flagellated with
a sprig of nettles; more and more abandoned becomes
the dance; through a dark opening which leads to the
garden advances a troupe of Pans and Satyrs under the
leadership of Dionysus himself: as they intone the hymn
to Bacchus: "*Evoe, evoe*," chants the infatuated roué,
and as the tones wax higher and higher they roll their
heads, and as they wane their heads droop: faster and
faster becomes the movement, the eyes of the dancer
sparkle with a brightness unhealthy and destroying, the
postures fade one into another like the everchanging
patterns in the brilliant skin of some viper that writhes
as it charms its victims: the tones ascend in a shrill
crescendo, a rocket of passion that expires in a thousand
brilliant sparks, and silence, exhaustion, and satiety! As
the dancer falls, she is caught by an attendant and carried
from the scene. Soon another will take her place: bring
stronger wine, on with the dance, let joy be unconfined.
Thus do the emotions of the audience run the entire
gamut of titillation, and soon, too soon, will vigor be
replaced by a softer and more treacherous substitute, and
the nation, suddenly confronted with an enemy that
knows only the ritual imposed upon those who are the
lawful spoils of war, will find its manhood impotent and
cowardly, and its daughters the willing prey of those

more worthy to work their will upon them. Thus did
Genseric glut his barbarian hordes, and thus did they in
their turn pay the ransom to an enemy more cunning
and virile than they. Thus and thus only has civilization
paid the wages of justice; the fittest survive, but the
term needs a proper definition. In the occident, three
dances such as we have described have come down
through the ages: they are the French chahut, the
Neapolitan tarantella (in its most abandoned form), and
the baji of the gypsies of Iberia and Balkan Europe.

Many of the poets of antiquity were smitten with the
charms of these sirens, but one citation from Gallus,
whose tragic fate has colored poetic legend, shall suffice:

"There was a young woman named Blanche; fair as
a lily was she, and her black hair was curled with an
artistic witchery. I saw her one day, and she had a
number of musically chiming little bells attached to her
garments, at her every movement they tinkled and the
tinklings multiplied themselves. When she snapped her
white fingers, or strummed upon a lute, she imbued the
chords with a sweet and haunting harmony foreign to
the instrument. She danced, and I was lost: I loved,
but in loving, I despaired. I suffered agonies from a
secret wound, but the agonies were sweet as the hope of
life itself. I have carried with me the memories of the
day I first saw her, every detail is perfect in my mind,
and the thought of her has filled my heart unceasingly,
I dream of her, day dreams too enchanting for expression,
and at night . . . ah, at night . . . I feel the fancied
touch of lips softer than the wing of sleep. I invent
imaginary conversations, intimate little confidences with
her, and yet in this dialogue, there is but one: question-
ings, doubts, fears; all that might have been, and I hum
to myself the soft airs she was wont to sing."

The dance is ended, and the Syrian follows it with

other diversions to amuse the wearied senses of an audience no less insatiable than she.

"Bring wine and dice," cries one, and now pure wine is served, "bring on the dice," is cried; "Death tweaks the ear and whispers low, live while ye may, I come!"

The dice are brought, they are contained in an ivory box, and in the hands of the revellers, hands no longer quite steady, they begin to roll and bound over the stone table top. The game, once begun, may continue without interruption for many hours, probably for two or three days and nights with varying fortunes and chances in the game of *senio* (game of six), and of *canicula* or *canis*, (game of the dog's ace), one of those games of chance in which the stakes were often enormous, and in which the Romans took such keen delight. The dullard Claudius was by nature a gambler, as both Suetonius and Seneca relate, and that the dice might not be disturbed by the movements of his litter, he had constructed a gaming table (*alveum*) so arranged that the dice combinations were not disturbed by the gait of the bearers. It is also reported that he wrote a treatise on dice games.

On this account Seneca, in his Apokolokintosis, can invent no keener punishment with which to plague the dead emperor than that of condemning him to an eternal game of dice with a dice box full of holes.

We need not occupy ourselves with the gambling propensities of emperors, however, nor with the weaknesses of the senators nor prostitutes: Seneca has dealt with them in a manner better than we could hope to rival:

> All ye, who owe your wealth's advance
> To games of skill and gambling chance,
> Though weighted down with treasure;
> Yea, iron-nerved gambler, risking all,
> Take heed, lest Death and Fire recall
> Your gold, at grim Fate's pleasure.

The scene depicted above is meant to represent a gambling party in one of the common inns: the players are probably knaves to a man; they have taken to gambling after having had a drinking bout, and will do the best that in them lies to cheat their way to victory, and the matter will presently end in a free for all fight. Plautus in the Curcullio has left us a graphic scene of this description. His hero was tempted to throw dice with a soldier, but he had not the slightest intention of losing; he relates his prowess and dexterity to Phedromos, another rapscallion of his own complexion:

"When we had eaten well and drunk our fill, he proposed a game of dice to me. I put up my mantle as a pledge, he places his ring in escrow, then he invoked Planesius . . . He brought in four blood-suckers. I took the dice for my turn and I invoked my wetnurse Hercules. "The Royal Throw," I whisper to the dice, "I present the soldier with a large throw, and his head falls heavily on the instant he sees it, and he falls asleep. I, I slip his ring off his finger and, for fear he may awaken, I slip under the bed, very quietly."

In 1877 archaeologists at work in the ruins of Pompeii uncovered a wineshop of the sort of which we have just spoken. The contemporary life is illustrated to admiration on the plaster in one of the front rooms: there are four scenes in all.

In the first scene, on the left, a young man is furiously kissing a slavey dressed in garish and hideous yellow garments. She is fighting him off and the legend belonging to the scene reads: *"NOLO CVM MVRTAL"* (I don't want you to, play with Myrtalis). In the second panel we see the same slavey in conversation with Myrtalis. Both are pointing their fingers at a third woman who staggers in under the weight of an immense wine jar; she also carries a glass. The legend says:

"*QVI VVLT SVMAT OCEANE VENI BIBE*," (Let him who wants take, I am here, Oceanus, drink). In the third panel are seen two gamblers. They are seated on opposite sides of a board which rests upon their knees. There are several *latrunculi* (counters) in rows upon the board: these counters are of different colors, some yellow, some black, and some are white. One of the gamesters has just thrown the dice: "*EXSI*," (I have won), he cries. The other points to the dice and says "*NON TRIA DVAS EST*," (Not three, it is two). In the fourth and last scene the battle is in full swing: "I did not throw two but three, I won," and the other answers: "You s . . . o . . . b . . . I won." The landlord has entered and is shoving both brawlers out into the street: "*ITIS FORAS RIXATIS*" (Outside to fight) is his valedictory.

Gambling was frowned upon by the authorities, except during the brief season of the Saturnalia, which corresponded more or less roughly with our Christmas holidays, except that the period was longer.

"Betrayed by the rattling of his dice-box," says Martial, "and dragged from the inn, the fuddled gambler begs mercy of the aedile." Great license was permitted slaves during this period of the Saturnalia; and unpalatable truths were told to masters under the immunity conferred by the season, infants were allowed the game of nuts, the game that ordinarily symbolized the temporary emancipation of the Roman patrician from some of those six unnatural things and his espousal of a relative degree of normalcy in his relations with society.

When the aedile sent his lictors to pay a call upon some tavern-keeper, it followed naturally that the master of the place was the first arrested, as he was by his very calling on the wrong side of the law; then there was the eternal suspicion of loaded dice. Martial speaks of one individual whose addiction to such lucrative pastimes was chronic: "Gambling with one or more loaded dice."

The society of the time was faced with the necessity of choosing between two evils: the villainy of the inn-keepers was traditional, but the inconvenience which would have resulted from the abolition of such establishments would have resulted in a still greater injury to society and commerce.

When Tarquinius Superbus decided that the knowledge and influence of Turnus Herodinus of Aricia might be fatal to his own interests, he bided his time with such patience as he could muster; waited until after the latter had denounced his imperialism and lack of faith to the allies, and then accused his intended victim of plotting his death. Witnesses were suborned and weapons secretly conveyed into the inn where Turnus lodged. By the treachery of slaves and circumstantial evidence his guilt was established and the Latin Assembly condemned him to death by drowning: he was confined in a basket weighted with stones and thrown into the Aqua Ferentia. (Livy, I, 50-1.) It goes without saying that the inn-keeper must have been one of the principals in this business, otherwise it would have been very difficult for his establishment to have been so well prepared as to entrap a man so honest and fearless as Turnus.

The murder of Clodius by the followers of Milo took place in an inn at Bovillae, but in this case the inn-keeper was also a victim without having been in the least involved in the affair. The wounded Clodius took refuge in this inn and the retainers of Milo attempted to force the doors. The place was well defended, however, but the besiegers finally forced their way in and murdered the innkeeper, who died toe to toe with them, fighting to the last. Clodius was dragged into the open, hacked into pieces, and left on the road. These details are mentioned by the scholiast on Asconius, but Cicero passes over them in silence; they are, in effect, a terrible indictment of Milo, who, if he had no actual part in the butchery, nevertheless gave the orders to force the barricades of the inn, that he might have Clodius at his mercy. His enemy was already seriously wounded and the result desired had been attained: it therefore looks as though the entire plan was the result of cold blooded malevolence, and Milo must have thought the campaign out and left the details in the hands of his officers. Nor does Cicero make mention of the fate of the innkeeper who died more gloriously than the majority of the members of his calling: he goes even further, for when Milo was placed in jeopardy by the evidence of Licinius, the tavern-keeper of the Circus Maximus, who had overheard the slaves of Milo plotting the death of Pompeius, the orator takes his revenge and makes light of the importance which might attach to evidence from a source so polluted, and ends by wondering how anyone can place the least credence in the word of a restaurant keeper (*popae credi mirabar*).

On this great road built by Appius Claudius, the same down which we have already chaperoned Lucilius and Horace from inn to inn and from tavern to tavern, we come at length, twenty-three miles from Rome itself, midway between that city and Capua, to a village in which three taverns were for many years the chief attraction, and probably the first buildings on the site. This hamlet bears today the name Tre Taberne, in classical times it was known as Tres Tabernae (Three Taverns). Because of its happy situation, a short distance from Lanuvium, and at most, ten miles from Aricia, at the crossroads where one could take carriage for Antium, it was an ideal situation for a post house, and it was the last stop of importance before the traveller reached the limits of the Eternal City itself. We need, therefore, manifest no surprise at learning that many an illustrious traveller stopped at Tres Tabernae, and that more than one plan of action which had a profound influence upon later history was outlined and developed in this little village named for the three taverns. Cicero made many stops here; rarely did he leave the Antium road to travel the Appian Way without first stopping to receive his letters or posting such as he had ready, and it is in this village, so little in keeping as to name with the meeting which follows, that we witness the first interview of the apostle Paul with the members of the new sect at Rome. After a vexatious journey, the apostle had arrived at Tres Tabernae, where he was greeted by the faithful of Rome, apprised, by rumor, of his arrival, and there he gave thanks to God for his care and protection as is related in the Acts of the Apostles. One must be struck with the singular destiny which gathered there, in the presence of their apostle, in a village of taverns, the first faithful of a sect whose God, born in the stable of an inn, reckoned Rahab the innkeeper or harlot among his ancestors, and whose first temple, as we shall see, was raised upon the same site as that of an inn at Rome, the violent objections of the tavern-keeper to the contrary notwithstanding. Could any illustration serve better to show the reasons that prompted the first Christians to subject themselves to that law of humility extending sometimes even to ignominy, and the observance of which was one of their first duties?

But this village, sanctified for cause, was later on to become the bloody theatre of signal crimes. The ruin of Maxentius and the fall of the pagan empire were to make this historic shrine a shambles, and its last days were to be as cruel as they were infamous.

CHAPTER XI.

*Death of Severus—Tavern signs—The gardens of Maecenus—
Intemperate drinking and religious festivals—Bear steaks—Corn mills—
Taverns and trap doors—Theodosius purges Rome of thieves and
harlots—The splendor and wickedness of the Roman Baths.*

Flavius Severus, an obscure Illyrian adventurer, was
invested with the purple in A. D. 305. He was the rival
of Maximinus and Maxentius, the son of the former, and
after his decisive defeat he fled to Ravenna for refuge,
looking forward in terror upon the gloomy prospect of
captivity or death. Maxentius, to expedite matters,
came to an understanding with Severus and the latter
surrendered under the most solemn promises of amnesty
and protection. He was conducted to Tres Tabernae by
the retainers of his captor and, without the slightest regard to promises, he was held in close captivity and
finally offered the choice in the manner in which he would
meet the grim reaper. He followed the example set by
Seneca and many others, and opened his veins.

There was also a quarter named Tres Tabernae in
Rome itself, and this is the probable reason for the error
in Victor the Younger, who has reported the death
of Severus as having taken place in Rome, despite the
evidence of Zosimus and others. Not a few of the quarters of the great city took their names from inns or taverns. The quarter known as the Vicus Ursi Pileati (The
Quarter of the Bear of the Skull Cap), for example,
which, according to Sextus Rufus, was found in the Esquiline, and which must have taken its name from the
sign of some inn or from some street performance with
a trick animal. The cap carried with it the implication
of freedom, and the curious antiquarian may easily sup-

pose that the original owner of such a tavern may have
been known by the name of Ursus (Bear), and that he
was probably a freedman.   Neither would it be difficult
to conjure from such a sign a picture such as may have
inspired Phaedrus the Fabulist to write his Battle Between the Rats and the Weasels.   It is also of interest
to note that today in the same quarter, there is an Osteria
del Orso (Inn of the Bear).   The curiosity of the pass-
erby would naturally be piqued by a sign so promising,
and rival establishments would scarcely remain long in
ignorance of the commercial value of such a tocsin.   It
is therefore not improbable that other Skull Capped
Bears were born in remote wards of the city, and other
signs no less piquant soon made their appearance.   Artemidorus mentions an inn which had a camel for a sign:
could he have anticipated that this grotesquely malodorous animal would, one day, come to play so important a
role in the national life of the greatest of republics?   The
inn of Sittius at Pompeii had for a sign an elephant in
the coils of a serpent, and the behemoth is led by a dwarf.
At Narbonne there was an inn which had a cock (*gallus
gallinaceus*) for an emblem, a fact that throws a little
light upon the continual employment of the same expression by Petronius.   Such an emblem was also used
by one of the stations between Utica and Carthage.
There were the Great Eagle, the Little Eagle, the Serpent, the Great Crane, the Sword, the Wheel, the Olives.
Such establishments often advertised their merits (or
lack of them) through the mouths of their owners and
sometimes such matter appeared upon the sign, or upon
a tablet which also set forth the prices demanded.   In
Italy the slogan was "service after the Roman fashion
and standard."   One heavily patronized commercial
hostelry at Lyons had Apollo and Mercury on its sign-
board and the inscription deserves quotation:

MERCVRIVS HIC LVCRVM
PROMITTIT APOLLO SALVTEM
SEPTVMANVS HOSPITIVM
CVM PRANDIO QVI VENERIT
MELIVS VTETVR POST
HOSPES VBI MANEAS PROSPICE

Mercury promises gain, Apollo health, Septumanus hospitality; whoever enters here will be the better therefor; stranger, watch where you lodge.

The fifth region of Rome, which was probably the Esquiline, was abundantly furnished with taverns because of the institutions in the vicinity: The Amphitheatrum Castrense, where the legions mustered to parade and drill and where gladiators sometimes trained themselves for their combats with man or beast, the vivarium, that huge menagerie where a number of slaves were always on duty looking after the animals destined for the games, and last of all, the praetorian camp with its perpetual garrison of well paid soldiers. The immense barracks in which the guard was quartered had been constructed under Tiberius, and they must have furnished the taverns with a steady custom which yielded the vintners a good profit. In addition to the foregoing, the gardens of Maecenas were situated on the summit of the Esquiline Hill, the loftiest site in Rome. From this lovely elevation the entire city was spread out to the view in a grand panorama. The idlers and transients in the city would necessarily visit a place so famous and their difficult climb would have made them ready and eager for refreshment in the taverns of the district, a factor which must also have weighed with the innkeeper when choosing his site.

Lastly, a short distance outside the walls, there was a temple of Bacchus. Many years later, Constantine erected on its foundations the mausoleum of his daughter Constantina, but at the time of which we are speaking,

the devotees of the god of drunkenness would have
naturally paid their compliments to the taverns after
having taken part in the ritualistic rites of the cult.   With
all the foregoing information before our eyes, we are
probably justified in assuming that of all the fourteen
regions of Rome, the fifth being most densely populated,
contained the greatest number of inns, because of economic
reasons furnished by the institutions grouped there.

In the earlier years of the city's history, such curious
sightseers as flocked thither from all over Italy at the
seasons given over to public jollification were unable to
secure quarters in the inns as there were not enough of
them for the purpose.   On this account it was customary
to erect tents in the public spaces and in the inclosures
of the temples.   Dionysius of Halicarnassus tells us of
an encampment of the Volscians in similar circumstances.
They could find shelter only in that manner.   On their
return to their own country, they went into camp along
the road as the inns were also scarce in the country.

But the sites around which the taverns and inns would
cluster most advantageously would, of course, be those
on which the temples stood, and wherever there was a
temple, there was almost certain to be a number of taverns, and why not, one would ask?   Did not intemperate
drinking have its origin in religious festivals?   According
to an authority well versed in ancient lore "it was not
the custom of antiquity to indulge in wine, or any other
luxury to excess, except, indeed, on the occasion of some
sacred festival: which is the origin of the terms *thoinai,*
thaliai, and *methai.*   *Thoinai* means that men thought
it right and proper to drink wine on account of the gods:
thaliai they assembled and met together in honor of the
gods, and the term *methai* is derived from the custom of
using wine after having sacrificed."*

*Athenaeus, Lib. I, 61, Yonge's translation.

Another reason for the close relationship which throughout antiquity subsisted between the public houses and the temples was that peculiar taste which the gods never failed to manifest in preferring for their ceremonies those parts of the sacrificial victim which were unfit for human consumption. The priests and their cronies, however, labored under no such handicap and merrily complimented Jupiter with the guts and garbage, in complaisant obedience to his orders. The meat, therefore, must be eaten, but before being eaten, it must be cooked, and an understanding and sympathetic inn-keeper and his menage were of the utmost service to the clergy in attending to this part of the ritual. This arrangement was equally convenient for the priesthood and the tavern-keepers, as the one was assured of the finest joint and the other of excellent meat at a moderate price. A funeral inscription preserved by Fabretti has perpetuated the name of a freedman of Q. Critonius, who made a business of carving such animals, and of his concubine Philenia, who, in her tavern, situated on the Isla de Tiberi, next door to the temples of Jupiter, Aesculapius, and Faunus, served her patrons with the meat from the animals slaughtered for her lord and master. The term *popa* (a priest's assistant), notwithstanding Forcellini's objections, must be taken as representing in its meaning the entire relation subsisting between the clergy, the innkeeper, and the victims, and Martial and Cicero furnish many passages in substantiation of this. As for *popina* (an eating-house) it is impossible that it should admit an etymology other than that inherent in *popa*.

If the modern reader could only place entire credence in certain of the writings of Tertullian, which perhaps are but moderately tinctured with hypocritical sanctimony, the innkeepers set up shop in the vicinity of the

circus with more than one end in view, and not because
the crowds flocking to that institution would be certain
to give them much patronage. Their reason, according
to the Christian father, was that thereby they would
be near an excellent source of supplies and raw material.
Our devout and rigorous censor of Roman morals and
manners implies that the savage beasts of the arena,
for all the majesty of their ferocious presence, had after
all an ending no more poetic than that accorded to the
common alley tom-cat, and garnished the stew-pans of
the Roman cooks. What an ending! And, to the felines,
at least, what a satisfactory and poetic climax! Bear
steaks are by no means a modern conception: Scintilla,
the mistress of Habinnas the stone mason, ate some
before coming to Trimalchio's table. It is true that she
indulged herself without knowing what she was eating,
and it must have been equally true that her reaction
when suffering from better information would, under the
circumstances, have pleased the victim best of all. These
inns and taverns near the circus were scarcely more than
booths or stalls, many of them being mere sheds in the
vicinity of the institutions. Such also were the *cenabae*
in which, later on, we shall see the wine merchants of
the Forum Vinarium establish their headquarters. There
were also the *cenabulae*, rustic ordinaries, located along
the banks of rivers; they were generally constructed
from light tiles and were covered with creeper roses.
Sometimes the *cenabulae* were also known as *tabernulae*.
It was in an ordinary such as this, close to the temple
of Concord, that, in the year 664 A. U. C., the praetor
Sempronius Asellio perished, a victim to the fury of the
debtor classes, and the precedent which is as old as time.
Inasmuch as the thing is exceedingly curious we shall
permit Valerius Maximus to relate the occurrence. After
having spoken of the period of reaction and deflation

which followed in the steps of the Marsic War, when property values fell and there was little money in circulation, when debtors were unable to discharge the claims of their creditors, and the situation was more dangerous than the authorities seemed to realize.

"Their animosity broke out with horrible fury against Sempronius Asellio, the praetor, for having favored the interests of the creditors. Infuriated still more by Lucius Cassius, the tribune, they fell upon the praetor when he was sacrificing in front of the temple of Concord, drove him from before the altars of the public place, ran him to cover in a little tavern, and mercilessly tore him to pieces." (Lib. IX, 7, No. 4.)

While it was to be expected that the taverns would nestle around the great public establishments, such as the circus, temples, and barracks, they were also partial to a site near each of the two hundred corn mills where the common people came to grind the corn issued to them from the granaries. The work incident to turning the huge mill stones, which beasts of burden found it difficult to move, was exceedingly trying and fatiguing, and the citizen was naturally averse to doing more than necessary. For this reason, the mills were sometimes idle because of lack of help, and the master millers were compelled to find such remedies as the situation afforded, often sentencing culpable slaves to serve out their time at the task of turning the mill stones. As one experience was generally enough for even the hardiest sinner, other means of supplying the demand had to be devised. In this forced recruiting of labor the inns and taverns played a very important part, and were out and out accomplices of the millers. Let us cite a passage from the Historia Ecclesiastica of Socrates the Scholiast which informs us as to the expedients which were invoked and, at the same time comments upon the

justice of Theodosius in dealing with the conditions
brought to his notice:

"Although the emperor Theodosius did not remain
very long in Italy, his stay was nevertheless productive
of great and solid advantages to the city of Rome, not
only because of the profusion of his pardons but also
through the repressing of disorders and the rooting out
of their causes. One infamous custom he abolished which
had been in force through a long period of years. The
great establishments where formerly the bread had been
made which was distributed to the people had, as the
years passed, become the haunt of thieves. A number
of taverns had been built adjoining the mills, and the
foresight of the tavern-keepers provided a number of
abandoned women to attract custom and patronage.
Trap doors were installed to permit those who had come
there for diversion to be taken by surprise, and by means
of a certain contrivance, such unfortunates were dropped
into the place where the corn was ground. There, help-
less and in confinement, many slaved away their whole
lives without their relatives or friends ever being able
to get news of them. It so happened that a soldier
belonging to the forces of Theodosius was trapped in this
snare: he drew his dagger, wounded those who attempted
to secure him, and made his escape. The emperor, when
apprised of the situation, punished the officials of such
establishments, pulled down the lurking places of the
thieves and harlots, and purged Rome of that filthy
infamy."

To enable the reader to grasp the details of the picture which we are tracing of the places of public entertainment, which, by the way, were always subject to the
authority of the aediles empowered to arrest trouble
makers (loca aedilem metuenda), as Seneca terms them,
we are compelled to give some little space and attention
to the baths of Rome.

During the earlier times of the Republic, the aedile had little cause to make official entry into such establishments: he contented himself and the public conscience by merely seeing that they were clean and comfortable, and kept himself informed as to the character of the patrons who came there. The latter cause was relatively unimportant because of the fact that luxury had not invaded the system. The bath keeper in those times was an honest man exercising an honest calling and one of some importance to the public weal, as Rome was never swept with such epidemics as those that scourged the boorish uncleanliness of the Middle Ages. The baths and the water supply were the causes of this long immunity.

But the corruption of manners was not long in eating its way through the social fabric and involving the bathing officials. From them it penetrated to every department of the institution, and whatever it touched, it corroded. The balneator became a fornicator, a word which indicates with sufficient force and precision the disorder which had invaded the baths and the calling which the expert had come to exercise so complacently. Respect for the law of decent propriety which had ordered the separation of the sexes in these institutions had long been a dead letter, and the law itself, a grisly spectre of the past, a nemesis no longer invoked by aedile or censor, had come to be regarded by the favored classes with that amused contempt which a later generation has held to be the just reward of a too zealous paternalism on the part of the authorities: it must have produced on their minds an effect similar to that produced on our own by the faces of the older and more barbarous reformers, and when one had the misfortune to be born in an age too crude to appreciate his merits at their true worth he might well have found himself in Dennis's shoes:

> But Appius reddens at each word you speak,
> And stares tremendous with a threatening eye,
> Like some fierce tyrant in old tapestry.

Usage is one of the most potent factors in affecting the moral status of a community, whether for good or for evil, and prostitution ran rife through the baths soon after people began to be admitted to them in a state of complete nudity. Instead of baths, they were transformed into immense lupanars, equipped, in later times, with every aid to comfort and to sensuousness. With the arrival of night, which cast a kindly shadow upon conditions such as these, licence raised its ugly head, and a troup of women of pleasure, well skilled in every specialty and refinement in their calling, arrived at the baths, loitered in the corridors and inside the doors, and the bath attendants, on seeing them, opened the cells and extinguished the outside lights. The thermae were open day and night, and the noise and bustle about them reminded an observer of the clack and clatter of a great restaurant. Here the soft and insinuating whisper of lust was heard, and the caressing blandishments of self interest had unrestricted play. The orgies carried on here were of every kind, and while Cotytto may not have presided in person, her pupils were scarcely less abandoned than their preceptress. The curious reader is at liberty to consult Boulanger for the particulars, and the works of Guido Pancirollus for the entertainment and dancing. All the world might have forgathered here to dine, and nearly all the Roman world did. The emperors were patrons, and Caligula was one of the most enthusiastic supporters of the comessationes, as well as one of the first to set the fashion by which he perfumed from head to heel, his body carefully depilated, and left reeking with the odors which exuded from his pores, for it was then the fashion to perfume the wine and thus enhance physical appeal by temporarily overcoming unpleasant body odors. Some of the essences used in this manner were cold, others were in the form of vapor which was inhaled and did away for a short time with the stench of impostumated lungs in a close atmosphere. Our modern Lysistratas have much to learn in the arts of the toilette. In the times of which we speak, particular and expert slaves were assigned to the care of every orifice and every feature, and they all had special terms to designate them and no others. A Roman dandy or even a Roman lady, preparing for a comessatio, might have even taught our own society misses a little lesson in the gentle art of waiting. Some of them took hours over the toilette.

After the death of Caligula the customs of the baths took on a more sombre tone; in the times of Seneca they were less abandoned, but the philosopher remarks scathingly that although the baths were now sweet and clean, the populace was only the more foul. Under Commodus, Caracalla, and Heliogabalus, however, they reached a state of depravity and luxurious refinement to which there is no parallel. It was in the course of one of these entertainments that Caracalla delivered himself from the menace of his brother and co-ruler, Geta, as well as dispatching Sammonicus Serenus and others hostile to his power.

Fastidious men about town often arranged love trysts with the ladies, and the scene of such tender encounters was generally laid in the baths: they used them as moderns do the institutions of our times. Ovid advises lovers to meet at the baths, in his Art of Love.

A check system was in force but theft of clothing was frequent nevertheless. Catullus mentions it, and in Petronius we find a slave serving the rarest vintages to Encolpius and his friends because they had intervened

to rescue him from the fury of the steward whose clothing had been stolen through the carelessness of that
same slave. Eumolpus philosophizes on the same subject. He had the greatest difficulty in getting possession
of his meagre wardrobe and had to be completely identified before the officious bath attendant would surrender
possession, although a rogue of a more sinister character
got attentive service almost at once by virtue of the
natural charm of his person—proof positive to Eumolpus,
that it was less advantageous to polish the mind than it
was to massage the body. All bath attendants were
soon regarded in the eyes of the law as either prostitutes
or procurers. The reason for such discrimination lay in
the demands to which their calling made them heir.
One of Martial's characters was "unable to return home
sober from the baths," and Seneca has not a little to say
upon the same subject. Nor have we yet reached the
most distressing phase of the situation. In order that
every possibility might be discounted and every taste
accommodated, huge dining-rooms, called Nympheae, were
maintained.   Here women emancipated by marriage
from the restrictions which had bound them while still
under the parental roof, amused their wearied and
voracious leisure by inviting all the gluttons and long
nosed parasites whom previously they had hankered after
in vain, probably the most striking manifestation of the
utter depravity which had invaded and corrupted the
entire fabric of the Roman civilization. A newly married
couple, on the day after the bride had been lifted across
the threshold of her husband's door, would celebrate
their nuptials in one of the magnificently sumptuous
dining rooms attached to the baths, amid surroundings
and schemes of interior decoration of the most graphic
and elevating kind, and amid scenes of artistic nudity
which we have no words to describe, although Juvenal

has done very well in the passage which he devotes to this subject. It was as though one were to enter an establishment in which the women, chosen for beauty, blondness, mentality, and the most exquisite and minute knowledge of all the demands to which their profession subjected them, and the most complacent skill in catering to these demands, were to entertain their guests between silken sheets of the deepest black! The practice has much to recommend it as man has been relatively blind since Lynceus, but such cannot be said of the state of mind which evolved so sensational a complex and studied with deliberation to solve it. Roman culture was little concerned with anything but the quasi-artistic atmosphere of such ritualistic orgies, and the time had long passed since Horace wrote the little ode to the simple country maiden, Phidyle, whose modest soul had felt misgivings at the poverty of her sacrifice:

TO PHIDYLE

If thou to heaven thine upturned palms shall lift,
Sweet Phidyle, when glows the crescent moon
With virgin splendor, and thy simple gift
Shalt offer to thy gods and ask thy boon,

Nor scorching drought shall smite thy fruitful vine,
Nor blight attack thy harvest in the ear,
Nor shall thy flock for lack of pasture pine
When Autumn comes and chills the dying year;

Yea, Wealth's fat victims feed in pastures lush,
Or graze in lanes of ilex or of oak
To stain the ax, amid the solemn hush,
And die beneath the consecrating stroke;

Thy little gods require not such of thee,
For Innocence hath little to atone,
And wreaths of myrtle or sweet rosemary
Are all they ask to make thy lot their own:

> The rarest gift that Riches can confer,
> From outraged heaven's justice less commands
> Than does the humblest sacrifice of her
> Who brings it to the fane with spotless hands.

A very curious passage in Pancirollus describes in some detail one of these great nympheae: "Besides these basilicae, there were also at Rome eleven other edifices called nympheae, as Publius Victor informs us. They were spacious halls, made use of for nuptials, by those that had no conveniency of their own for such solemnities. And for this end (as Zonaras declares in the Life of Leo the Great) these nympheae (I suppose) were supported with pillars. They were built with kitchens, parlors, closets, and the like, wherein they laid towels and napkins, bowls and dishes, and other utensils, and were called nympheae because the Greeks called the bride a nymph. Capitolinus tells us the Gordian the emperor joined baths to his nympheae, for the ancients did frequently bathe before supper; and 'tis easy to gather as much from two laws of Theodosius and Valentinian. Suidas saith, that the water was brought to these bridal-houses from a fountain, called now, Enneacrunos, and formerly, Callirrhoe.

"These nympheae had also most stately and ample piazzas, large enough to walk in; one whereof Augustus built in the place where the house of Vedius Pollio (whose heir he was) was ruinated, and inscribed it with the name, not of Pollio, but of Livia, as Dion writes. And many others built glorious porticos." In the 1715 English translation of this old antiquarian is the following:

These were large and capacious Fabricks, design'd for the celebration of Nuptial Solemnities, and us'd only by those who had no Houses of their own: But this is contradicted by Alciatus and Beroaldus; who think it to be a very foul Error to imagine these Nympheae to be Genial Apartments appointed for marriages.

Some take them for Baths built by Princes for the sake of Posterity; wherefore Julius Capitolinus saith, that no Works of Gordian are remaining, besides the Nympheae and Baths. So that these Nympheae seem to be Tepida Lavacra, Warm Bagnios, and used for Pleasure, but not for Health.

But where is the Absurdity, if we affirm with our author, that Gordian did only adorn his Bridal-Houses with Baths adjoining? And what Soloecism is it to say, that by these Nympheae, we understand as well Baths for Women, as Nuptial Chambers?

Some say that brides were called Nymphs, apo to nun proto phainesthai, because they now expose themselves to open View, whereas formerly they appeared covered with a Veil. Nay, the Greeks call Matrimony itself Nymphaeum, because (as 'tis thought) Religion and Piety were propagated by Nymphs to Mankind, in regard no Rite or Worship was ever perform'd without their being mentioned. The Deities that presided o'er the Waters, were call'd Naiades; and because these Naiades were Nymphs in Corpora Tendentes, therefore Sobolis propagandae causa, New-marry'd Girls were term'd Nymphs.

CHAPTER XII.

Cato and the Sumptuary Laws—Contempt for the Law enforcers—
Orgiastic dances—Prices of foods and wines controlled—More of Nero's
slumming escapades—Julius Capitolinus, Commodus and Heliogabalus,
the most dissolute of all, patrons of the low taverns—Aurelian cleans the
Augean stables—Virgil pays court to the divinities of hospitality—
Horace the man about town.

We have already had occasion to speak of the gyne-
comus at Athens and the power invested in the office, a
power that prevented gatherings and picnics which comprised more than thirty individuals: we now find the
Roman law favoring a regulation almost the same, but
applying it to the entertainments in the nympheae. With
the individual guests invited, the law did not concern
itself further than to limit the maximum number that
could be in attendance. But an ancient proverb, a
joyous and spirited double entendre, took a sprightly
revenge upon the rule limiting the number of guests to
seven:

Septem convivium . . . novem convicium

a play on sound and sense, signifying a convivial party
of seven, may result in anything from a new meeting
to a recognition of hostility, or nine critics. Varro was
a trifle more indulgent in his estimate, for Aulus Gellius
quotes a passage from the Menippean Satires in which
the following passage occurs: That though the number
of guests should not be smaller than the number of
Graces, yet should it not exceed the number of the Muses.

However, there was still another reason for the surveillance maintained by the authorities, an inspection
that often invaded the home and the tavern. Among
the Romans some of the more austere citizens, such as

Cato, saw in the increase of luxurious appetites the seeds of ruin, and for this reason, they passed certain sumptuary laws designed to curtail the expenses which could be incurred in private dinners. As prodigality would increase the prices of commodities and place a hardship upon the shoulders of the common people, such laws, though opposed during their passage through the senate, were generally passed, but, like many of our own, soon fell into neglect, and were invoked and revitalized from time to time. Such powers were placed in the hands of the censors, who were better prepared to enforce them because of the nature of the office they held. One of the first regulations promulgated after the passage of the earlier sumptuary laws was to the effect that the citizen must eat his meals in the first room of the house, and leave his gates and doors wide open to make inspection easier and more rapid. "And this," says Pancirollus, whom we shall have frequent cause to cite in dealing with the bypaths of antiquity, "was to enable the censors passing by to ascertain whether the citizen living there was complying with all the provisions of the law and keeping within the limits prescribed. According to these laws, it was not legal to serve more than one hen; no poultry should be specially fattened for the table; on wedding days not more than two hundred asses could be expended on the entertainment, on certain festival days named in the Fannian Law, one hundred asses could be expended, on ten other days in each month not more than thirty asses could be lavished, and on all other days not more than ten asses could be spent. There were several of these laws, passed at different times, but all of them fell eventually into neglect."

The Licinian Law also provided that on ordinary days not more than three pounds of fresh meat should be served, and not more than one pound of salt meat.

Extravagance in funerals had been prohibited by the Twelve Tables, and a law of the dictator Sulla revitalized this ancient regulation and limited also the amounts that could be expended upon monuments: precepts which we today might imitate and follow to advantage.

Needless to say, the sumptuary laws were the occasion of some dissatisfaction, and the pride of the individual who successfully evaded them was commensurate with that of our own citizens in dealing with certain of the amendments to the American Constitution. In order that they might have finer and more caustic sport at the expense of the censor and his assistants, his living effigy was present at entertainments during the saturnalia, the seasons of the greatest licence and drunkenness, and filled the role of master of the feast, a toastmaster charged with the authority of regulating the drinks and prescribing the rules to be followed under a satiric and mocking exterior, the very personification of Folly in a merry mood. The regulations prescribed by him were a parody of the laws and mannerisms of the censor in office. He was chosen by lot after a throw of the dice. The so-called Cast of Venus (do not our own dusky experts at African golf continually call upon Little Joe from Kokomo or Little Dick from Boston?) decided his election and crowned him king of the revels. Once named, he threw himself heart and soul into his task, he impersonated the censor to admiration, and if the latter happened to be a martinet his vagaries and mannerisms were imitated and the mirth ran high. With all the gravity with which a little responsibility always invests a light weight, this pseudo-censor would take from the hands of the obsonator and the vinerius the lists setting forth the dishes and the vintages, and should they prove too numerous and extravagant, it boded ill for the host! This little satire on manners and customs

must have been highly diverting to the other guests
and might even be said to approach in subtle delicacy
our own "ain't prohibition grand," heard so frequently
when the juniper and the coriander begin to get in their
insidious work. The principal charge, however, a thing
that occupied the serious attention of our toastmaster,
was fixing the number of bumpers to be tossed off by
each guest: the bigger the bumper the oftener it came
around, and they were good drinkers in those days. This
mock-heroic monarch, personification of contempt for
law, this index to a state of mind that considered nothing
but its own amusement and convenience, carried matters
to the very heights of sardonic banter by promulgating
outlandish orders among the guests, who were duty
bound to obey them with a smile even as the serious
orders of constituted authority provoked sorrow and
tragedy more frequently than joy. He could command
a guest to vilify himself, as being the best possible authority upon the subject; another would be ordered to dance
in a state of nature and to sing a song, a third would
take the nude flute girl upon his shoulders and lead the
orgiastic procession through the whole establishment, the
customary number of tours being three:

> Thy praises shall be sung
> By youths who thrice shall dance around thy shrine,
> Happy in youth and full of this year's wine.
> —Petronius, Hymn to Priapus.

Another might be called upon to blacken his face
with soot, another to leap into a pool of water chilled
with December's rigors. Those most successful in execut-
ing the letter and spirit of the orders received were
awarded as a prize a magnificent sausage or other appropriate trinket no less recondite.

Such is the nature of the "so-called human race,"
that so fine an example as that set by the wealthy liber-

tines would never have been lost upon the lower orders, and burlesques of a more revolting character took place in the inns and taverns, especially in those which lay beyond the city walls, although the eating-houses and pot-houses of such districts as the Esquiline, Velabri, Suburra, Trans Tiber, and, on a more elaborate scale, the Peace Ward (Vicus Pacis) must also have celebrated the Saturnalia in a lively and lubricous manner. The more the observer gets down to brass tacks with the commoners, the deeper one descends through the various social strata, the more he will encounter satire, acrid and mordant, merciless to those in power; it is a very natural revenge; they who suffer most and oftenest will always be found ready and eager to pay off their grudges when license and usage counter a temporary immunity. When the Saturnalia had passed, however, the Roman landlords were very chary of permitting the authorities to be complimented in such a manner; freedom of speech was punished severely whenever it became a menace to official peace of mind, and even at that early day, it was a case of the greater the truth the greater the libel. The aedile and his four myrmidons were empowered by the laws to inspect all places where food, wine, beer, and other luxuries and necessities were sold. He could order merchandise thrown into the river and the magistrates would sustain him in all his official acts, though there are instances on record where this official has permitted his zeal for reform to outrun his common sense, and then he has become a trifle lumpy in spots, as when the prostitute Hostilia drive the aedile from her establishment when he had no right of entry. She used bricks and stones with telling effect and the authorities reprimanded the aedile as being in the wrong in going to the place with his lictor.

The taverns were always under the eye of the police

and the regulation of such establishments was never a
task to be undertaken lightly. Some, which came within
the meaning of the term lupanar, he was not supposed
to enter because of the sacredness of his office and the
example he might thus furnish others. He could enter
the taverns and inspect them, however, see that the
prices were not too high, and cast the cold eye of official
formality upon the weights and measures to see that
they were not fraudulent, but conformed to the standards kept in the temple of Ops or in that of Jupiter
Capitolinus. Measures found dishonest were summarily
broken in pieces on the spot, and the tavern-keeper or
retailer was in for a crowded half hour if his case could
not be compromised in some manner. This law pertaining to weights and measures was enforced in every
part of the empire; it applied in an equal degree to the
Roman landlord and to the poor scullion who conducted
a pitiful stall amongst the Volscians, as Juvenal informs
us, and, according to Persius, to the retailers even at
Aratium.

We do not know whether the official authority of the
aedile was broad enough to include wine in its scope;
thus permitting him to condemn adulterated or diluted
products and order them dumped into the river, but we
do know that the vintners from Gades to Cappadocia
were past masters in adulterating and diluting. In
Petronius, Trimalchio classes all the bartenders under
the sign of Aquarius, and Martial has something to say
of those who diluted and those who did not.

> The vineyards are swamped with continual rains,
> But my innkeeper, will'e or nil'e
> Serves wine undiluted and won't take the pains
> To water my draught though it kill me.

Although the vigilance of the aedile had little to
reward it in dealing with the subtlety of the Roman

landlords and adulterators, it could, nevertheless, take
certain indirect measures against the former. Several
of the emperors promulgated decrees empowering the
aediles to arrest those selling certain commodities mentioned by name in the instrument, such, for instance, as
pastry. Some even went so far as to ban the sale of
every article of food except peas and pulse and other
vegetables, and this may throw a dim and flickering light
on the date of the Satyricon, as Encolpius and Ascyltos
had only a two as piece with which to purchase pease
and pulse when the necessity of redeeming the lost tunic
with the gold pieces in the hem suddenly confronted
them. Such decrees must have gravelled the tavern-
keepers especially when they had ready money in sight
if only they could furnish victuals; by feeding their customers they sold them drink, and by selling rum they
got the profits. Taverns were the perpetual cockpits
where the disorders and breaches of the peace had their
origin and frequently their solution. This would not
have been so bad, but unfortunately, such brawls were
carried out into the streets and resulted sometimes in
riots requiring the services of a maniple of praetorian
guards to quiet the mob and restore order. Tiberius
was the first to issue such an edict and it was extremely
severe in the penalties it provided.

The attitude of Claudius is more difficult to gauge.
At one time we find him confirming the severity of
Tiberius, as Dion Cassius reports, and at another he
speaks in the house in defense of these establishments,
and removes them from the surveillance of the aedile.

Nor was Nero less inconsistent than Claudius in his
persecutions of the innkeepers. He was one of the principal actors, in fact he played the stellar role, in the
orgies of the ganea at Baiae and along the coastline of
that lovely gulf; he spent his days in diversions such as

these, and at night he covered his head with a freed-man's cap or a mantle and made the rounds of the free-and-easies in the city, insulting those whom he met returning from supper, striking them and laughing the while as they were stripped of their cloaks; entering the smaller cabarets by force, pillaging wherever he went and sharing his booty with his confederates. Yet this same emperor who had roistered it merrily in every low dive and cabaret in the city did everything in his power to control the traffic of the innkeepers and keep them within bounds. Nor were his marauding expeditions the worst services he did the tavern-keepers; the decree of which we had spoken above as from Petronius, was of Nero's sanction and was signed by him; it prevented the sale of any cooked foods in the taverns and restaurants, save only vegetables, notwithstanding the fact that usage had long compelled them to serve delicacies of every sort before his time.

Vespasian's attitude toward public houses was no less severe, but he was parsimonious and austere by nature and when he levied war against these middlemen there were none who could accuse him of double dealing.

Many of the emperors followed the examples set by Claudius and Nero in their social habits and debaucheries, but none exceeded these two odious tyrants in the harshness and injustice meted out to the innkeeping classes. These must have resulted from their orgies. For example, we know that Verus was given to the frequenting of public houses, and spent his time there day or night, but we know nothing of any decrees promulgated by him against them or their owners; those who had amused his love of excess were safe from whatever spleen he might feel as the result of a big head, and his repentance, if he manifested any, did not take the form of proscriptive edicts and cruel and unusual punishments.

Julius Capitolinus does not leave us in ignorance of Verus's predilection for taverns and restaurants, nor does the malignity of the chronicler gloss over the excesses committed there.

"Emulating the examples set by Caligula, Nero, and Vitellius," says mine author, "he frequented the taverns and haunts of vice at night, his head enveloped in a cowl such as is worn by vagrant wayfarers; disguised in this manner, he mixed with the brawling roisterers and bullys, took part in their battles, and came home with his face and body a mass of bruises and contusions. In spite of his disguise, he was well known in these taverns. Sometimes he amused his ennui by throwing heavy pieces of money at the vases and porcelains, to break them."

By instinct, this emperor was devoted to low amusements. The achievements of a Caligula seemed common and ordinary to him, and he would have fallen asleep over them. Caligula established a lupanar in his palace; Verus set up a tavern in his. Caligula served his familiars as bogau and water-boy; Verus beguiled his in his capacity of tavern-keeper and entertainer: a sort of chaperone to predaciousness, as it were: in other words, he exercised all three callings at the same time.

"His manners," to quote again from Capitolinus, "his manners were so dissolute that on his return from Syria he set up a tavern in his palace, whither he betook himself as soon as he could leave the table of Marcus Aurelius; here he rendered services and extended a hospitality which out-rivalled all the infamies of Rome."

According to Trebellius Pollio, the habits and inclinations of Gallienus were closely akin to those of Commodus, of whom we have just spoken. Of him also it was said that "he passed all his nights in the taverns, and lived and amused himself with all the go-betweens, mimes, actors, and actresses and witty rascals," whom he could meet. And as for Heliogabalus, we need not stay our progress to relate his exploits when Saltus in his Imperial Purple has done us that favor. Had there been no English translation of the Augustan History, we might still have gone into his career, but the need, if it exists, has been nobly met. Suffice it to say that Heliogabalus was probably the most dissolute androgyne that ever dishonored the throne of any nation. Compared to him, Sardanapalus was an immaculate conception. This emperor was a constant frequenter of cafés and all they stood for in an age whose unbridled viciousness has never been approached in public. Commodus was the incarnation of evil, a brutish and uninstructed evil, his influence could scarcely have corrupted the minds of those about him, on the contrary, he filled them all with the most raging contempt, as is shown in the manner in which his body was dragged with the hook: Heliogabalus, however, more abandoned than the son of Marcus Aurelius, had, withal, a certain refined charm; he could appeal to the better feelings of strangers upon first meeting them; he was physically very handsome, and, on occasion he had the capacity for wit without cruelty. Such a character may be a frightful menace to an entire city, especially if its owner is invested with absolute power and inviolability. This is especially the case when the individual is disposed to use his power to minister to the self interest of others. Under Heliogabalus every order of society was affected by the festering contagion induced by an utter lack of all moral values, and it is left to the melancholy historian who wishes his race well and to the malignant chronicler who perhaps has suffered under a tyranny no less bitter in that its mandates were couched in gentle terms and soothing phrases, to comment upon conditions which surround them.

It is with relief that we turn this filthy page and

come at length to the age of Aurelian, that stern re-
storer of character and discipline who only preoccupied
himself with inns long enough to instruct one of his
lieutenants to see that the soldiers did not lavish upon
the eating-houses and taverns the pay from the money
belts worn by them. The same thought must have animated Hadrian in the sparkling retort courteous which
he sent to Florus. Aside from the fact that he was a
poet and a friend of Hadrian, we know nothing of Florus:
some authorities have been inclined to attribute the
Copa to him. He had written in a bantering style to
Hadrian:

> No Caesar would I want to be,
> Inspecting Britain's wastes,
> Lurking in savage (Germany)
> No Scythian frosts would suit my tastes. . . .

And Hadrian answered him:

> No Florus would I want to be,
> Inspecting bar-maid's waists,
> Lurking in a hostelry,
> No fat round insects suit my tastes.

The inns play a greater part in public life than ever
before, some are sumptuous, but the majority must still
have been tawdry and repulsive. Yet Florus did not
stand alone in paying his court to the divinities of
hospitality. Many of the finest poetical geniuses of all
ages were similarly smitten. We have already called
attention to Virgil's Copa, that lithe and sinuous purveyor of sensations; we have seen Lucilius react to the
advances of another of the same species; and Horace in
his writings speaks of many affairs with innkeepers.
The epithets which he bestows upon them are generally
sarcastic, auguring unpleasant experiences and dissatisfaction with their customary hardihood at impudent

repartee, which was more in the style of the bludgeon
than the rapier.   "Yon vintner, an exceeding knave,"
says our author, in instructing neophytes in the rhetorical
art of treating subjects in a manner natural to themselves
and to human experience.   Elsewhere he speaks of the
greasy eating-house, though the passage may mean the
reverse as he is remonstrating with his steward who is
totally lacking in appreciation for the rustic life on the
Sabine farm, and has requested a transfer:

> A wench,
> The greasy luxury of a tavern bench,
> 'Tis this I see, that makes you long for town,
> And you on that dear nook of mine look down;
> Because the spice of Eastern climes you know
> As soon or sooner, theme than wine will grow;
> Because too there's no tippling house hard by
> To drop into whenever you feel dry;
> No piping jade your heavy heels to set
> Jigging and jumping to her flageolet.
>   (Martin's Translation.)

In another passage he uses the term caupona and
again it is to express dissatisfaction; he advises his friends
Scaeva to go to Ferentinum for rest and relaxation as
the noise of Rome is scarcely less nerve wracking than
that of an inn:

> If what you lack be sweet unbroken rest,
> And sleep till after dawn; if you detest
> Worry, and dust, and smother, and the din
> Of cars and carts, and of a noisy inn. . . .

However, Horace was too much of the man-about-
town not to have regaled himself many times in the
taverns of a gayer aspect: more than once, as he tells
his steward, he had tasted the delights his steward craves,
but he was ever a critic denouncing the uproar of the

inns and taverns as one of the plagues with which Rome was afflicted.

Martial expresses himself more freely; he delights in taverns and avows it without the least restraint:

"An innkeeper, a butcher, baths, a barber, a well furnished exchequer, a few books of my own choice, a friend not too ignorant, a young lady who is pleasing to my slave, a huge fellow of a slave, not too lively, but of an age which will permit him a long life; give me these, Rufus, and let them even be at Byzantium, but I will cede you the baths of Nero with all my heart."

Sometimes he wets his youthful muse with wine of Crete, country of Minos, that wine which is the nectar of poverty:

"The vines of Crete, country of Minos, produce that liquor, the ordinary wine of the people."

Again he may have felt impelled to take a meagre repast from one of the peripatetic stalls which a yelling cook pushed from tavern to tavern. This may not have satisfied the inner man, but, nevertheless, he got some of his finest touches from surroundings and contacts such as these.

> Syriscus has run at so rapid a pace
> 'Tween the benches of tavern and stew
> That he's now neck and neck in a bankruptcy race
> And the million he had is run through;
> "A million devoured! What a glutton," you'll say;
> Aye, a gulligut glutton, to do it that way!

CHAPTER XIII.

The literati—Philostratus's beautiful tribute to a cabaret girl—Nero as a cabaret singer—Catullus flays the lewd taverns—Juvenal's description of the lupanars—Patricians liberal patrons, many being tavern owners—Trimalchio speculates in wine—Plutarch tells of the baseness of the inns.

The literati and declaimers of the times, the rhetoricians and out at elbow philosophers and intellectuals, made the taverns and thermopolia their headquarters: here they gathered to gossip and discuss affairs of everyday life, and they were probably no vainer or more verbose than the expatriated sophists who came from Greece in the times of the Scipios under the pretext of refining the local customs and social usages, and giving a rhetorical and artificial polish to the rude vigor of the old Latin tongue.   In reality, however, they set a fine example of tavern swilling and wenching, and the term pergraecari (to drink like a Greek) was coined to describe their cultivated avidity in this exercise.

Plautus, who was contemporary with them, has drawn a picture which enables us to see them as they were, enveloped from head to heel in their cloaks, which were equipped with cowls to cover the head.   They stagger under the weight of the books they are carrying, on their way to the tavern, there to drink themselves into a state of philosophical abstraction which will make them for hours immune to all the crudities with which they are surrounded.   Let one of them catch the scent of wine and he becomes prudent, simulating the countenance of a drunken man under a thoughtful mien of philosophy. Under the emperors they are still the same, displaying the same old vices and masquerading under the same

philosophy. One of them, however, has avowed his
intimacy and has immortalized the object of his adora-
tion: I speak of Philostratus, a Greek sophist of the
deepest dye, yet who did yeoman service in refining the
crudities of a language already effeminate, a language
degenerating under the subtleties of a philosophy of
decadence. His example was one that others could
follow: he frequented taverns as he chose. If he permitted sentiments so exquisite to flow from his pen it
must have been because he was more moved by love
and artistic appreciation than by drunkenness. A girl
of the cabarets has attracted his glance; probably to
order something to drink: he sees her eyes, and, like
Catullus translating Sappho,

> A-down my limbs flows subtle flame
> My ears are ringing with her spell
> My eyes see naught but night!

Yes, the glance of an eye weaned him away from the
fetishes of a lifetime; he ceased scoffing at chastity, and
wrote three little letters, one might almost be tempted
to call them madrigals, that contain the finest essence
of worshipful appreciation. These resulted from the
spell which the tavern Hebe threw over him and were
born of the inspiration with which she fired his soul.
They are sincere, they voice a refined passion, they
have survived the ages, and they are of the very stuff
of the gallantry not only of Greek antiquity, but of the
gallantry of all time.

Charmingly simple, they must have been addressed
to a character no less lovely.

TO A CABARET GIRL

"Everything about you delights me; to me your robe
of linen is the peplum of Isis; your tavern the temple of

Aphrodite, your chalices so round and shining the eyes of Hera, your wine has the bouquet of ambrosia itself, and the three fingers you extend to take up the cup are like the triple rose entwined in the sacred chaplet.

"I tremble lest the cup shall fall, but no, it is as firm in your hand as a sun dial on its base, and reminds me of a flower pushing out and growing from between your fingers.

"If you would touch the cup lightly with your lips and warm the wine with your breath it would be sweeter than nectar. It would run through every vein and every nerve would tingle. It would be more than wine . . . it would be a draught of kisses.

"Your cups are of glass. In your hands they become silver and gold and your touch communicates to them I know not what of softness and gleaming charm. Yet it is a transparence dull and without reflection, like that of a sleeping lake. Ah, how it differs from the radiance of your eyes sparkling with the joyous spirit of your countenance. What sweetness they convey to me, with what a thirst for kisses they inflame my senses!

"The cup is fragile and easily broken, place it upon the table; with such eyes as yours, I have no other need.

"Your glances alone intoxicate me even as do those of the adorable child, the cupbearer to the god of gods, under whose soft glances Zeus brings on his drunkenness.

"Yea, serve me no more with that flavorless nectar, water alone shall suffice; bring but the cup to your lips, implant thereon your kisses, and when I would drink present it to me. Where is the man who could demand wine, the gift of Dionysus, when Aphrodite offers him her ambrosia?

"Your eyes are more transparent than the crystal of your cups, and they mirror your soul. The color of your cheeks is more brilliant than that of the wine itself.

The whiteness of your linen robe is reflected in your face, and your lips are tinted with the blood of roses. Your eyes, humid and lovely, are like those of the statues adorning our fountains; they weep with the joy of living. Yea, you are one of the nymphs.

"And they whom you cause to halt in their course, who remain when their intention was to pass by without, yea, you know how to invite them without speaking a single word.

"As for myself, what a thirst I had the first time I saw you. The cup remained immovable in my hand in spite of my unwillingness. I could not bring it to my lips. I drink to your eyes."

Any and all of these little pastels might have been odes of Anacreon to the nymphs of the vintages, and they have immortalized a hostess whose exquisite simplicity and loveliness could only detract from itself by adornment. With such a subject poetic enthusiasm and lyric rhapsody cannot be out of place, whether it be a tavern girl or a geisha, and, as we have remarked, many of the classical poets and many that have come after them gained their finest inspiration from the girls of the cabarets. The Syrian *ambibia* has danced for us, we have been enthralled by the rustic flute that enchants the echoes of garden and tavern, and, if we search diligently enough, perhaps we shall find the material with which to complete our picture of the olden time, the lyric and poetic side of the tavern life of Rome. It is not our intention to introduce our readers to any ordinary songbird such as is to be met with in our own cafés chantants; nor shall we inflict the falsetto screechings of a cabaret lizard upon the unwilling ears of our patrons and torture their patience with doubtful and obscene double entendres. For lack of a performer more illustrious, we shall introduce Nero himself; Nero, whose joy and pride lay in singing in the taverns, garbed as an entertainer, and who decreed a fête day whenever he thus distributed his largesse. Philostratus has related a very curious fact. He is speaking of the exile of Demetrius, a cynic philosopher contemporary with himself, but less addicted to questionable places and more restrained and austere in his manner of speaking and writing.

"One day Demetrius was ranting in the gymnasium, the object of his scorn was the institution of the baths. He characterized them as places which catered to extravagance and which served all the effeminates who went there for the purpose of polluting their bodies under the pretext of washing them. It so happened that on that very day Nero was singing in a cabaret next to the gymnasium, and had surpassed himself. He was clad like any innkeeper, in a pair of drawers and the rest of his body was naked. Tigellinus, the praetorian prefect, informed him as to what Demetrius had said and construed the words as a satire directed against Nero's conduct in the cabaret. Nero was furious and deported Demetrius, 'as though,' says Philostratus, 'the baths might have tumbled down before the breath caused by his words." This anecdote is curious not only because of what it teaches us of Nero, but also because it bears out what we have said of the understanding which existed between the baths, gymnasia and the taverns. According to Isadore of Seville (Origines, Lib. XIV, Chap. 2), the taverns adjoining the baths went under the name *popinae*, but Lefebre (Agnostiques Lib. III, Chap. 28), remarks that the cabarets operating with the gymnasia at Rome were called *ebeterion*.

We should not be astonished at the praise lavished by Philostratus upon the cabaret girl: the Roman innkeepers were not blind to beauty, nor were they oblivious to the

effect of exquisite loveliness upon trade. Twenty centuries later we shall see Madame Bourette, the Muse of
Lemonade Sellers, enthroned in her café in the rue Bour-
bon-Villenueve: the goddess who reigns in the café du
Bosquet does so by virtue of her beauty and charm; and
many another Hebe shall officiate in establishments where
sherbet is sold, or chocolate, where the prices are high but
the buying public is more than anxious to bask in the light
of the beauty's smiles; to court her favors, and press a
fortunate moment for all it is worth. In them is the
origin of the charming cashier system.

They knew well that a pretty face, animated with the
joy of living, is a finer appeal to good-will than the most
subtle and piquant sign; a glance of the eye was more
potent than all the haranguing of an obsequious and
fawning predaciousness at the threshold of the tavern, as
for instance we find in Juvenal:

"And when it pleases Lateranus to go back to the all
night tavern, some Syro-Phoenician runs forth to meet
him—some denizen of the Idumaean Gate perpetually
drenched with perfumes—and salute him as lord and
prince with all the airs of a host; and with him comes the
venal Cyane with her robe tucked up, carrying a flagon
of wine." (Sat. VIII, 158 et seq.)

And then again we may take the case of Aulus Binnius, the jolly tavern-keeper, of whom Cicero speaks so
slightingly in what is probably the finest defense for the
wild oat fields sown by the exuberance of youth:

"And it is also reported to us that you suborn an
entertainer of many guests, a certain Aulus Binnius, an
innkeeper on the Via Latina, to say that violence was
offered to him in his own tavern." (Pro Cluentio,
ch. 59.)

The women of the common people well knew what
success would wait upon their charms if they became

cabaret girls: therefore, when they abandoned their status of virtuous mediocrity where virtue was too often its own reward, it was with full knowledge of what to expect and a willingness to pay the price necessary; to marry a tavern-keeper was the goal they set themselves to reach. They generally consulted some oracle or other as to what the matrimonial future had in store for them:

"The woman who displays a long gold chain on her bare neck inquired before the pillars and the clusters of dolphins whether she will throw over the tavern-keeper and marry the rag man." (Juvenal VI, 589 et seq.)

Custom and good-will flowed into taverns such as these where pretty young women were in attendance; but their morality was in inverse ratio to their business and the very nature of the calling augured complaisance. See what havoc two beautiful eyes can make! How powerfully they attract custom! When the mistress whom Catullus loved so deeply ran away from her house to the tavern near the temple of Castor and Pollux, see how the patronage increased: two hundred customers at the very least, but such customers! All more or less hardened. And see how well the tavern deserved to be flayed by the indignant poet in the injurious epithet with which he salutes it: *Salax taverna*—lewd tavern:

"Lewd tavern, the ninth sign-post from the pileated brothers' temple, and you, its frequenters, do you think that you alone have the attributes of manhood? That you alone are licensed to kiss the girls all and sundry and hold all other men at naught, you rank he-goats? Is it because you sit there night and day, a hundred boobies or two, that you think I will not venture to tackle the whole two hundred of you at once? Aye, but you may think it, and I will write inscriptions all over the front of your tavern. For my girl who has fled from my bosom, my girl, whom I loved as woman was never loved

before, for whom I have waged great wars, has sat herself
down there; and now you all make love to her; pleasant,
comfortable fellows, and—what is really too bad—all of
you pitiful knaves, gallants of the by-streets, and you,
Egnatius, above all, one of the long haired race from the
rabbit warrens of Celtiberia, you whose merit consists
in a bushy beard, and teeth bleached white."

Catullus complains bitterly of the injury done him,
but he makes no allowance for the fact that he had taken
her from a similar place when he came to an understanding with her. That was the usual custom, and all the
women who have been loved and immortalized in the
couplets of the Latin poets probably came from places
such as the one spoken of above. They were daughters
of *lupanar* or tavern. In writing of the Syrian hostess
Virgil did not stoop, he merely followed the example set
by Catullus and Lucilius before him. Horace flirted
with the *mendax puella* (lying jade) in the smoky house
at Trivicum, and the calling she exercised made not the
slightest difference to him. Propertius had an inveterate
passion for intrigues such as these, and whenever his
trifling with Thais or Phyllis threw Cynthia into trans-
ports of jealous rage her fury spent itself on his devoted
head: she would rush with dishevelled hair into the rustic
arbor in which Propertius had abandoned himself to
drunkenness under the charm of their dances and the
blandishment of their caresses. Where, then, could they
find sanctuary, except in the tavern that knew them first?
And Cynthia, or, if we are to believe Apuleius, Hostia,
was always too faithless herself to have been permitted
to exercise the rights conferred by honest jealousy.
Whither then could she betake herself when pride demanded that she abandon her lover? To an inn on the
Appian Way, the retreat of others no less disorderly,
where she was free without reproach to enjoy the em-

braces and lavish favors of some new admirer, or some
libertine who had introduced her into his silken litter.

Shall we longer remain in doubt that the taverns of
Rome were lupanars? Perhaps the only difference lies
in the fact that they were completely open to the public
gaze, they were located on the forum and in conspicuous
places where all the world could see what went on and
hear the brawls and uproar. The lupanars, however,
were hidden away on dark and narrow alleys which
Plautus calls angiporta. The taverns were entered openly
without attempt at concealment, and through the front
door; whereas in the case of the lupanars prudence veiled
its head and waited till night to glide into them. From
this the term latebricolae (they that dwell in lurking
places, or, if you prefer, friends of darkness) was derived:
it was used to characterize those who frequented the
lupanars. Aside from what has been said above, the
two institutions were almost identical; whatever was
found in one could be had in the other, good cheer and
luxurious debauchery. A passage in the Poenulus of
Plautus is very much to the point and furnishes a vivid
scene. I refer to the entry of the slave Syncerastus into
the house of his master the procurer. There is little room
for error here. He always speaks of tavern and lupanar
as synonyms, a propriety which would have included
the guests as well. Syncerastus arrives upon the scene
with his arms laden with vessels for sacrifice and orgy;
all this paraphernalia he has brought to Rome and he
begins by speaking of his worthy master and the establishment conducted by him:

"It's very clear that gods and men neglect the benefit
of him who has a master with a character like my master's. There's not another person anywhere in the whole
world more perjured or more wicked than my master,
nor one so filthy and so defiled. So may the gods bless

me, I'd rather pass my life either in the stone quarries or at the mill, with my sides hampered with heavy irons, than pass this servitude with a procurer. What a race this is! What corrupters of men they are! Ye gods, by our hopes in you, every kind and condition of men you may see there, just as though you had come to Acheron—horse and foot—a freedman, a thief, or a runaway, if you choose, one whipped, chained or condemned. He that has got the wherewithal to pay, whatever sort of person he is—all kinds are taken in; throughout all the house, in consequence, are darkened spots, hiding-places; drinking and eating are going on just as in a cook-shop, and in no less degree. There may you see epistles written in letters inscribed on pottery, sealed with pitch: the names upon them are a cubit long, such a levy of vintners we have got at our house." (Plautus, Poenulus, Act IV, Scene ii.)

Were we to take a trip through our own cabarets we would not fail to recognize the types of Plautus, and we mention these types in order that we may fill in all the details and make a complete picture.

With this in view, let us then cite a passage from Juvenal, to give the finishing touches to the votaries and the establishments we have been describing. The passage is from Satire VIII, line 146 et seq.:

"The bloated Lateranus whirls past the bones and ashes of his ancestors in a rapid car; with his own hands this muleteer consul locks the wheel with the drag. It is by night, indeed, but the moon looks on; the stars strain their eyes to see. When his time of office is over, Lateranus will take up his whip in broad daylight; not shrinking to meet a now aged friend, he will be the first to salute him with his whip; he will unbind the trusses of hay, and deal out the fodder to his weary cattle. Meanwhile, though he slays woolly victims and tawny

An Innkeeper

steers after Numa's fashion, he swears by no other deity before Jove's high altar than the goddess of horseflesh, and the images painted on the reeking stables. And when it pleases him to go back to the all night tavern, a Syro-Phoenician runs forth to meet him—a denizen of the Idumaean Gate perpetually drenched in perfumes—and salutes him as lord and prince with all the airs of a host; and with him comes venal Cyane, her robe tucked up, carrying a flagon of wine for sale. An apologist will say to me, 'we too did the same thing as boys.' Perhaps: but then you ceased from your follies and let them drop. Let your evil days be short; let some of your misdoings be cut off with your first beard. Boys may be pardoned; but when Lateranus frequented those hot liquor shops with their inscribed linen awnings, he was of ripe age, fit to guard under arms the Armenian and Syrian rivers, and the Danube, and the Rhine: fit to protect the person of his emperor. Send your legate to Ostia, O Caesar, but search for him in some big cook-shop. There you will find him, lying cheek by jowl beside a cut-throat, in the company of bargees, thieves, and runaway slaves, beside hangmen and coffin makers, or of some eunuch priest lying drunk with idle timbrels. Here is Liberty Hall! One cup serves for everybody, no one has a bed to himself, nor a table apart from the rest. What would you do, friend Ponticus, if you chanced upon a slave like this? You would send him to your Lucanian or Tuscan bridewell. But you gentlemen of Trojan blood find excuse for yourselves; what would disgrace a huckster sits gracefully on a Volesus or a Brutus!"

At last the tableau is complete; not a thing has been omitted nor a type overlooked. You have beheld every variety of eating-house glutton or tavern parvenu; the *tricones*, and, as Seneca has called them, in speaking of their wine swilling, *scordali*. We have beheld the priests of Cybele, fat and thick set, who fraternize with the Syrian *ambubia*, and the thieves who are doubtless as well received there as at the public baths, if we may place credence in what Seneca has to say: and, in addition, the pack of idle and slanderous slaves who have come here in attendance upon their masters and who occupy their leisure by getting drunk and gossiping. Who knows but they may have been sent here to get them out of the way?

"While the performance is going on," says Plautus, in the prologue to the Poenulus, "you lacqueys make an onset on the cookshops; now, while there's an opportunity, now while the monogrammed tarts are smoking hot, hasten there."

The tavern-keeper, well posted in every detail, knew the secrets of every customer of importance who patronized him—a splendid chance for blackmail and a fruitful source of profit, favor, and immunity. Ammianus Marcellinus remarks that no matter how haughty the patrician of his times was to provincials bearing letters of introduction, no matter how studied his insolence to those from whom he had nothing to gain, whenever he met at the baths with any of the ministers of his pleasures, he would become gentle courtesy itself and his condescension was not that of noble to commoner or slave, but that of friend to friend.

"Close the doors and windows," says Juvenal, "extinguish the lights, stop up all the cracks, dismiss all the witnesses, and though the noises of the neighborhood prevent things from being heard, before dawn, before the cock crows for the second time, the tavern-keeper will know not only everything that was said, and everything that was done; and not he alone, the cook, and the staff of the establishment."

Thanks to Plautus and Juvenal we have been able to

see the patrician in his relationship to the taverns and inns, we have also followed the footsteps of other less exalted disciples of the same cult, and why should we manifest astonishment, when even the emperors set them all an example? But we shall be astonished at learning that the Roman nobles, not content with merely haunting the taverns, sometimes turned taverner on their own account. The thing is so strange, and the Roman patrician was so jealous of his standing, that we would not believe it possible were it not for the testimony of such a witness as Pliny:

"In the ninth year of the reign of Tiberius, the equestrian order was brought together into a single organization. The formulae giving the right to wear the ring were drawn up, in the consulship of C. Asinius Pollio and C. Antistius Vetus, in the year of Rome 775, and, a thing very remarkable, an instance of futility caused the change.

"C. Sulpitius Galba, seeking to conciliate the good graces of the prince by decisions of a young man, had established penalties for the infractions to which tavern-keepers were liable. He complained to the senate of great opposition to his plans. 'The proprietors of illegal establishments,' said he, 'evaded these penalties, thanks to their rings.' It was enacted that no person should wear the equestrian ring, whoever he might be, unless his father and his father's father before him had been free, and furthermore, unless he possessed 400,000 sesterces, and unless he could be admitted to sit in the first fourteen rows of the theatre, according to the provisions of the Julian Law." (Pliny, Hist. Nat. Lib. XXXIII, ch. 8.)

Such legislation would have been futile had it not been fortified with other measures which nullified any possibility of a tavern-keeper's being able to scale the social and economic ladder and rise to a position which entitled him to rank with the patrician. While these measures dealt the whole innkeeping class a severe blow, they were by no means prostrated; and though the lowly wine seller might not aspire to the rank of a knight, the processes of economy enabled him to sate his ambitions along other lines: his vanity made him ape the fads and fashions set by the nobles, and his wealth placed the necessary means in his hands. The most outstanding instance of bigoted arrogance, yet kind hearted, withal, is the character of Trimalchio. Martial in several of his epigrams has summed this situation up and in one, especially, he has left us nothing to be desired:

"Cultured Bononia, a cobbler gave you an exhibition, and a fuller gave one to Mutina. Where, now, shall the tavern-keeper give his?" (Lib. III, 59.)

In Petronius we find Norbanus using this means to political affluence and position, and it is well known that Julius Caesar used the same device upon an unprecedented scale in preparing the minds of the people to take his yoke upon their necks.

The tavern-keepers and the callings allied to that of innkeeping were prosperous, as a rule, as they tempered their trust to the necessities of a given situation; where credit would do them good they sometimes extended it, where failure to extend credit was likely to procure mine host a sound drubbing, he was liberal, but generally speaking we believe the attitude of Cleoereta, the *laena* in Palutus's Asinaria, is more in keeping with the tenets of the past:

"Daylight, water, the sun, the moon, the night, these things I purchase not with money; the rest, whatever we wish to enjoy, we purchase on Grecian trust.*

"When we ask bread of the baker, wine from the wine-shop, if they receive the money they give their wares.

*Cash in hand.

The same principle do I go upon, my hands always have eyes in them, they believe what they see; there's an old saying: 'Trust is good for nought,' you know whose it is, I say no more." Act I, Scene iii.

There was great profit in selling wine: Trimalchio remarked that he had laid the foundations of his fortune by a lucky speculation in wine and foodstuffs. There was also a fine profit in selling food products to be consumed where sold: although the landlord had the right to retail all sorts of vintages, Falernian, Caecubian, Setian, his real profits were derived from the sale of inferior products, and then, as always, the public suffered as a consequence. Adulteration, artificial fortifying, synthetic ripening: all these arts were generally practised by the vintners and soon brought some of the finest wine producing provinces into a disrepute which they little merited. This was especially true with certain portions of southern France.

As far as the innkeeper went, however, the beggars of the Porta Trigemina and the Velabrum had a finer opportunity to taste the wretched Laletanian vintage and get from its cloudy harshness all the kick that could be desired. Martial, who must have known this wine well, recommends it to Sextilianus:

"Sextilianus, you yourself drink as much as five rows of benches; you could get drunk drinking as much water. Not only do you take the tokens of your neighbors, but you ask, also, the bronze coins of those farther from you. This vintage is not from Pelignian wine presses nor was the grape juice born on Tuscan hillsides; you drain dry a jar of ancient Opimian; Massic stores furnished the blackened jars. If you must have more than ten drinks, Sextilianus, go and get cloudy Laletanian from the innkeeper." (Epigr. Lib. I, 27.)

Tavern-keepers were so accustomed to serving base

and inferior vintages without discussion, and without
even ascertaining whether the customer had any preference in the matter of drink, that when some guest did
demand better wine it was the cause of some surprise and
sometimes got the would-be purchaser into difficulties.
Mine host was forward to require an explanation of such
an anomaly on the part of some slave or some lowly
commoner, and the rumor would soon filter out that some
lord or high official was lodged there for the time being.
The Roman orator Marcus Antonius, grandfather of the
triumvir, would not otherwise have been dragged from
his hiding-place in the proscriptions of Marius.   And so
it has always been: the insatiable curiosity of a tavern-
keeper and the gossipings of some slaves have often been
the causes which have led to discovery and to murder.

Plutarch has related the episode with all his verve
and realism, and the facts speak for themselves in utter
condemnation of the baseness of the tavern-keepers, and
their addiction to delation; their malignant espionage,
and their perpetual league with the slaves and des-
peradoes:

"Marcus Antonius the orator, though he, too, found
a true friend, had ill fortune.   The man was but poor
and a plebeian, and as he was entertaining a man of great
rank in Rome, trying to provide for him with the best he
could, he sent his servant to get some wine of a neighboring vintner.   The servant, carefully tasting it and bidding
him draw better, the fellow asked him what was the matter, that he did not buy new and ordinary wine as he
used to do, but richer and of a greater price; he, without
any design, told him, as his old friend and acquaintance,
that his master entertained Marcus Antonius, who was
concealed with him.   The villainous vintner, as soon as
the servant was gone, went himself to Marius, then at
supper, and being brought into his presence, told him

he would deliver Antonius into his hands. As soon as he heard it, it is said he gave a great shout, and clapped his hands for joy, and had very nearly risen up and gone to the place himself; but being detained by his friends, he sent Annius and some soldiers with him, and commanded him to bring Antonius's head to him with all speed. When they came to the house, Annius stayed at the door, and the soldiers went upstairs into the chamber; where, seeing Antonius, they endeavoured to shuffle off the murder from one to another; for so great, it seems, were the graces and charms of his oratory, that as soon as he began to speak and beg his life, none of them durst touch or so much as look upon him; but hanging down their heads, every one fell a weeping. When their stay seemed something tedious, Annius came up himself and found Antonius discoursing, and the soldiers astonished and quite softened by it, and, calling them cowards, went himself and cut off his head."

The strangest thing about this murder is that the facts as elegantly related by Plutarch are in exact agreement with Voltaire's relation of the death of Coligny in the massacre of Saint Bartholomew's eve. Stranger still, the manner in which the hiding place of Antonius was discovered was identical with that of General Pichegru's betrayal—always in the place of a tavern-keeper who may or may not be involved in the plot. As the story of Pichegru's betrayal is an excellent commentary upon that of Antonius we shall introduce it here, with apologies to Merimée. The speaker is Madame Leblanc, the principal actress in the affair and one of the staff of the theatre Clara Gazul:

"Ah, Elisa," says the spy, speaking to her daughter, "in affairs such as these nothing can be neglected. It was by means of a roasted chicken that I was enabled to discover the hiding-place of General Pichegru; and without boasting, the affair did me great honor, to say nothing of the profit it provided. Here is how it all came about. Your father was alive then, Captain Leblanc. He had returned from the army; he had wealth. We had a good time of it and lived brilliantly. One day I went to my caterer and demanded a roasted fowl of him. 'My God, madame,' he replied, 'I am greatly distressed, I have just sold my last one.' As for myself, I knew the entire quarter and I wished to know to whom he had sold it. 'Who got it,' I demanded of him. 'Such and such an one,' he replied, 'he treats himself very well, too, and every day for the past three days he has had a fowl of me for his dinner.' Note well that it had been just three days since we had lost all trace of General Pichegru. I turned the matter over and over in my head, and I said to myself, 'The devil, neighbor, you have got an appetite, you are famishing.' Finally, I came back the next day and purchased some partridges which were not yet cooked done, remarking at the same time that I would send my scullion for them when they were ready. Then my man of the great appetite entered and bought a roasted turkey, and a fine turkey it was, too, take my word for it. 'Ah,' said I to him, 'what a thing, you surely have a great appetite, enough for two persons for a week.' He winked his eye at me and replied, 'Yes, I have appetite enough for two.' A Frenchman must always make the best of an opportunity for an epigram. I watched him with both eyes; he turned away, mounted his horse, and set off. He did not mislead me to his advantage, I knew that he knew General Pichegru. My man is apprehended and he surrenders up my general with right good will as an honest recompense, and I for my part, six thousand francs' worth of gratification."

Proof positive that even a conspirator should have due regard to the finer points of diet and that one should by all means avoid transgressing the proprieties whatever they may be locally. Eating roast fowl or drinking rare wines in neighborhoods in which such luxuries are not common articles of table or cellar is the very height of stupidity.

As for the taverns and inns of classical Rome, we have long held the opinion that the institutions which resembled them most strikingly, were the cabarets of papal Rome, and we have the evidence of William Savage in our favor.

"The disposition of these cabarets," says he, "is uniform, they are long chambers with a vaulted ceiling, a sort of shed and kitchen combined.

"Long tables are found here, and the benches, mere trestles, evilly constructed and crude in the extreme, have little but strength to recommend them. The master of the place is seated upon a kind of chair or on a platform, the serving boys are in the most complete negligee, the walls are coarsely painted, some bearing inscriptions such as the following:

" 'QVANDO QVESTO GALLO CANTARA, ALLORA, CREDENZA SI FARA.'

" 'When that cock shall crow then credit will be given.' Above the inscription is a rude likeness of the gallus gallinaceus or dunghill cock, and the emblem is surely the very pink of propriety; a pithy commentary upon the honesty of the host and the trade which he has gained."

That little platform on which the host is seated is but a repetition of the older one on which the bar-maid took her ease and the trestles or benches were also copied from originals more ancient, as a well known scene from Pompeii proves. Martial speaks of a bench ridden tavern (*sellariolae popinae*), and the miserable mural decoration might well have inspired Phaedrus to excel

himself, as we have said above. Catullus has spoken of
writing with burnt sticks upon the walls of an infamous
tavern, and Juvenal speaks of the awnings of linen inscribed *inscripta lintea*. When Savage speaks of the
negligée of the serving boys he means to indicate a picture such as Nero must have made when harping in a
pair of drawers. The resemblance between the two
institutions so widely separated in point of time is strikingly close in every detail.

A little further on, Savage speaks of the signs of the
merchants and says: "Brandy and wines sell themselves
without any sign," and this was generally the case in the
ancient world as well. Publilius Syrus, the mime, has
preserved in his Sententiae one ancient proverb which
does justice both to the situation and to human nature:

"*Vino vendibili suspensa hedera non opus est*" (a wine
good enough to be sold needs no garland of ivy to garnish
it), which is the same as the ancient French, *bon vin
point d'enseign* and the biblical, a good wine needs no
bush. In connection with the term *hedera* (ivy) it should
be remarked that a tendril of ivy was an attribute
of Dionysus, even as the bush became traditional with
our own cabarets and taverns. Many a vintner dis-
pensed with such a sign because of the truth of the
proverb, deeming a sign almost a confession of selling
inferior vintages. The ivy, however, sacred to the god,
was often used either as it was brought in or else in the
form of a painting over the door. Sometimes we find
bas-reliefs in which the ivy is the motif. A vintner's
establishment was found at Pompeii: it had a very
poorly executed sign on which were depicted two men,
probably slaves of the establishment, clad in drawers,
carrying an oblong amphora which hangs by a thong
from the middle of a long pinga pole the ends of which
are supported upon the shoulders of the two slaves.

CHAPTER XIV.

Display of foods in restaurants—Profuse in their use of garlic—Kitchen utensils—A Roman plebe—All night taverns—Romans fond of mellow wines and sweetened liquors—"A hot drink's as good as an overcoat"—Hot water drinks become popular—The murrhine vase—Refrigeration—Snow and ice—An Athenian debauch—Age of gluttony—Cooks and scullions.

The restaurants often displayed their wares in the manner in which ours do today. Seneca uses the term *oculiferium* in that sense. Here they laid out the finest samples of their wares to catch the eyes and stimulate trade. Eggs, goose liver patés, sow vulvas, fowls, game, and the like, and they practised a refinement which is not appreciated amongst us, in that their samples were sometimes put together in a glass vase full of clear water or other crystal menstruum. The optical effect, as it was tortured by magnification or diminution, was sometimes startling to say the least, and Macrobius has devoted some little space and trouble to explain the various illusions and effects thus produced. We come at last to the quarters where foods, more or less fresh, were on display. It may be a goat, and the customer would be asked to believe that the poor beast had browsed in a pasture of myrtle and eucalyptus leaves, and was saturated with that relish because the bleeding cuts of meat are skewered with a branch of that wood, even as today some of the rural butchers in France, and in modern Greece as well, adorn with laurel some meat of dark and doubtful ancestry, and retail it to their credulous customers as the finest delicacy. Hence, in Greece, at least, it is always well to insist that the butcher produce the hide and hair of the animal in question, and thus save future complications and dietetic regurgitations.

Bits of pork and cheese are also displayed by the
Roman eating-house keepers, even as was the case with
Philemon and Baucis, and in the Moretum of Virgil.

"Quarters of pork (hams) salted and drying hang
above the hearth, a rounded cheese with a blade of
esparto grass run through its centre hangs suspended
from the rafters and with it a bundle of fennel, well
tied," and we may add to this little picture the scene
from Petronius in which Oenothea mounts upon the
rotten stool to take down a piece of dried hog's cheek,
scored by a thousand slashes of a knife proverbially dull,
a commodity coaeval with herself.

However, let us pass by the display at the doors of
the restaurant and enter the interior where we shall
probably find little in keeping with the display outside.

"No regard should be paid to such displays," remarks Seneca, "mere bait thrown to the buyer who
enters the place but once before he finds that the merchandise offered by the establishment is not at all in
keeping with the samples hanging from above the doors."

A glutton might have been well satisfied to have
dined upon what was shown outside, but only a slave
or some poverty stricken artisan would have been tempted
by what was served inside—an excellent commentary
upon the character and commercial honesty of the exhibi-
tionists. Everything to put up a front—show without
substance. The kitchens of these restaurants were, of
course, under the supervision of slaves, and the menu
was neither delicate nor various. They served, for
example, lupines for the Greek cynics, a variety of coarse
peas which were boiled in a great quantity of water, the
resultant mess being an agglutinous substance of so
peculiar a consistency that the patron might have been
equally correct in his table technique whether he drank
it or whether he ate it. They also had *cicer* (chick-peas),

a variety of vegetable sold either in porridge or fried. These latter were held in great esteem by the commoners, and candidates for the higher political offices frequently served them on the streets, hoping thereby to influence the political destinies of their parties. It is probable that from this custom we have derived that villainous delicacy known as the campaign cigar, which, but for the smell when ignited, might have been mistaken for tobacco. Such services in old Rome were often provocative of more black eyes than votes. The small peddlers sold chick-peas under the arcades and porticoes and at the games, as ours today sell popcorn and peanuts. Horace mentions a fellow who devoured chick-peas and nuts during a performance at the theatre. The customer in the eating-house need not confine himself to the humble chick-pea, however, he could have a plate of beans served in their pods, raw cabbage, or even worse, cabbage which had been cooked twice (*crambe recocta*) or (*repetita*), plenty of raw vegetables reeking with vinegar, and, on days of splendid extravagance, he might even establish contact with a boiled sheep's head. Delicacies such as these, as Juvenal has informed us, were consumed in the riotous company of cobblers, hog reeves, and the like, characters of the sort to round out the society of the place and give it the spice of infinite variety. Sometimes there were beets, the unsavory tang of which had to be tempered with a sauce made from pepper and wine:

"To give the flavor to the wallowish beets, the food of artisans, the cook always asks for wine and pepper." Martial Epigr. Lib. XIII, 13.

Everything was highly seasoned, and rare indeed was the occasion when one would not almost have gagged himself with garlic and onions or some other garnish of an acid or peppery savor; some used asafoetida to fortify their meats, but all were profuse in their use of sauces.

Everything was prepared by the cook, the master of the house, his woman, or by a special servant known as the *focaria* (from *foca*, a hearth), as the Digest informs us. A kitchen furnace, set up against one of the walls of the establishment, served the purposes of a modern range, while four great vases or urns of baked clay were mortised into a space behind the table which formed the front. They contained the cold foods prepared in advance and kept for any and all occasions. Behind the furnace, where the *focaria* labored at her tasks, were a series of stone or marble steps or terraces, three in number: on these steps were ranged the vases and measures used in the inn. The Digest contains a list of these vessels in which are found the following:

Calices, round cups, *ancones*, vases shaped like a cone, *trullae*, ladles or scoops, the *sextaria* were vessels which contained the sixth part of a *congeum;* Plautus refers to them in the Pounulus.

There were two back stalls in the establishment uncovered at Pompeii. Mazois has made an exhaustive study of it and we avail ourselves of his labors and scholarship. It is possible that these rooms were designed for vessels too huge to keep in the front, such, for instance, as the *dolia, congiaria*, and the like; diners were served there at two asses per capita, and all the idlers loafing about the establishment and rendering the proprietor an allegiance almost feudal had their reward of virtue in sitting down to table, welcoming the end of a perfect day, and spending a night in watching the posturings of a demi monde demi blonde dancer, sometimes to the harp, sometimes to the flute, or indulge their imaginations with obscene stories and puns. In the age of Ammianus Marcellinus (A. D. 360 circa), the cabaret was almost the only pastime of the proletariat at Rome. "The populace," says he, "had no

other shelter at night than that of the taverns, or the
awnings stretched before the theatres; they gambled
furiously with dice and made filthy noises with their
nostrils."

Let us conjure a picture of a Roman plebe out of the
mists of the past; let us strip him of the glamour with
which legend has invested him and see him as he actually
was: he spent his nights on the wet straw of the Velabrum, or in the Esquiline or the Suburra, and when
morning dawned, he came shambling along to the stone
benches at the gate, to shake off his dull torpor along
with his vermin. The heat in the inns and lodging-
houses was suffocating, and more comfort was to be had
in the streets; the plebe was insufferably filthy in spite
of the magnificent baths: here you see an exemplar of
the rulers of the world! What then must have been the
pot-houses which they frequented? The answer is easy:
they swarmed with flies and mosquitoes, kept in motion
by branches of laurel or palm, but the worst plague seems
to have been the fleas. The gentle and soft spoken Pliny
says, with becoming euphemism, "the insects jumping
so during the summer, rendered the taverns unendur-
able," and of course he refers to the flea. Still, Pliny
would never have entered such sanctuaries as those that
shielded the proletariat. There were also "all night
taverns" which Juvenal designated by the term *pervigiles*.
We must remember that the ancient cities were unlighted
by night, and their streets were generally narrower than
civic pride of today would countenance: the satirist counts
the doors of these all night taverns, the lights of which cut
into the murk and bloom of the outside like a friendly
beacon on a rocky lee shore. Their watchful windows
saw everything that passed in the night, some unwary and
unsuspicious loiterer saluted with chambered bile from
a second or third story window; it is like the old times in

Edinburgh when *garde lieu* was the password to dry
immunity. Did Strap find it so, or had Smollett read
Juvenal's third satire? The taverns were always furnished with substantial shutters, as were also the other
shops at Rome; features which are still characteristic
of all the native shops in romantic countries and their
colonies. By means of these heavy shutters the owner
could make himself and his reasonably secure against
the night and the menaces it held over him. The doors
were exceedingly heavy and were fastened by means of a
system of chains and bolts: a small trap-door served as
a peep-hole. Juvenal has described these fastenings in
his third satire:

> And all is silent
> When the grating chains have clanked into place
> And the tavern is closed.

Mazois, however, after an exhaustive study of the
Pompeian inn of which we have already spoken, is far
more minute in his descriptions: "The gate of the place,"
says he, "was made fast in a manner very like that in
which the storehouses at Paris are secured: by means of
a groove in the threshold of the door and of another
complementary to it in the lintel of wood, they introduced bars whose ends glided at once into these two
grooves; a wooden bar was then placed behind the other
bars to hold them immobile; and lastly, as the door
turned upon a pivot, fastened itself in that manner and
closed the opening into the place."

There were certain police regulations which forbade
the taverns to remain open before certain hours or after
a specified hour. Ammianus Marcellinus cites one such
order issued by Ampelius, praefect of the city: in this
instrument, the tavern-keepers are ordered not to open
their places before the fourth hour.

On days of religious feasts, joyous festivals, or occasions of public mourning, the taverns were compelled to remain closed. We know of few particular instances in which this was the case; we do not know the precise terms in which such injunctions were couched, but we do know that upon the occasion of an emperor's death, or that of any member of his family, these injunctions were especially severe and those who evaded this rescription were sometimes punished with death for their pains. Cassius Dio, the malignant historian of the senatorial order, has informed us that Caligula thus rewarded the supplications of a poor devil who had kept a hot drink emporium open on the day set aside for the funeral of the emperor's sister. The police made no distinctions between the tavern-keeper and the keeper of a *thermopolium* or hot water establishment. The regulation of Ampelius makes not the slightest distinction between them, and the restrictions which bound the tavern-keeper were no less binding upon the hot water seller; neither could open before the fourth hour.

The *thermopolia* which we have already seen established in Athens came to Rome along with the rest of the Greek world and when they came they also brought their own particular customs and usages. Their proprietors conducted a sort of acid drink emporium, they might, in fact, almost be called lemonade sellers, sellers of decoctions of liquorice or other sweet flavors, and it is highly probable that there was a special local name for each class of drinks and for the establishment in which they were sold. A painting in color at Pompeii represents one of these drinks and it is distinctly yellowish in color.

The Romans were always fond of mellow wines, and also of other sweetened liquors, some of which were distilled. From the beginning they were favorably disposed towards *thermopolia*. In the time of Plautus such establishments were heavily patronized, not only by philosophers but also by all sorts and conditions of society. Nearly every character in the old dramatist may be said to have been at some time or other a guest of one of the *thermopolia*. In the Rudens, for instance, he makes one of his heroes, still dripping from ship-wreck, say: "By Castor, but Neptune is a bather of the coldest. It's certain he had no hand in inventing *thermo-polia* because his drinks are salty and cold as ice."

In the Pseudolus, a glutton cries out: "In drinking, there is so much spiced wine, so much boiled wine, so much must and hydromel that I commence to make an out and out *thermopolium* of my stomach."

And in the Three Penny Bit (*Trinummus*) another, after having swilled the same beverages to excess, re-marks: "You have made a *thermopolium* of my gullet (*thermopotasti guttur*)."

These passages should suffice to show how the stalls of the venders of hot drinks were patronized, but in addition we may also cite one from the Cena Trimal-chionis: "A hot drink's as good as an overcoat." The wines were often toned down with honey, perfumed with myrrh and spices, or fortified with some feebly acidulous excipient, as, for instance, the flavor of cedar, so much in favor in the France and Italy of the seventeenth cen-tury. The lemonades still to be had in Naples, efferves-cent or flat, were also to be obtained in the ancient *thermopolia*. While such beverages are not specifically mentioned by the classical authors, there are passages in Pliny and Martial which furnish inferential evidence that they were sold, and we possess one bit of evidence which is beyond challenge: the traces of liquor remain-ing on the stone steps and in the vases in a hot drink emporium uncovered at Pompeii. Mazois speaks thus:

"Just within the great gate of the building where the traces of the vessels still remain upon the marble of the counter, and the steps upon which rested the measures; here we have evidence as to the real nature of the beverages sold. In bringing the services of chemistry to our aid our doubts have been resolved. Such analysis points to acidulous drinks. At the door of the *thermopolium* are two benches exposed to the noonday sun to offer a comfortable loafing place in winter to the frequenters of the stall."

The innovation of hot water drinks had not been long introduced in Rome before it became very popular with both patrician and plebe. The patrician affected to perfume his drink with spices, such as myrrh, cinnamon, saffron, and the like, and a very curious passage in Lucan's Pharsalia speaks of the jets of such perfumes (saffron), which spurted out and perfumed not only the air but also the breath of the theatre patrons. The patrician wanted his water hot, and, though he did not, and would not, demean himself by drinking from vessels other than the most expensive and beautiful, the commoner contented himself with the kernel of the matter by having recourse to common clay. The patrician had a decided preference for artificially cooled beverages and made use of snow for refrigerating purposes. There is a supposition that the rarest of these vases, I refer to the murrhine, which Petronius Arbiter is said to have smashed to prevent its falling into the hands of Nero after its owner's suicide, had, within itself, the property of communicating some exquisite essence to whatever decoction was being digested in its opalescent depths, and some are of the opinion that there is a connection between the myrrh of antiquity and the properties said to have been inherent in this vase. There seems to be little doubt that the vase derived its name from the

myrrh of antiquity. It is composed of three huge
sections of opal: the first forms the cup, the second
the stem and the third the base. The cup is about nine
and one-half inches high and about six inches in diameter at its greatest measurement. An exquisitely carved
swan's head dips into the bowl, a lovely allegorical allusion, and the bottom is chased with geometrical designs
perfect throughout. The Prince of Biscari has written
a monograph on the cup, which merits the study of all
experts in porcelains and vessels. If we are safe in
assuming that this exemplar is in fact genuine, the long
mooted question of murrhine vases may be regarded as
settled: they were of opal, and not of sardonyx or chal-
cedony, and they may have been steeped for years in
tincture of myrrh to give them the exquisite qualities
with which tradition has endowed them. In bringing this
brief dissertation on murrhine vases to a close, I should
add that the base of the exemplar described is about
four inches in diameter, the stem about two and one-
half inches in length, and the greatest diameter of the
stem is about one and one-quarter inches.

Nor should we omit mentioning the hot drinks which
were served in the thermopolia at Rome as well as at
Athens, drinks which derived their names from Hellas.
This was one of the first indications of their commerce
and its scope. This hot drink service had not been long
introduced at Rome before it had become as popular with
the patrician as with the plebeian. The nobleman
affected to perfume his posset with spices such as myrrh,
cinnamon, saffron, and the like, and two very interesting
passages attest the importance which had come to be
accorded these adventitious excipients. Lucan in his
Pharasalia speaks of the jets of saffron which spurted
from devices in the theatres and perfumed the foyer and
the breath of the patrons of the establishment, and

THE HOSTESS OF APULEIUS

Petronius speaks of cinnamon as having displaced essences far more worthy, if a trifle more domestic. The patrician wanted his water hot and he rarely demeaned his dignity by drinking from vessels other than the most costly, whereas the commoner had to content his inclinations with mugs of clay baked to the hardness of tile. The wealthy also had a decided preference for cool beverages and used snow for refrigerating purposes. Huge pits were dug and the snow was stored up against the arrival of the hot season. A Roman, to get the right temperature, would mix very hot and very cold liquids, in accordance with Greek usage, and he imagined that by this technique, he was enabled to get the finest and subtlest tang which could be extracted. Aristaenetus has elegantly described the practice which, to modern tastes, would seem to be unhygienic, to say the least.

Ice or snow was heaped up upon the tables beside the steaming drinks, and Pliny the Elder, in one of those phrases of ostentatious antithesis which he loves to use, remarks, with epigrammatic force: "Snow they drink as well as ice, and their voluptuousness imposes a punishment upon mountains." Seneca, in his Questiones Naturales, speaks in the same manner and to the same purpose. "See them, they are feeble, wrapped up in their mantles, sitting in the hall, pale and sick, not only drinking the snow, but eating it as well, and throwing the lumps out of their cups when they can drink no more."

With such a demand it was but natural that there should arise at Rome a retail trade in refrigerants. They had an excellent example on which to go, if we are to believe Athenaeus.

"Charles of Mitylene, in his History of Alexander, has told us how we are to proceed in order to keep snow, when he is relating the siege of the Indian city of Petra. For he says that Alexander dug thirty large trenches close to

one another, and filled them with snow, and then he
heaped on the snow branches of oak; for in that way snow
would last a long time." (Lib. iii, 97.)

A passage in Seneca also deals with the early history
of refrigeration and refrigerants: "The Lacedaemonians," says he, "hunted down the perfumers and ordered
them to quit their territories without delay, because they
had spoiled the oils, they who had operated these store-
houses, these snow depots, these beasts of burden employed to transport the aqueous blocks whose savor and
color suffered from the straw that covered them! So easy
it is to assuage the thirst of health!"

There is little doubt that the wealthy had their icemen
and their dealers in fresh sea foods who insured the quality
of the product sold, and we ought not to be astonished
that refrigeration had come to play an important part in
domestic life when we reflect that rare fish were transported immense distances in the water of their native
haunts and arrived at the table alive and in perfect condition. What applied to the establishments of the
wealthy would also perforce apply to the sumptuous
dining-rooms which they frequented, and if we find scanty
mention of such refinements in the inns and taverns it is
to be attributed to the haughty exclusiveness of the
patrician class that entertained its cronies and the instruments of its pleasure and lubricity in its own sumptuous establishments where there were no ten command-
ments and where the most voracious thirst could and
would be quenched temporarily by complete coma, an
utter disgust for food and wine, a feeling that included
women, and life itself. When a parvenu such as we
have in mind uses his peacock feather to permit further
exercise of the sense of taste it is either at home or in the
house of a friend or host.

Let us examine a portrait of the indulgence of a great

noble, which Lycon has drawn for posterity. Our
Athenian, as was the case with many of the senators at
Rome, was what we would call in modern times a solitary
drinker, although he frequently debauched himself in
company. He would totter from the chamber where he
slept to the chamber where he drank, and back again.
To have gone to a cabaret would have been wearisome
and a disgrace. He spared himself the trouble of coming
home, and by so doing, saved his vanity from the contempt and the grins of the populace as well.

"Stupefied by excesses," says Lycon, "the dreamer
slowly awakens from the torpor which indigestion and the
incontinence of his waking hours have prolonged until
noon; his eyes puffed with wine, clouded with humors, are
scarcely able to endure the light of day for some little
time after his discomfort has aroused him. He is sensible
of extreme faintness as though his veins contained wine
instead of blood, and he finds it beyond his power to lift
himself up without support. At last, leaning upon two
slaves, faint as though worn out by his slumber, he dons
a simple tunic without an outer robe; clad in slippers as
though just getting out of bed, his head wrapped up to
protect him from the cold, his neck stooped, knees weak,
color pale, he sets his yawning course from the bed
chamber to the hall in which he will recline to banquet
his friends and drink with them; there he will find certain
convivial familiars of whom he is the chief, and who are
animated by the same passions that move him. He
hastens to expel by drinking some of the collywobbles
with which his black melancholy has been deepened and
embittered; he strives to regain a little of the animation
and spirit of the rest, provoking them to drink and mocking their lack of capacity, believing that as much credit
is to be had from such an engagement as from one on the
field of battle. Time makes no account of drinking, it

comes and it goes, the fumes of the wine obscure all eyes
and sets them all to weeping; every guest is drunk, recog-
nizing neither himself nor anyone else; without the slightest cause one gets into an altercation with his neighbor,
another would sleep but is forced to remain awake, a
third, 'even as was the case with the heroes of Petronius,'
attempts to make his escape and evade his troubles and
his tormentors only to be brought back by the porter who
has prevented him from leaving.   By and by, another is
ignominiously thrown out of doors; he totters, but his
slave catches him and leads him off, and as he staggers
along, he lets his cloak fall into the mud of the street.   At
last, our guttler is left alone in the room, monarch of all
he surveys, nor does he quit the cup until he falls asleep
with it in his hand or at his mouth, then weaving drunk-
enly, he has escaped from himself, and is asleep."

Vastly different, this illustrious glutton who debases
himself in secret orgies, from the man of the people,
whether at Rome or elsewhere.   The politician, if he
indulged himself at all, would do so in the taverns and
inns, where he could cater to publicity by treating.   There
his wit and good nature would have free scope, his delight
lay in numbers, he is a past master at putting indigence
at ease and winning the confidence of the out-at-elbow
rabble; blustering and roistering fit well into his designs
and further his interests.   Such a politician would hold
his daily banquets in the popinae, on the occasion of a law
suit, an election, and the like, to the accompaniment of
the thousand noises of the Forum.   At night he might
indulge in one of the nympheae, in the name of the
republic or the emperor, and lastly, on those occasions
when the members of a century came together at table
the scene was usually laid in one of the fine and sumptuous
public halls set aside for the purpose.   There he could
comfort his poverty by a brief sojourn amid scenes of

decorative splendor, a willing worshiper of the god of things as they ought to be. These were great days for the commoner; his entertainment cost him nothing and he revelled in luxury and riot at the expense of policy. On occasions such as these, he could compare his lot to that of the great patrician, and the silver from which he ate and drank was but an added sop to political indirection and expediency. There is a passage excellently to the point in the Treatise on Rhetoricians, addressed to Herennius, and attributed to Cicero, though it scarcely seems worthy of the best powers of that orator. We have here a very curious adventure, such an example of ostentation and bigoted vanity as Shakespeare or Molière might have envied. As a portrayal of Roman false pretenses it has few equals and it must have been traced by the hand of a master. In translating the episode we wish to call attention to the fact that it is a mine of information upon our subject and it may have been in Quevedo's mind when he drew his Hablador. The character is the true and unmistakable ancestor of all the poseurs who have come after him. An advocate is speaking, probably one of the lumpy faced vulture species who haunted the Forum or the Market for Stolen Goods. Petronius has furnished us with an exquisite portrait of such a lawyer in his story of the stolen mantle. He it is who dresses down our fine gentleman, a debtor unable to pay, and certainly in no frame of mind to discuss the obligation, especially with such a specimen of humanity. The battle between Shylock and D'Artignan will ever be one of the most amusing and instructive.

"Look at the fellow," says the lawyer, "he wants to pass for a rich man. How proud he is! See how he looks down on us, as if to say: 'If it is not too much trouble I may give you what you want.' And when he takes his mantle up with his left hand he imagines all the world is

dazzled by the gleam of his jewels and the glitter of his
gold ring.   Then he calls the only slave he owns, I know
this, but you do not, he calls him first by one name and
then by another.   'Here, Sannio,' says he, 'come here,
see to it that these barbarians don't annoy me by crowd-
ing around'; he would have strangers think that he has
chosen his slave from a crowd of them.   He orders him
to place couches before the tables, he tells him to go to
his uncle and demand an Ethiopian to accompany him
to the baths, or to lead a fine saddle horse to his door, or
to prepare some fragile and tinselled pomp for his false
glory.   Then, in the hearing of all present, 'make sure
the silver is all accounted for before night, if possible,' and
the slave, well knowing the character of his master makes
answer, 'If your highness wants the stuff counted in a
single day, you should send several slaves.'   'Very well,
go and attend to it and take Libanus and Sosia with you;
I want the thing done.'   It once came about that certain
gentlemen waited upon him, gentlemen who had entertained him handsomely when he was travelling.   He was
a little put out because of this, but even then he did not
recede from the evil propensity of his nature.   'You have
done well to come,' said he, 'but you would have done
even better had you come to me straight away.'   'We
would have done that,' was the reply, 'if we had known
where your house was.'   'That is easily remedied, come
along with me.'   They followed him.   In the meantime,
all his talk was taken up with ostentation and boasting.
He lectured them on the state of the crops and informed
them that he no longer went to his country places because
all the houses were destroyed and he had not ventured
to rebuild at Tusculum where he was even then restoring
an ancient villa on its old foundations.   As he was telling
them this, he led them into a house where he was known
to the owner and where he knew there was to be a ban-

quet. 'Here's where I'm staying,' he informed them. Then he fell to examining all the silverware in sight, he inspected the table which was ready set and expressed his satisfaction with everything. A slave came and informed him privately that the master had arrived, and asked him to go about his business. 'Well, come along, friends,' said he, 'my brother has just arrived from Salernum, and I want to meet him on the road. Please be good enough to return at the tenth hour.' The strangers took their departure and he hastened away to hide in his own house. Then, at the appointed hour, as he had stipulated, they returned. They inquired for him and learned who really owned the mansion. They retired, in confusion, to an inn. Next day they found the fellow. They told him what had happened. They expostulated with him. They accused him. He made answer that they had mistaken either the house or the street and that he had waited for them till far into the night. He then commissioned Sannio his slave boy to get vases, vestments, and slaves together. The little servant, who did not lack ability, acquitted himself nobly and his master led his guests home. One of the finest houses was being prepared for a wedding and he told them he had loaned it to a friend who was to be the groom. His slave demanded the silver, for he was terrified at having acceded to the request. 'Away with him,' said he, 'I've loaned him my house, I've given him my slaves, does he want my silver into the bargain? notwithstanding the fact that I too have guests? Well, let him have it, we will be beautifully served on Samian ware in spite of him.' " (Lib. IV, 50 and 51.)

Mention should also be made of the fact that the caterers of such banquets as those of which we have spoken were no less vain and boastful, no less difficult to manage than the parasite whom we have described. For

many years they had little or no consideration, but with
the decline of republican severity and austerity, the calling
which had formerly been regarded as vile (vilissimum
antiquis mancipium is the expression used by Kivy),
came more and more into prominence with increase of
luxury and the questionable refinement of the standards
of living, and the haughty patrician was compelled perforce to put up with more abuse and insolence from his
cook and his caterer than would have been thought possible. Insolence was the order of the day, but a good
cook, then as now, was difficult to obtain and it was
thought worth all the inconvenience if he could be held.
The stern age that had produced a Cincinnatus or a
Fabius was above giving the slightest consideration to
such matters, but when Rome had succumbed to the tastes
and refinement of Lucullus, and the age of gluttony had
dawned, slaves who were specialists in catering and cook-
ing were very costly, more so in fact than those serving
as short-hand writers or copyists. One hundred thousand
ases was by no means an exorbitant price for a slave
with such qualifications, in witness whereof I would
cite the figure at which Sallust purchased the famous
Dama, who had formerly been the property of Nomen-
tanus. Whenever an elaborate entertainment was in
prospect it was necessary to procure the services of some
such caterer at once, and by any means necessary to
insure the desired result, and the host often had to bear
in silence the insolence of a specialist who knew his craft
was indispensable. It was never the custom to haggle
over the price which such a culinary artist set on his
services, and this was especially true if the prospective
employee had received the title "archimagirus," carried
in his belt the traditional carving knife, and commanded
a numerous horde of scullions. Those who haggled, or
refused to pay the amount demanded, were reduced to the

lowest terms by some cook of nine days' experience, and the waste accruing from his ministrations was staggering.

As Plautus has it:

"That fellow's a nine-day cook; on the ninth day
He will go about his business—cooked."

The explanation lies in the Roman customs at funerals. The scullions prepared the lentils and porridge on the ninth day after a funeral, and another explanation a trifle more recondite is that they were competent to prepare the repasts during the nine days following a funeral when their employers would not be so testy as usual. On the tenth day, however, tragedy was certain to stalk abroad in the land, and the consequences of red-eyed fury suffering from indigestion could only be prevented by the hasty departure of the entire kitchen staff.

We need not speak of the cooks and scullions in the establishments of the small vendors of sausages (botularii) who ran hither and yon with their smoking ovens (tomacula fumantia), as Martial aptly calls them:

"You are a buffoon, Caecilius. You are like the fellow who sells pea soup to the idle crowd, like the vile boys of the sellers of salt, like the hoarse cook who carries smoking sausages in his pans." (Lib. I, 42.)

Hawkers of short-order food stuffs went among the crowds in the streets, in the porticoes and arcades, in the tiers of seats in the amphitheatre, in fact, wherever there was a prospect of business, and peddled their wares. There were also portable ovens for bread, and one of the keenest memories which the writer has of old Seville and other Spanish cities is the high, resonant singsong cry— P—A—N, that echoed and re-echoed in the dim darkness of the narrow and crooked streets where the acoustics were excellent and the echoes persisted long after their cause had vanished in the distance. It is as much a survival of culture as is the custom of advertising lodgings by twining palm fronds or newspapers around the baranillas under Spanish windows; a usage which goes back to the Middle Ages and which, in its primal simplicity, meant sanctuary. Had one but the leisure and the space, he could write an entire chapter on such survivals as had their inception in taverns and inns.

As such peddlers continually encroached upon the preserves of the proprietors of eating-houses and thermopolia there was perpetual hostility between the factions they represented. No gathering could escape the attentions of these peripatetic hucksters, who promptly betook themselves and their stocks in trade to the meeting. The eating-house keeper and his vassals would then make a sortie upon the enemy and attempt to drive them to a stand in front of the inn or tavern. It might have been thought that these petty dealers were in Seneca's mind when he coined the term "institores popinarum," hawkers of the eating-houses. The strident cries of these retailers in merchandising their wares were among the causes which contributed to the perpetual noisy uproar of Rome. And in all this garish hurlyburly not the least strident were the cries of the ragged old hags who sold herbs, she who led Encolpius into evil ways, as described by Petronius, and she of whom Persius speaks en passant—crying her herbs to attract the slaves.

CHAPTER XV.

The adventure of a Roman parasite—The age of gluttony—Hawkers of food everywhere—Caesar Germanicus suppresses the traffic—The wines of Italy sold by the slaves of the producers—Lucullus distributes 100,000 casks of wine—Roman rogues—Aurelian takes charge of wine markets—Dilution of wines—Women condemned for drinking during Early Republic—Barber shops as meeting places.

The baths were always in a state of turmoil and uproar, due to the limited space and the numbers congregating there. For a long time Seneca lodged in the first story of one of these establishments, and, amongst a myriad of discordant sounds, he was never able to forget the cries of the eating-house keepers and their rivals, and he has informed us with a certain touch of grim humor that their calls topped the very gamut of discord. "There are," says mine author, "the diverse clamors of the pastry sellers, the pork butchers, the confectioners, and also the yells of all whose trade was based upon tavern patronage, and each and every one to sell his wares affected a particular tone and modulation." These petty merchants of ancient Rome have perpetuated their calling to our own times. We see them in Naples, selling macaroni, ravioli, and other food pastes; we see them after nightfall in the British Isles, selling fried potatoes and fish, each commodity in its greasy wrapper of brown paper; but in some cases the peripatetic oven has been mounted upon wheels. One who has lived in Naples, especially in bohemian quarters in the art colony, needs only to cast a glance at the picture reproduced at the end of this chapter to see that, aside from changes in raiment, Herculaneum and Parthenope (the ancient name for Naples) differed but little from the modern city in the

matter of selling food stuffs. The dealer is seen, standing
in front of his smoking utensil which is mounted upon a
tripod; he is a macaroni vendor to the life in everything
except clothing, and, were his hands tied. he. too, would
be dumb.

We do not know whether the delicacies esteemed by
the inhabitants of the realm of Naples were a happy
importation, or were naturalized at Rome, nor do we
know whether the petty dealers held their stocks in
common, and sold them to the men on the street; nor do
we know whether they had a guild which would have given
them enough power to meet the competition of their
rivals; but one thing is certain: their industry was rewarded and their patronage extensive, their wares were
exhibited in every quarter of the city.

Some chose stations under the porticoes, near a pillar,
and, to advertise their presence, they garlanded the
column with bottles fastened to a chain. This, in impudent defiance of the tavern keeper and his modest
branch of ivy or bush. Others of greater hardihood, who
were not afraid to beard their enemies even more openly,
betook themselves to the Cupedinarum forum (the forum
of the confectioners) and braved without blenching the
fury of the greater merchants, laying hold of their customers like any Bleeker-street vendor of second-hand
clothing. They ran about in the crowds before the booths
of the fishmongers, butchers, sellers of sweetmeats,
poultry merchants, inviting their customers to come and
sample their wares, and, according to Terence, they
found, in each calling, a means to advance their own
interests.

There must have been cause for great rejoicing among
the tavern keepers and other retail dealers when, in the
times of Martial, Caesar Germanicus, under pretext of
clearing the streets of impediments to traffic, promulgated

RETURNING FROM THE TAVERN

a decree which gave the death blow to all peddlers who had fattened at the expense of established business. Martial has addressed an epigram to Germanicus on this occasion, and given us much information on Rome and the conditions in that city:

"The audacious shop-keepers had robbed us of the entire city, usurping even our thresholds. You, Germanicus, have ordered the narrow streets to be widened, and former paths to become roads. Now, no pillars are draped with chained bottles, nor is the praetor obliged to walk in the midst of the mud. No razor is rashly wielded in the midst of a crowd, nor are the public ways cluttered with kitchens. Barber, tavern keeper, cook-shop and butcher-shop keep on their own thresholds. Rome exists now: formerly, it was simply a huge shop." (Lib. VII, 61.)

This epigram of Martial has been taken seriously to heart by the authorities of other cities, and all have profited by the example.

One usage there was, which has become obsolete in France except in such wine producing provinces as Champagne, but which persists to this day in Italy and Greece, and that is a method of disposing of the vintage by means of a slave or servant of the proprietor, at the house of the latter, and under his supervision.

Such establishments are to be seen at both Naples and Florence, often as an important adjunct to the most impressive properties. The servant stands in his little stall and sells the wine which belongs to his master. You do not enter as though it were a tavern, but come to a wicket through which you pass your empty bottle and your money; a few moments later your bottle returns to you full. According to Savage, Leo XII was of a mind to set this fashion of wine selling in Rome because of the practises of the innkeepers, but the effort came to nothing

as it was bitterly opposed.   The Romans under the popes
were not desirous of being reminded in that manner of
their republican ancestors and of those under the empire.
In ancient times the bulk of the vintages of Italy was
retailed in the manner which we have just described.
Many such places have been uncovered at Pompeii.
The booth communicated with the house of the owner
and the latter exercised his authority and superintended
the business carried on.   The slave in charge of such a
booth was called "caupo" just as was the tavern keeper.
A wealthy property holder might have several such
booths on his premises, and the amount of the vintage
was considered in rating him commercially for credit.
In the case of the very rich landowners, inns were maintained on an elaborate scale and in places such as these the
traveller could find food and lodging as well, and he was
safer than in establishments not under the patrician's
control.   Martial, writing to Bassus concerning the
country place of a nobleman, adduces as a bit of evidence
showing the prosperity of the owner, that the slave who
sold wines had no leisure in which to pine away in sloth.
Hence it follows that such stalls must have been highly
profitable to the owner.   The great proprietors rarely
permitted themselves to be annoyed with all the petty
details of business.   It is true that Trimalchio's coadjutor
read aloud at table the various business undertakings in
course of completion, and the gossip pertaining to the
estates, but this was satire of the finest.   Trimalchio did
not even know that the Gardens of Pompeii had been
purchased for his account and demanded to be kept
better informed in the future, a wonderful touch of realism.   Nevertheless, the great landowners did take a keen
interest in property titles and heavy transactions in
wines and foodstuffs, and the procurer in the Pseudolus
of Plautus sends a wealthy merchant to his Hedyle to be

fleeced. Alciphron has several such passages to the same purpose. We are justified in suspecting that Crassus was engaged in huge deals in which wines and commodities were involved. The edict promulgated by him two years before the death of Marius, during his censorship with Lucius Julius Caesar, prohibiting thereafter the sale of wine of Amineum, one of the finest vintages of Italy, and those of Greece, at the low price of 8 ases the amphora, bears eloquent testimony of the statement made above. Whether the decree was inspired by local producers in league with the authorities, producers whose products could not compete with better merchandise at such a price, or by farsighted political expediency designed to enable the master politician to outrival the luxuries of Lucullus after his return from Asia, is not known. We do know that Lucullus distributed 100,000 casks of wine to the people when he returned to Italy; and we also know that Crassus was instrumental in having the import tax law passed, and it is axiomatic that imposts are never free from self-interest, at bottom.

Cato himself, notwithstanding his austerity, was involved in certain business transactions, but anonymously; he acted through a freedman in his dealings with the greatest rascals in Rome, and it is to be hoped that his factor was their equal in finesse.

> "And of old Cato the tale is told
> That often his virtue he warmed with wine,"

says Horace. More power to him, says the author. There are not lacking features of the traffic in wines and foods that convince an impartial observer that the Arbiter may have had two strings to his bow in satirizing the aediles for their collusion with the bakers. Freedmen acting in the interests of powerful patricians enjoyed a degree of immunity which left them little to fear. The

churlish gate-keepers (portitores) of Rome took careful
precautions against inconveniencing such gentry by an
over-meticulous scrutiny of garment, person, or cart, and
the lure of gold quieted the uneasy suspicions of official
authority.   One might almost compare an inexperienced
gate-keeper of old Rome with a young naval officer
exercising his first commissioned authority as officer of
the deck on a battleship.   There the watchword is "do
not molest the admiral's domestics."   Mercury was the
god of thieves and diplomats, and he had also enrolled
many officials in the lists of his priesthood.   The spectacle
afforded by the rigid censor on the one hand and the
rascally vintner on the other, each, perhaps, playing into
the other's hands, each holding a club over the other's
head, must have afforded the keenest humor to any
bystander knowing all the facts.   The wine sellers and
oil vendors suffered alike for their pains, although the
rigor of authority was directed principally against the
latter, as they had less protection.   Their improbity has
passed into a proverb: they were hand and glove together.
"They all make a compact like the oil sellers in the
Velabrum."

The aediles punished smuggling, but the cultus of
Mercury also dealt with malefactors, and the penalties
imposed by the latter were inflicted upon all who trafficked
in flagrant and fraudulent offenses: on cabaret keeper
and oil seller alike, although the latter frequently revisited
their reputation for commercial malfeasance on the heads
of the innkeepers.   A passage in the Captivi of Plautus
will enable us to judge of the punishment inflicted by the
priest of Mercury upon a rogue more indurated still.   It
ended with a proverb which pilloried public morality,
and the ends of justice were rarely reached.   The practise developed the Lex Talionis to a high degree of effi-
ciency.   The punishment actually consisted of a denun-

ciation at the hands of the priest of Mercury. The
tavern keeper, a shameless adulterator, a vendor of more
commodities than the vintner, was punished, therefore,
because he had sinned. But the evil, the inadequateness
of the penalty, remained, and our retailer finds himself
purified after the ewer has been emptied over his head,
even as the sinner after baptism. He was then ready to
begin all over again. Ovid describes this purification in
his Fasti, and quotes the prayer of the penitent during
the imposition of the sentence. After having besought
Mercury to pardon him for having misrepresented his
wares, he begs the god to pass upon whatever he sells so
he can lie again:

"Purify me of perjuries past, that the gods may not
occupy themselves with my concerns if I lie but a little;
vouchsafe me certain profits, and when they shall have
accrued, permit me to enjoy them, and make my patrons
believe my words when they buy."

The public complained for years of the dearness of
wine and its vile quality. Mercury did not punish the
vintners. He found his godhead in a difficult situation.
To have penalized the guilty would have resulted in a loss
to his priesthood, as their emoluments would have been
curtailed. Under Augustus, matters such as these were
taken to the emperor, but little account was made of
them. The sarcastic banter of Octavian was equal to any
occasion and it is reported that he answered a thirsty
plebe that Agrippa, his son-in-law, had already taken
active measures to avert death from thirst in watching
carefully over the spouts of the public fountains, and
that consequently the complaint could not be based upon
fact. Tiberius, Claudius, Nero, and Domitian paid more
regard to the exactions of the vintners, and under Pescen-
nius Niger the legions voiced their complaints against
being deprived of wine. "What!" says he, with biting

sarcasm, "you demand wine with the Nile at your feet!"
The troops which were defeated by the Moors had met
the situation as follows: "We have not been provided
with our rations of wine; we cannot fight." The response
this time was more mordant still: "You should blush
with shame, because those who have taken your measure
drink only water."

During the reign of Aurelian these complaints persisted and that prince at last made it a point of law.
He decreed wine should be placed on the free list with
bread, oil, meat, and pork. He ordered the vast and
well wooded plains which extended to the maritime
Alps be acquired and cleared; that the hillsides
might be set with vines to be cared for by numerous
familia of slaves to be established in the country. The
wine produced by this experiment was to be disposed of
only by the public treasury, and disbursed, free of imposts, to the people. After this, it was merely a question
of computing the daily rations, "facta erat ratio dochae,
cuparum, navium, et operum," remarks Vopiscus: when
Aurelian listened to the wise advice of his praetorian
praefect, who told him: "If we issue wine to the Roman
people today, we shall be forced to serve them with geese
and chickens tomorrow." The advice was prudent, and
the gratuitous distribution was thereupon suppressed.
Thereafter Aurelian contented himself with selling in the
porticos of the temple of the Sun such vintages as had
been exempted from imposts or seized by the Roman
customs officers as the result of fraud or smuggling
(fiscalia vina). Although his biographer tells us nothing
on the point, he doubtless sold the merchandise at prices
lower than the market. When an emperor puts the
government in business, the chief loser, aside from the
government, would, of course, be the tavern keeper,
and the people had every reason to be content, as they

were thus able to purchase better wines at a lower price; and Aurelian, to indemnify them for not making free distribution of such commodities and thus putting a premium upon nonproduction, issued to them white tunics of African cloth and Egyptian linen, and, perhaps, handkerchiefs, such as had not been seen until then.

The place given over to the sale of wines, in ancient towns, in Italy and France as well, in Rome and in Lyons, was a large empty space surrounded with little buildings (cenabae), in which the merchants did business. The wine market at St. Bernard, with its little booths, each numbered and bearing on its façade the name of the merchant occupying the premises, is an ideal illustration. The forum vinarium of ancient towns differed little from this example. All that is conveyed to a Frenchman by the term "Marchè au Vin" (wine market) would have been found in the Roman forerunner of that institution of the middle ages, little larger than was necessary to house the press.

The wine merchants, whose corporation was reconstituted by Alexander Severus, upon what grounds we do not know, used these little cenabae as the centres from which they did their business. In them lay the origin of those shops of Italy which we now know as canove or cantine. An inscription in Gruter's collection informs us as to their establishment in Lyons—in cenabis consistentium. In the same collection there is another further along in which mention is made of the cenabenses, the loafers around wineshops; the inscription deals with a temple consecrated to the fortune of the emperor and the protecting genius of the vintners' gild:

Fortunae Augustae sacrum, et genio canabensium
Sacred to the inperial fortune and to the genius of
    the vintners.

The affairs transacted in these cenabae at Rome were of considerable magnitude, for there was much wine drunk in Italy, and the vintages numbered about eighty. Without taking count of the synthetic products, such as mulsum (a mixture of Falernian and honey), Italy alone produced about fifty varieties of wine. We do not include within our estimate the spiced beverages and aromatic drinks, nor those perfumed with verbena, calamus, myrrh, aloes, and the like, or even those vile mixtures such as blitum which were made on the spot by the landlord.

Some of these which we have seen flowing in torrents in the taverns, where the art of the vintner had rendered them even viler than they were before, were of a detestable quality. Their bitter taste in the mouth, the tongue thickened by their acridness, they could be freely damned even as the Greek Cineas, in observing the loftiness of the trellised vines by which they were produced, remarked: "They would do well to hang the mother of such wines as high." Others there were, however, which differed greatly from these vile plebeian vintages; among such were the wines of Vaticani or of Nomentani, in which qualities no less rare than exquisite were inherent; tartness, highly flavored and haunting bouquet, and a tempered ardour. With Falernian every reader of Horace and Martial has been long familiar; there was also Caecubian no less generous and no less celebrated, although greater pains had to be taken with it and it had to be aged more to get the finest results; the true imperial wine of Italy, however, was the Setian, which was also a better stomachic than either of the preceding and was long the favorite at the court of Augustus and probably of Tiberius and Caligula as well. The wines of Sorrentum were long esteemed as tonics for disordered stomachs and very helpful as an aid to digestion, but which, worse luck, had

to age for about twenty-five years before they were at
their best maturity; and lastly the sweet wines of Alba
esteemed for frayed nerves. They were dry wines and
were better than Falernian, and agreeable and gentle
tonics for the stomach and digestion.

These were the precious wines, the vintages which
required careful nursing, and which would bear not the
slightest neglect from the time of picking the grapes till
the moment when, gushing and foaming from the pressure
of the press and turned into the huge dolia, remaining
therein thirty days, stirred without intermission with rods
of elm to prevent the lees from depositing on the inside;
lastly drawn off to clarify and often rendered more limpid
still by the aid of pigeon eggs broken into them.

Thus prepared, thus placed in the best state for
preservation and keeping, they were decanted, not like
inferior wines into leathern bottles and wineskins (culei),
but into puncheons (cadi) of terra cotta which probably
had a capacity of about six and one-half gallons; into
amphorae of a like capacity, or even into little vessels
(graeca testa) as Horace calls them (Lib. I, 20) which,
on account of their elegant form, added on that account
to the price of the wine which they contained. Such
vessels were hermetically sealed with a cork which had
been first dipped into boiling pitch. There was usually
an inscription on the neck of the vessel which told the
year of the vintage, and usage gave the name of the consul
of the year in which the wine was made to the wine itself.
Petronius speaks of Opiniam and Horace of wine of
Manlius's consulate, incidentally giving us at the same
time the year of his own birth (Lib. III, 21). After the
vessels had been carefully stoppered, the casks and
amphorae especially, they were deposited carefully on
end on a bed of fine sand in the cella vineria, a sort of
little cellar, or in a cool shed (horreum). If they were all

small and of equal capacity, of an elegant and graceful
form like the testa graeca for example, they were kept
under guard in the hall or house, disposed in niches
arranged in the walls, even as we have seen in the taverns
and pimping houses in Plautus, where we were reminded
that the pitch legends could sometimes serve as love
letters.

In the taverns, therefore, we need feel little surprise at
failing to discover such niches holding vessels such as we
have spoken of; because, ordinarily, such establishments
were not frequented by the classes who could afford to
purchase vintages so rare and costly, but by the poorer
elements who had little opportunity to taste the Setian
or Caecubian wines but who, on the other hand, were
habituated to the cheap concoctions and synthetic forti-
fications which the landlord provided.   The patrician
left the plebe to wallow in his own drunkenness and filth
in these public houses, but for himself, his house was well
furnished with everything his tastes could remind him of,
and his cellar abounded with the rarest and costliest wines
of Italy and the Grecian archipelago.   His stock of wines
was not limited to his cellars but often took up more room
still and was stowed in ranks and rows even in the atrium
of the house.   Rank and quality in wine was carefully
noted by ticket, pitch legend, and by the position in which
it was placed.

One apartment in the house there was, however,
where wine was interdicted.   I refer to the suite occupied
by the women of the establishment.   There it was not
only a vice to drink, it was a crime.   It was always thus.
Under the kings and during the first years of the republic,
though Rome was gross and barbarous, the severity with
which such drinking was punished and the horror with
which it was regarded was more severe than under the
civilized regime of the emperors.   Romulus placed wives

who drank wine in the first rank of culpable women, along with those getting caught in adultery. In the opinion of the ancient legislator both offenses merited the same punishment. A husband who killed his wife drinking or drunk would have been absolved by Romulus. It was left to the women to have charge of the keys to the storehouse or cellar and have access to them. A young girl who placed them in her closet was condemned by parental authority to starve herself to death. It further appears that the Roman woman, according to Cato, was supposed to embrace her husband, his parents, and relatives on first seeing them each day, and this not so much in sign of love and amity as to assure them by her breath that she had not tasted wine (had the temetum in mind), for in ancient times this was the word used to convey that meaning and the later derivation temulentia had come to mean drunkenness.

The women, menaced by such severe precautions depriving them of wine, made the best of the matter and contrived to content themselves with liquors less stimulating. For instance, they were permitted to take passum, a wine made from dried grapes and thin anodyne, which people used to garnish their delicacies and flavor them much as we used brandy or hard cider to fortify mince meat, or preserved fruits. Martial speaks of this beverage as also does Columella, who intimates that it is new wine copiously steeped and having its savor augmented by virtue of passing this produce through a bed of raisins which have been dried by the sun. This must have been one of the beverages which Plautus had in mind when he puts into the mouth of one of his characters the following words: "Prepare the honeyed wine (commisce mulsum); make ready the quinces and the pears, that they may warm well in the pans; throw in the cinnamon," and so on. This must have been real pear cider as that which is extracted from the same fruit in Asia Minor, according to Artemidorus, and such as that made from apples, of which Plutarch speaks.

Women, in addition to these beverages so innocuous were also permitted a liquor called defrutum, which was derived from the lighter vintages, adulterated with water and reduced to a third of its original volume by long boiling.

How many of the Greek wines were interdicted we cannot say, but we suspect that the number was great, and especially did this apply to those vintages which did not arrive in Italy diluted with water in a proportion which would render them, according to belief, improper for secret libations. Notwithstanding this dilution, which proves less, as we see it, the fidelity of the Greek vineyard keepers for the ancient usage of sobriety, than that their wine merchants followed an ancient custom of cheating, they were, as we would have you see, the vintages preferred by the gluttons; they were always dear, but their high cost added only to the merit of the wine. The impost (*portorium*) which they had to pay as luxuries, elevated the price still higher. Always, one might say, this was a contribution not excessive. It did not exceed the fortieth part of the value of the object sold; but the moderateness of the impost was not always the real reason which caused the high price to be sustained. Smuggling operations were very frequent—many a merchant, even as we have pointed out in the case of Cato, engaged in traffic of this sort with impunity; and you must know that if the contravention required courage, the Roman impost must have been rigorous.

All merchandise, and wine especially, which was imported in a province which also exported, whether by land or water, had, without exception, no privilege to evade the law.

It is true that a traveller might import merchandise for his own particular use and needs, but for more the tax was applied always without prejudice at the toll house, which as a general thing was located near one of the bridges. One was bound to declare himself at the bureau of customs the objects designated by the law. If he made a false declaration and the misrepresentation was discovered, confiscation followed.

Those who complained against the contribution were not less numerous than those who avoided it, which was the cause of the exaction, and especially when a collector of customs bestirred himself, as, for instance, Verres or Fonteius. These reclamations were not left without authority. The latter was vehemently accused, for example, of having unlawfully levied excessive contributions on wines while in command of Gaul, and it required nothing less than all the eloquence of Cicero to dissipate the grief caused by the grave charges brought against the governor. And what brought all this about? A levy of four denarii at Toulouse on each amphora, under the pretext of customs duties (*portorii nomine*) and of certain other smaller imposts levied by the agents of Fonteius, which seemed outrageous to the wine merchants of certain French towns. Pletorius, the principal accuser, would have it believed that this levy was but a link in a system of fraud powerfully organized, and pretended that Fonteius had not conceived in Gaul this detestable idea of levying an excessive impost on wine; that he had worked out the project in Italy, and that the plan had also its agents and ramifications in Rome. Nothing is more redoubtable, in an affair of thievery, than for one thief to accuse another. Unfortunate Fonteius! to have been placed in the position of having been accused by vintners.

We have already passed in review a goodly number of

gluttons; we are able likewise to say that in our painstaking visits to the inns of the environs of Rome and to the taverns of the great city which we have visited on foot, we have seen all that was vile in the Roman dregs without having entered as yet the stalls more shameless, which we shall later throw open to the light of the sun; and we shall know intimately the élite of the vagabonds, the fine flower of the ancient rascals. Some may resent a graphic picture of the scenes to follow before the close of this chapter, but we shall draw them still. It is no part of our plan to describe to the readers those places of public reunion, which people were accustomed to frequent without distinction to rank, but because of the relation they bore to hospitality, we find ourselves compelled to introduce our readers to the barber shops where the man about town, the beaux-brummels and the novelists, made their headquarters. Here luxury grew to an unprecedented height and when we reach the age of Julian, we find that emperor greatly incensed at discovering that society had so degraded itself that barbers had become an important part of the cosmos. We shall begin then with that institution of many professions, the female barber, well skilled in her trade of hair-dresser, barber, masseuse, manicure, and prostitute. In her shop gathered the slaves to homage and gossip, to sleep on the benches while waiting to conduct their infant charges, then at school, home when the master had terminated his lessons; and we shall find here plausible scoundrels working out their plans of campaign and preparing their snares even as in the cabarets, effeminate sissies such as Martial's Priscius who dreaded wind and dust, dandies (*belli*) always occupied with comb and mirror (*inter pectinem speculumcue occupati*) as Seneca has said so spiritually.

The barber at least ought to be worthy of our observation. Why, you will ask? Because he is a gossip and for that reason alone is well worthy to figure in our gallery. Have not gossips and curiosity always been considered a crime, especially on the part of barbers? Has not tittle-tattle always been the very letter and spirit of that calling? And the anecdote of the barber who demanded of an unknown customer "How shall I shave you?" received in response these words of Spartan brevity: "Without speaking." Is this not vouched for by no less an authority than Plutarch, and is it not always as new as the latest gossip in the corner barber shop?

In connection with the barber shops, we are also bound to mention the stalls of the perfumers (*nyropolia*) and also those of the doctors (*medicinae*). There also among the Roman empirics, who did not content themselves with prescribing drugs, but who also prepared those which they sold, with their own hands. There, I repeat, in the stalls of the doctors, like those of our apothecaries, dudes, dandies, and novelists congregated. And we may also suspect that other frequenters, more sombrely intentioned, were to be found there. Did not they sell, in fact, poisons which were sometimes used as remedies, but which could bring death as well as health? "I will go to the doctor," says a character in the "Mercator of Plautus," "and there with poison I will buy death for myself."

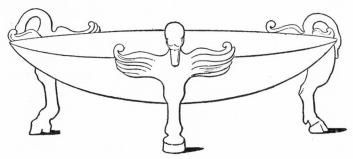

CHAPTER XVI.

Meritoria in relation to lupanar—Inns respectable and otherwise—Nero again—Apuleius' spirited account of an adventure in an inn of the second century.

Next we shall visit the *meritoria*. They are places, I assure you, which you will never be able to know well, no matter how keen your curiosity, except at the expense of your modesty. These are inns of which the most respectable savor somewhat of our family hotels, but of which the worst could scarcely be placed upon the same level as the *lupanars*. In fact, the terms came to be almost synonymous. A passage in the Digest enlightened us completely as to the difference between the *meritorium*, and the ordinary lodging house (by *meritorium* we refer to the honest establishment). "There," says Ulpian, "lodgers remain for a long time and are persons known and respected, (*in longum tempus, certisque personis*)." In the other the lodger is a transient from day to day (*ferre in dies*) and is a person unknown and uncertain. Other places there were which belonged to this latter class but which were of a lower order in which chance guests could rent a furnished room for the night. These places were almost invariably dangerous. They were evilly constructed and were several stories high; more crowded even than our tenements, and filthy beyond description. The characters of their lodgers were usually in keeping with the proprieties of the place. In these *meritoria*, poverty stricken families were accustomed to live from day to day, paying for their lodging for a short time and at a high rate and when they were unable to amass the funds necessary to maintain them, the pro-

prietor ejected them without scruple, to rent another
lodging or to huddle in the streets or in the dank cold
passageways. There flocked always the vagabonds which
are to be found at all times in all the great cities—a
class without fire or roof (*sine lare certo*) as Horace says
of them, who roosted where they could but lodged no-
where. The women and the children of Vitellius were
reduced to such straits. According to Suetonius, ruined
by the gormandising of that glutton, abandoned by him
at Rome without other resource than the house in which
they lived, they left it and went to lodge in furnished
lodgings. They did not leave it until they went to live
in the imperial palace when Vitellius became emperor.

Tenants such as these, however, were rare in such
lodgings. Ordinarily, the classes who lived in the *meritoria* were so poorly dressed and so unsociable and so
pitiably degraded that the legislator implicitly declared
it fatal to propriety to live in such a situation, and in the
Codex a defence is based upon the premise that a house
was to be transformed into a *meritorium* or lodging house
with small bedchambers.

For us, and without doubt the legislator took the
same view, that law is more than a civil law, it is also a
moral law: the chief reasons for its passage were those of
propriety, as the population common to these *meritoria*
was degraded and good manners had to be safe-guarded,
which could be done by preventing the erection of establishments where scandal and crime were sure to originate.
The *meritoria* were in effect infamous refuges where vice
and vicious practices flourished and crimes of luxury
found here the shadow of oblivion and the secrecy without which they could not flourish. Especially were such
lodging houses the ordinary refuges of adulterers. The
scandalous usage which was made of these commodious
retreats became at last so general, and little by little they

assimilated to themselves so completely the other places of debauchery, that finally, as we have said, the two words *meritorium* and *lupanar* came to have the same meaning. When Vopiscus said that the emperor Tacitus gave orders as to certain bad places of the city he refers to the *meritoria;* with Sparianus it is the same, when he cites the letter of Severus reproaching Rogonius Cellus because the tribunes of his army ate in the cook shops but slept in the taverns he uses a significant phrase, "*pro triclinus popinas habent, pro cubiculis meritoria.*" Lodging houses, as was but natural, took also sometimes at Rome the name *meritorium*. Certain verses of Juvenal do not permit us to doubt this. He shows us a poor devil of a traveller who, ill in a lodging house in the most noisy quarter of Rome, where the uproar is torture, dies then from lack of sleep; and another who, tormented by his indigestion, caused by the meal which he had taken in that inn, lies upon his stomach and cannot sleep peacefully.

To designate these inhospitable retreats, the word *meritoria* is used by the satirists.*

That which is decisive proof that by *meritorium* was meant a hotel at Rome is the fact that one does not call otherwise the immense asylum, a veritable hotel of disabled soldiers in which at the expense of the state the old wounded veterans were maintained. This *meritorium* stood upon the site occupied today by the church of Santa Maria in the Transtiber.

However, the inn in Rome as well as along the roads was generally called simply *caupona*, whether it savored of the cabaret or not; again, the term *diversorium* was applied and sometimes *diverticulum*, because, forsooth, they were found upon the side streets and not upon the

*See page 128 (See Juvenal Meritoria).

public ways but at crossroads. Tacitus has represented
Nero as running about in the habiliments of a slave,
the streets of the city, the red light district, and the
taverns and inns; and the term which he applies is
diverticula.

An epigram of Martial has lent color to the charges
frequently preferred against the innkeepers, charges
accusing them of all manner of theft including even that
of robbing the pack animals, owned by their guests, of
their grain and fodder.

"Muleteer, accept what thou dost not give to the
uncomplaining mules as, though I do not wish to give
you a present, neither do I wish to give it to the landlord."

The Roman inn, fairly well provided along the great
routes, could lodge beast and men at the same time;
could give shelter at the same time to the host, to the
guest, servants and baggage. In the Menaechmi of
Plautus the hero arrives at Rome with a considerable
equipage which he sends on ahead of him to an inn
under the guard of one whom he can trust and also of
his other slaves; nor did he retain those things esteemed
of greatest value in his baggage, and we shall find it
also very imprudent to thus rely upon the honor of an
innkeeper and of his slaves.

All these lodgings came at a high rate, but were not
worth what they cost. Stratilax, in the Truculentus, a
man well informed, prevented such treatment for himself.
"Hold," said he to his guide, "I would be led into a tavern
where I would be received badly for my money." And
it was worse in the suburbs. Judge by what Harpax says
of the hag Chrysis, the toothless and greasy hostess
whom he met, "I will go and lodge outside the gates,
at the third tavern, with the old woman Chrysis, gross
as a hogshead, lame and greasily fat."

From the propriety of this hostess, judge well that of the lodging.

In the city or in the suburbs, the majority of the inns were uncleanly, frequented by peoples of all sorts and conditions, a medley of thieves, debauchees, and unsavory lodgers, and the eyes of the prudent aedile and praetor were always on them. Every day a lictor visited suspected inns where espionage was thought to be carried on.

Many a passage in Petronius has recorded perhaps too faithfully the doings and life of institutions such as these, and Eumolpus and Encolpius were as well qualified to speak of the things which went on under their eyes as they were to take part in them. Marcus Manicius, that hardy type of landlord, is as universal as self-interest, and who shall say that the sweet predaciousness of designing widowhood is more frequently imposed upon today than it was in the reign of Nero, when the laws did not protect it so thoroughly. Apuleius has preserved a spirited account of an adventure in an inn of the second century. He had arrived at Hypatia, in Thessaly, and being a mystic, devoting much attention to witchcraft and magic, made the best of the story he puts in the mouth of Aristomanes. The passage occurs in the first book of the Metamorphosis and runs as follows:

TALE OF ARISTOMENES, THE COMMERCIAL TRAVELLER

"I am a native of Ægina, and I travel to and fro through Thessaly, Ætolia, and Bœotia, for the purpose of purchasing honey of Hypata, as also cheese, and other articles of traffic used in cookery. Having understood that at Hypata,* which is the principal city of all Thes-

---

*Hypata.—This was a famous city of Thessaly, situate on the banks of the river Spercheus.

saly, new cheese of exquisite flavour was to be sold at a very reasonable price, I made the best of my way to that place, with the intention of buying up the whole of it. But, as generally is the case, starting unluckily with the left foot foremost,* all my hopes of gain were utterly disappointed. For a person named Lupus, a merchant in a large way of business, had bought the whole of it the day before.

"Weary with my rapid journey, undertaken to so little purpose, I proceeded, early in the evening, to the public baths, when, to my surprise, I espied an old companion of mine, named Socrates. He was sitting on the ground, half covered with a sorry, tattered cloak, and looked almost another person, he was so miserably wan and thin; just like those outcasts of Fortune, who beg alms in the streets. Consequently, although he had been my friend and particular acquaintance, I yet accosted him with feelings of hesitation.

" 'How now, friend Socrates,' said I, 'what is the meaning of this? Why this appearance? What crime have you been guilty of? Why, you have been lamented at home, and for some time given up for dead.† Guardians have been assigned to your children, by decree of the provincial magistrate. Your wife, having fulfilled what was due to the dead,‡ all disfigured by grief and long-continued sorrow, and having almost cried herself blind with excessive weeping, is being worried by her parents to

---

Left foot foremost.—To start on a journey by putting the left foot foremost was considered to be especially significant of ill luck; so much so, that the expression came to be generally used to denote a bad omen.

†*Given up for dead.*—"Conclamatus es." After a person was dead it was the custom of the Romans to call on him by name, for the purpose of recalling him to life, in case he should be only in a trance. This ceremony was called "conclamatio," and was generally performed while the body was being washed, once a day for seven days; after which period the body was burnt.

‡*Due to the dead.*—Ovid, in his Fasti, b. i. l. 36, mentions ten months as the period assigned by Numa for widows to mourn the loss of their husbands.

repair the misfortune of the family by the joys of a new
marriage. But here you come before our eyes like some
spectral apparition, to our extreme confusion.'

" 'O Aristomenes!' said he, 'it is clear that you are
ignorant of the slippery turns, the unstable freaks, and
the ever-changing vicissitudes of Fortune.'

"As he said this, he hid his face, which was crimsoned
with shame, in his cobbled covering of tatters, so that
he left the rest of his body naked. At last, unable to
endure the sight of such a miserable spectacle of woe, I
took hold of him, and endeavoured to raise him from the
ground. But, with his head covered up as it was, he
exclaimed, 'Let me alone, let me alone; let Fortune still
enjoy the trophy she has erected.'

"However, I prevailed upon him to accompany me: and
at the same time pulling off one of my own two garments,
I speedily—clothed, or covered him, shall I say? immediately after which, I took him to a bath, and, myself,
applied to him the requisite anointing and scrubbing
processes, and laboriously rubbed off the coat of filth with
which he was defiled. Having paid every attention to
him, though tired myself, I supported his enfeebled steps,
and with great difficulty brought him to my inn; where
I made him rest on a couch, gave him plenty of food,
cheered him with wine, and entertained him with the
news of the day. And now our conversation took quite
a merry turn, we cracked jokes, and grew noisy in our
prattle; when, heaving a bitter sigh from the bottom of
his breast, and violently striking his forehead with his
right hand:

" 'Miserable man that I am!' said he; 'to have fallen
into these misfortunes while intent on gratifying myself
with a famous gladiatorial spectacle. For, as you are
very well aware, I went to Macedonia on an affair of
business; and after being detained there for the space of

ten months, I was on my return homewards, having gained a very pretty sum of money. I had nearly reached Larissa,* which I had included in my route for the purpose of seeing the spectacle I mentioned, when I was attacked by some desperate robbers, in a lonely and rugged valley, and only effected my escape, after being plundered by them of all I possessed. Being thus reduced to extreme distress, I betook myself to a certain woman named Meroë, who kept a tavern, and who, though old, was remarkably engaging; and to her I related the circumstances of my lengthened absence, of my earnest desire to reach home, and of my being plundered of my property on that day. After I, unfortunate wretch, had related such particulars as I remembered, she treated me with the greatest kindness, supplied me with a good supper, all for nothing. But from the very moment that I, unhappy man, first saw her, my mind contracted a lasting malady; and I even made her a present of those garments which the robbers, in their humanity, had left me to cover my nakedness. I likewise presented her with the little earnings I made by working as a cloak-maker while I was yet in good condition of body; until at length this worthy partner, and ill fortune together, reduced me to that state in which you just saw me.'

" 'By Pollux, then,' said I, 'you deserve to suffer extreme misfortunes, if there is anything still more extreme than that which is most extreme, for having preferred the pleasures of dalliance and a wrinkled harlot, to your home and children.'

" 'Hush! hush!' said he, raising his forefinger to his mouth, and looking round with a terror-stricken countenance to see if he might speak with safety; 'Forbear to revile a woman skilled in celestial matters, lest you do yourself an injury through an intemperate tongue.'

*Larissa.—A city of Thessaly, situated near the river Peneus.

" 'Say you so?' said I. 'What kind of a woman is this tavern keeper, so powerful and queenly?'

" 'She is a sorceress,' he replied, 'and endowed with powers divine; she is able to draw down the heavens, to uplift the earth, to harden the running water, to dissolve mountains, to raise the shades of the dead, to dethrone the Gods, to extinguish the stars, and to illumine the depths of Tartarus itself.'

" 'Come, come,' said I, 'do draw asunder this tragic curtain* and fold up the theatric drop-scene, and let's hear your story in ordinary parlance.'

" 'Should you like,' said he, 'to hear of one or two, ay, or a great many of her performances? Why, as for making not only her fellow-countrymen love her to distraction, but the Indians even, or the inhabitants of both the Æthiopias,† and even the Antichthones‡ themselves; these are only the leaves, as it were, of her art, and mere trifles. Listen, then, and hear what she has performed in the presence of many witnesses. By a single word only, she changed a lover of hers into a beaver, for having been connected with another woman. She likewise changed an innkeeper, who was her neighbour and of whom she was envious on that account, into a frog; and now the old fellow, swimming about in a cask of his own

---

*Tragic curtain.—The "siparium" was a piece of tapestry, stretched on a frame, and, rising before the stage, answered the same purpose as the curtain or drop-scene with us in concealing the stage till the actors appeared. Instead of drawing up this curtain to discover the stage and actors, according to our present practice, it was depressed when the play began, and fell beneath the level of the stage; whence "aulæa premuntur," meant that the play had commenced. "Aulæa" seems here to mean the stage curtain, which divided in the middle and was drawn aside: while the "siparium" would more nearly correspond with our drop-scene.

†The Æthiopias.—The eastern and the western, separated from each other by the river Nile, which the ancients (as we are informed by Strabo, Geograph. lib. ii.) considered as the boundary of Asia and Africa.

‡The Antichthones.—So called from inhabiting the earth contrary to that on which we dwell. Hence they are either the same with the Antipodes, or, at least, are those who dwell in the inferior hemisphere which is contrary to ours.

wine, or buried in the dregs, croaks hoarsely to his old customers, quite in the way of business. She likewise transformed another person, an advocate of the Forum, into a ram, because he had conducted a cause against her; and to this very day that ram is always at loggerheads.* Then there was the wife of a lover of hers, whom she condemned to perpetual pregnancy, when on the point of increasing her family, by closing her womb against the egress of the infant, because she had chattered scandal against the witch.

" 'After this woman, however, and many other persons, had been injured by her arts, the public indignation became aroused against her; and it was determined that on the following day a most dire vengeance should be wreaked upon her, by stoning her to death But, by the power of her enchantments, she frustrated this design: and as Medea, having obtained by entreaty from Creon the truce of a single day, prior to her departure, burned his whole palace, his daughter, together with the old man himself, with flames issuing from a garland, so, likewise, did this sorceress, having performed certain deadly incantations in a ditch,† (as she herself lately told me in a fit of drunkenness), confine all the inhabitants of the town, each in his own house, through a secret spell of the dæmons; so that for two whole days together, neither could the bars be wrenched off, nor the doors be taken off the hinges, nor, in fine, could a breach be made in the walls; until, by mutual consent, the people unanimously cried out, and swore in the most sacred manner, that they would not lift a hand against her, and would, in case any one should think of so doing, afford her timely assistance.

*Is always at .oggerheads.—"Causas agit." This Sir G. Head cleverly renders, "and gives rebutters and surrebutters as he used to do."

†Incantations in a ditch.—Sacrifices to celestial gods were offered on raised altars; those to terrestial gods, on the ground; those to infernal gods, in a pit or ditch.

Being after this manner appeased, she liberated the whole city.

"'In the middle of the night, however, she conveyed the author of this conspiracy, together with all his house, that is to say, with the walls, the very ground, and all the foundations, close shut as it was, into another city, situate at the hundredth milestone hence, and on the summit of a craggy mountain, in consequence of which it is deprived of water. And, as the dwellings of the inhabitants were built so close together, that they did not afford room to this new comer, she threw down the house before the gate of the city, and took her departure.'

"'You narrate,' said I, 'marvellous things, my good Socrates, and no less terrible than marvellous. In fine, you have excited in me too, no small anxiety, indeed, I may say, fear, not inoculating me with a mere grain of apprehension, but piercing me with dread as with a spear, lest this old hag, employing in a similar manner the assistance of some dæmon, should come to know this conversation of ours. Let us, therefore, with all speed, betake ourselves to rest, and when we have relieved our weariness by a night's sleep, let us fly hence as far as we possibly can, before daylight.'

"While I was yet advising him thus, the worthy Socrates, overcome by more wine than he had been accustomed to, and by the fatigue of the day, had fallen asleep, and was now snoring aloud. Shutting the door, therefore, securing the bolts, and placing my bed close against the hinges, I tossed it up well, and lay down upon it. At first, indeed, I lay awake some time through fear, but closed my eyes at last a little about the third watch.*

"I had just fallen asleep, when suddenly the door was burst open with too great violence for one to believe that it was robbers; nay, the hinges being entirely broken and

*Third Watch.—The beginning of this would be midnight.

wrenched off, it was thrown to the ground. The bed-stead, too, which was but small, wanting one foot, and rotten, was thrown down with the violence of the shock, and falling upon me, who had been rolled out and pitched upon the ground, completely covered and concealed me. Then was I sensible that certain emotions of the mind are naturally excited by contrary causes. For as tears very often proceed from joy, so, amid my extreme fear, I could not refrain from laughing, to see myself turned, from Aristomenes, into a tortoise.* And so, while prostrate on the floor, peeping askance to see what was the matter, and completely covered by the bed, I espied two women, of advanced age, one of whom carried a lighted lamp, and the other a sponge and a drawn sword. Thus equipped, they planted themselves on either side of Socrates, who was fast asleep.

"She who carried the sword then addressed the other, 'This, sister Panthia, is my dear Endymion,† my Gany-mede,‡ who by day and by night, hath laughed my youthful age to scorn. This is he who, despising my passion, not only defames me with abusive language, but is preparing also for flight—and I, forsooth, deserted through the craft of this Ulysses, just like another Calypso, am to be left to lament in eternal loneliness.'

"Then extending her right hand, and pointing me out to her friend Panthia; 'And there,' said she, 'is his worthy counsellor Aristomenes, who was the proposer of this flight, and who now, half dead, is lying flat on the ground beneath the bedstead, and is looking at all that is going on, while he fancies that he is to relate disgraceful stories of me with impunity. I'll take care, however, that some

*Into a tortoise.—From his bed and bedstead being turned over him.

†My dear Endymion.—Alluding to the secret of Diana and the shepherd Endymion, on Mount Latmus.

‡My Ganymede.—Called "Catamitus" in the text; by which name he is also called in the Menæchmi of Plautus.

day, ay, and before long too, this very instant in fact, he
shall repent of his recent loquacity, and his present
inquisitiveness.'

"On hearing this, wretch that I was, I felt myself
streaming with cold perspiration, and my vitals began to
throb with agitation; so much so, that even the bedstead,
shaken by the violence of my palpitations, moved up and
down upon my back.

" 'Well, sister,' said the worthy Panthia, 'shall we hack
him to pieces at once, after the fashion of the Bacchanals,
or, shall we bind his limbs and hold him prisoner?'

"To this, Meroë replied—for I perceived from the
circumstances, as well as from the narrative of Socrates,
how well that name fitted her*—'Rather let him live, if
only that he may cover with a little earth the body of this
wretched creature.'   Then, moving the head of Socrates
to one side, she plunged the whole sword into him up to
the hilt, through the left side of his throat, carefully
receiving the flowing blood into a small leathern bottle,
placed under it, so that not a drop of it was anywhere
to be seen.   All this did I witness with my own eyes;
and, what is more, the worthy Meroë, that she might not,
I suppose, omit any due observance in the sacrifice of the
victim, thrusting her right hand through the wound, into
the very entrails, and groping among them, drew forth
the heart of my unhappy companion; while, his windpipe
being severed by the thrust of the weapon, he emitted
through the wound a voice, or rather I should say, an
indistinct gurgling noise, and poured forth his spirit with
his bubbling blood.   Panthia then stopped the gaping
wound with the sponge, exclaiming, 'Beware, O sea-born
sponge, how thou dost pass through a river.'

*How well that name fitted her.—Ausonius, Epigram xix., explains this allusion.
    You are named Meroë, not because you are of a swarthy complexion like one
born in Meroë, the island of the Nile; but because you do not dilute your wine with
water but are used to drink it unmixed and concentrated.—K.

"Hardly had they passed over the threshold, when the door resumed its former state; the hinges resettled on the pannels; the posts returned to the bars, and the bolts flew back once more to their sockets. But I, left in such a plight, prostrate on the ground, scared, naked, cold, indeed, I may say, half dead, but still surviving myself, and pursuing, as it were, a posthumous train of reflections, or, to say the least, like a candidate for the cross, to which I was surely destined: 'What,' said I, 'will become of me, when this man is found in the morning with his throat cut? Though I tell the truth, who will think my story probable? You ought at least, they will say, to have called for assistance, if you, such a stout man as you are, could not resist a woman. Is a man's throat to be cut before your eyes, and are you to be silent? How was it you were not likewise assassinated? Why did the barbarous wretch spare you, a witness of the murder, and not kill you, if only to put an end to all evidence of the crime? Inasmuch, then, as you have escaped death, now return to it.'

"These remarks I repeated to myself, over and over again, while the night was fast verging towards day.

"It appeared to me, therefore, most advisable to escape by stealth before daylight, and to pursue my journey, though with trembling steps. I took up my bundle, and putting the key in the door, drew back the bolts. But this good and faithful door, which during the night had opened of its own accord, was now to be opened but with the greatest difficulty, after putting in the key a multitude of times.

" 'Hallo! porter,' said I, 'where are you? Open the gates of the inn; I want to be off before break of day.'

"The porter, who was lying on the ground behind the door of the inn, still half asleep, replied, 'Who are you, who would begin your journey at this time of night?

Don't you know that the roads are infested by robbers?
Ay, ay, though you may have a mind to meet your death,
stung by your conscience, belike for some crime you have
committed, still, I haven't a head like a pumpkin, that
I should die for your sake.'

" 'It isn't very far from day-break,' said I; 'and
besides, what can robbers take from a traveller in the
greatest poverty?   Are you ignorant, you simpleton, that
he who is naked cannot be stripped by ten athletes even?'

"The drowsy porter, turning himself on his other side,
made answer, 'And how am I to know that you have not
murdered that fellow-traveler of yours, with whom you
came hither last night, and are now consulting your safety
in flight?   And now I recollect that just at that hour I
saw the depths of Tartarus* through the yawning earth
and in them the dog Cerberus, looking ready to devour
me.'

"Then truly I came to the conclusion that the worthy
Meroë had not spared my throat through any compassion,
but that she had cruelly reserved me for the cross.†
Accordingly, on returning to my chamber, I thought about
some speedy mode of putting an end to myself: but as
Fortune had provided me with no weapon with which
to commit self-destruction, except the bedstead alone—
'Now, bedstead,' said I, 'most dear to my soul, who hast
been partner with me in enduring so many sorrows, who
art fully conscious, and a spectator of this night's events,
and whom alone, when accused, I can adduce as a witness
of my innocence, do thou supply me, who would fain

---

*Saw the depths of Tartarus.—Of course in a dream. Just at that hour:—He
knows all about it, even to the precise time. The promptitude with which the porter
decides from the evidence of his dream that the murder had been actually committed, and at the very moment when the dream occurred, is a fine touch of
nature.—K.

†For the cross.—The cross was the instrument of punishment for slaves and
foreigners, especially in cases of murder.

hasten to the shades below, with a welcome instrument of death.'

"Thus saying, I began to undo the rope with which the bed was corded, and throwing one end of it over a small beam which projected above the window, and there fastening it, and making a strong slip-knot at the other end, I mounted upon the bed, and thus elevated for my own destruction, I put my head into the noose. But while with one foot I was kicking away the support on which I rested, so that the noose, being tightened about my throat by the strain of my weight, might stop the functions of my breath; the rope, which was old and rotten, broke asunder, and falling from aloft, I tumbled with great force upon Socrates (for he was lying close by), and rolled with him on to the floor.

"Lo and behold! at the very same instant the porter burst into the room, bawling out, 'Where are you, you uneasy traveler who were in such monstrous haste to be off at midnight, and now lie snoring, rolled up in the bed-clothes?'

"At these words, whether awakened by my fall, or by the discordant notes of the porter, I know not, Socrates was the first to start up, and exclaim, 'Assuredly, it is not without good reason that all travellers detest these hostlers. For this troublesome fellow, intruding so impertinently, with the intention, no doubt, of stealing something, has roused me out of a sound sleep, by his outrageous bellowing.'

"On hearing him speak, I jumped up briskly, in an ecstasy of unhoped-for joy: 'Faithfullest of porters,' I exclaimed, 'my friend, my own father, and my brother, behold him whom you, in your drunken fit, falsely accused me of having murdered.' So saying, I embraced Socrates, and was for loading him with kisses; but he, being assailed by the stench of the most filthy liquor with which those

hags* had drenched me, repulsed me with considerable
violence. 'Get out with you,' he cried, 'for you stink
like the bottom of a sewer,' and then began jocularly to
enquire the cause of this nasty smell. Sorely confused, I
trumped up some absurd story on the spur of the moment,
to give another turn to the conversation, and, taking him
by the right hand, 'Why not be off,' said I, 'and enjoy the
freshness of the morning on our journey?' So I took my
bundle, and, having paid the innkeeper for our night's
lodging, we started on our road.

"We had proceeded some little distance, and now
every thing being illumined by the beams of the rising
sun, I keenly and attentively examined that part of my
companion's neck, into which I had seen the sword
plunged. 'Foolish man,' said I to myself, 'buried in your
cups, you certainly have had a most absurd dream. Why
look, here's Socrates safe, sound and hearty. Where is
the wound? where is the sponge? where, in fine, is the
scar of a wound, so deep, and so recent?'

"Addressing myself to him, 'Decidedly,' said I,
'skilful doctors have good reason to be of opinion that
it is those who are stuffed-out with food and fermented
liquors who are troubled with portentous and horrible
dreams. My own case is an instance of this: for having
in my evening cups exceeded the bounds of temperance,
a wretched night has been presenting to me shocking and
dreadful visions, so that I still fancy myself besprinkled
and defiled with human gore.'

" ' 'Tis not gore,' he replied with a smile, 'you are
sprinkled with, but chamber-lye; and yet I too, thought,
in my sleep, that my throat was cut: some pain, too, I felt
in my neck, and I fancied that my very heart was being

Those hags.—"Lamiæ" were enchantresses, who were said to prowl about at
midnight to satisfy their lustful propensities, and their fondness for human flesh.
They correspond very nearly with the "Ghouls" mentioned in the Arabian Nights'
Entertainments.

plucked out: and even now I am quite faint, my knees tremble, I stagger as I go, and feel in want of some food to refresh my spirits.'

" 'Look,' cried I, 'here's breakfast all ready for you;' and so saying, I lifted my wallet from off my shoulders, and at once handed him some cheese and bread, saying, 'Let us sit down near that plane-tree.'

"We did so, and I also helped myself to some refreshment. While looking at him somewhat more intently, as he was eating with a voracious appetite, I saw that he was faint, and of a hue like box-wood; his natural colour in fact had so forsaken him, that as I recalled those nocturnal furies to my frightened imagination, the very first piece of bread I put into my mouth, though a very tiny bit, stuck in the middle of my throat, so that it could neither pass downward, nor yet return upward. And then besides, the number of people passing along increased my apprehensions; for who would believe that one of two companions could meet with his death without any harm done by the other?

"Meanwhile, after having devoured a sufficient quantity of food, he began to be impatient for some drink; for he had voraciously eaten a good part of a most excellent cheese; and not very far from the roots of the plane tree, a gentle stream flowed slowly along, just like a placid lake, rivalling silver or glass in its lustre. 'Look,' said I, 'drink your fill of the water of this stream, bright as the Milky Way.'

"He arose, and, wrapping himself in his cloak,* with his knees doubled under him, knelt down upon the shelving bank, and bent greedily towards the water. Scarcely had he touched the dewy surface of the water with the edge of his lips, when the wound in his throat burst wide open, the sponge suddenly rolled out, a few drops of blood

---

*In his cloak.—"Palliolo" seems a preferable reading to "paululum."

accompanying it; and then, his body, bereft of life, would have fallen into the river, had I not laid hold of one of his feet, and dragged it with the utmost difficulty and labour to the top of the bank; where, having, as well as the time permitted, lamented my unfortunate companion, I buried him in the sandy soil that eternally begirt the stream. For my own part, trembling and terror-stricken, I fled through various and unfrequented places; and, as though conscious of the guilt of homicide, abandoning my country and my home, and embracing a voluntary exile, I now dwell in Ætolia, where I have married another wife."

One must realize that in accounts such as these, circulated in the conversation wherever people met, an author such as Apuleius would revel, and his fiction is founded upon such episodes, tinctured perhaps by lore from the Levant, or from the more remote hamlets of his native Africa. The perseverance with which such peoples adhere to the customs of primitive hospitality has much to commend it, and the bandits and beauties in distress whom he has introduced were as characteristic of his age as they are of our own.

EPILOGUE

During the interminable number of years which comprised the life of the Roman world and through which we have conducted our readers, we have met always the same abuses; whether in tavern, inn, or cabaret, always have the scandalous contraventions of honesty and morality intruded themselves into our speculations and forced themselves upon our notice.

Lechery in silk, lust in rags, vice generally unpunished and always open, and unbridled orgies that transcend belief, infamy and robbery—all these things taken together may be said to have formed an integral part in the calling of the innkeeper.

The spread of Christianity, the invasion by savage barbarians, whose morals were at first purer than the effeminate serfs whom they subjugated, the slow strangulation of internal commerce; these three things may, in the largest sense of the word, be said to have caused innkeepers and innkeeping to decline to a degree which would have scarcely been deemed possible, and forced the refectories of the various religious orders to take upon themselves the duties of a hospitality well-nigh Grecian in its purity and its freedom from self interest.

The innkeepers at Rome during the age of Alexander Severus were engaged in open warfare with the Christians and sought by every means possible to give the death blow to the new religion which seemed designed to destroy their calling by its austere and moral precepts of sobriety. But these precepts were the main factors in the destruction of the inns and innkeepers of the early Middle Ages, and it is scarcely too much to say that such institutions during that period were to be found in numbers only in the great sea-ports and centres of trade, designed upon the one hand to serve the interests of such mariners as were lucky enough to escape the pirates, and on the other to cater to the appetites of such country rustics and louts as were able to run the gauntlet of mediæval highwaymen and assassins on market days and occasions of fêtes and fairs.

We shall bring our account of the inns of Greece and Rome to a close by relating, along with a few other incidents, an early chapter in the history of Augusto-dunum, now known as Augsburg, and the martyrdom of Affre, its patron saint.

The Rhetians as a people remained unconquered for many years, but we cannot escape the suspicion that that German province had acquired the corruption of Rome before it was subjected by her arms. Vice marching ahead had undermined the barbarian vigor and had prepared its votaries for the sacrifice. One lone tradition has come down to us dealing with this country in the Roman epoch, and that, alas, is a scandalous tradition and deals with the histories of infamous taverns even as we have already dealt; nay more: it shows us an admirable illustration of the power and example exerted by those same precepts of austere and moral sobriety which were the cornerstones of primitive Christianity, ere it had come to purify by fire and sanctify by blood.

Let us then suppose ourselves in the last year of the reign of Galerius, and in the midst of the last persecution brought about to subjugate the Christians. Gaius is vested with the imperial authority of Augsburg, the tribunal before which must appear all those confessing themselves Christians and refusing to sacrifice to false gods. Among the women identified with the cults of shameless divinities which were anathema in the nostrils of the new faith we find the daughter of Hilaria, born, as

was her mother, in Cypress. Affre, for that was the name
of the future martyr, was, we regret to say, a prostitute.
But what of that; what was one to expect of a priestess of
Aphrodite?

With the aid of three young women who came, doubtless, either from Cypress or Greece itself, Affre and her
mother opened at Augsburg a cabaret on the order of
those gay establishments conducted by Thracian girls in
Athens, or, a finer comparison still, like those tasteful
retreats conducted at Rome and its suburbs by Syrian
harp-girls. Hilaria managed the house, Affre and her
companions ministered to the wants of the patrons.
"Affre," according to Tirardin, who has been instrumental
in preserving this legend in its entirety, "Affre was, I
suppose, the Phryne and the Aspasia of the municipality
of Augsburg. One may easily conjure up a picture of the
opulent young Romans who came to Augsburg in their
tour of duty; whether as praetors or in other official capacity, sighing for the flesh-pots of Italy, and looking
forward with disgust to a period of barbarous and horrid
isolation and dreary boredom. What must have been
their surprise at finding in this forbidding province a
retreat which would have charmed Cypress and hostesses
in whose company Pericles would have been delighted?"

One day there arrived at the door of this abandoned
retreat two men of forbidding mein and grave countenance. One was the bishop, Narcissus, and the other was
his deacon, Felix. They found here a refuge from the per-
secutors put upon their track by the minister of Galerius;
they had seen this hostelry, and not believing it as
infamous as it really was, they had entered. Affre
received them, "and as the legend had it, believing them
to be two travellers inflamed with impure desires, she
invited them to supper and prepared everything in the
manner usual and convenient to such occasions; but the

bishop, when he approached the table, began to pray and
sing hymns to the Lord. Affre, stupefied by these words,
the like of which she had never heard before, demanded of
him who he was, and he apprised her that he was a
bishop of the church. Immediately she cast herself at his
feet and cried out, "Lord, I am unworthy to receive you,
and in all the town there is not a single creature more vile
than I. I am not worthy to touch even the hem of your
garments." "Fear nothing," the bishop responded, "the
Saviour was touched by impure hands and remained un-
stained. Does not the light of the sun shine equally upon
sewers and immodest places and is it contaminated
thereby? Therefore, my daughter, receive in your soul
the light of the faith that you may be purified from all
your sins, that you may rejoice to have received me in your
house." "Alas," responded Affre, "I have committed
more sins than I have hairs on my head. How shall I be
able to wash away the spots?" "Believe, receive
baptism, and you shall be saved," answered Narcissus.
At these words, which promised hope of salvation even in
this house of shame, Affre, radiant with joy, called in the
young women who lived with her, her companions in
luxury, whom she wished also to make her companions in
a life of purity. They entered, and viewed with pious
respect the holy man in their shrine. "This man who has
come among us," she told them, "is a bishop of the
Christians and he has said to me if you will believe in
Christ and receive baptism, all your sins shall be forgiven
you. What do you think?" And the three priestesses,
Digna, Eumenia, and Euprepia, responded, "you are our
mistress; we have followed you in vice, why should we not
follow you to procure pardon for our sins?" And after
these words, that night, which as all the others would
without doubt have been passed in an orgy, was passed
by these repentant daughters in all the fervors of prayer,

under the eyes and extended hands of the bishop. The morning came, Affre apprised her mother, Hilaria, of the presence of the holy man, she experienced the charm of his conversation and the old courtesan was filled with grace, and placed all her hopes of heaven in the blessings of the bishop. Not only did she consent to give him sanctuary in a house which she possessed near the inn, but when Affre said to her, "It is well, tonight I will bring you to him," she cried out full of joy, "bring him immediately lest he refuse what thou askest."

Thus it was that day, Narcissus, conducted by Affre to the house near the infamous resort which his presence had so miraculously sanctified, was brought into the presence of Hilaria to whom he brought an equally poignant gladness. The old Cyprian fell at his knees and during three hours, so says the tale, she made the curtain hoops ring with her cries, "I pray you, O Lord, vouchsafe that I shall be purified of my sins."

Here the legend, as is customary in these sorts of tales, introduces the devil, who is to strive to annul all that the bishop has accomplished and to prevent Narcissus from obtaining such rich prey as the four friends whom he had uplifted in a single night in the inn of Affre, by insinuating the advisability of spending another night alone with the four friends in that retreat of pleasure. Narcissus refused, fearing lest the sinners, with difficulty brought into the faith, should backslide in the hours of darkness devoted ordinarily to impurity, and the demon, vanquished, took his departure.

On the following day Affre, her servants and her mother, were baptized.

But all too soon the soldiers of Gaius surrounded the inn of Affre, seized the new Christian, brought her before the Roman commander, who threatened to have her burned to death unless she sacrificed to the gods. She refused, and was taken to an island in the Leκ, where, lashed to a stake, she died, praying to her God.

"During all this, Digna, Eumenia, and Euprepia, who had been slaves, sinners, even as she, and baptized with her by the holy bishop Narcissus, were down at the river. They passed over to the island and found the corpse of the holy Affre unmutilated. A boy who was with them recrossed the river by swimming and carried the news to Hilaria, the mother of the martyr. She went at night with the priests of God, took up the body and interred it two miles from the town in a sepulchre which she had built for herself and hers. Gaius, who had been apprised of this, sent her a messenger with orders to persuade her to sacrifice if it should be possible; if not, to slay her in the same sepulchre. The soldiers, after having employed in vain promises and threats, and finding them firm in refusing the sacrifice, filled the sepulchre with fagots and dry pine cones, set them afire, and departed. Therefore the same day which saw the holy Affre canonized, witnessed also the martyrdom of her mother and her three servants," as Fleury has related.

A little after this same epoch in which the martyrdom of the holy Affre, hotel hostess and courtesan, prepared the way by her pious example for the conversion of the German provinces, there was born and grew up in a little inn in Sicily a holy woman who was able more than any other to serve the cause of the faith and to open the road even to the imperial throne. I refer to the holy Helena, the mother of Constantine the Great. She was born in the third century in the village of Drepanum, a village which Justinian in memory of her so richly embellished and which he called Helenopolus. Her father was an inn-keeper. Some historians, by no means satisfied with so humble an origin for the mother of the first Christian emperor, have attempted to cloud the issue and to secure

for Helena a more noble parentage, but the birth of
Helena in the little inn at Drepanum cannot be disputed,
as it has been established by the evidence of Orosius, who
wrote in good faith, and thanks also to Entropius, who
though less explicit, has remarked that Constantine the
Great was born of a very obscure marriage contracted by
Constantius *ex obscuriore matrimonio*. After them
Gibbon has confirmed what we have said of the origin of
Helena: "We are obliged to confess that Helena was the
daughter of an innkeeper," and he adds in a note, "It is
indeed probable enough that Helena's father kept an inn
at Drepanum and that Constantius might lodge there
when he returned from a Persian embassy in the reign of
Aurelius."

In discussing the decline of innkeeping, and the
change which the rites of hospitality underwent, as a
necessary corollary, we must give some consideration to
one of the most curious social conditions with which the
world has ever been confronted. On one hand, we have
the movement of the Christian revolution, operating in
favor of liberty, enfranchising poverty, and extending the
protection of the laws to it; on the other, the political
chaos brought about by barbarian invasions, operating to
install new authority, the parent, as it were, of a new
slavery. It was not a case of action followed by the
inevitable reaction, for the two contrary movements were
simultaneous, and the singular combination born of that
contradiction has never been thoroughly studied and
understood by historians. The masters of Rome became
the slaves of their conquerors; the classes who had known
nothing but slavery passed under the authority of new
masters, and the ancient slaves of the Germans and the
Goths attached themselves to the destiny of their latest
owners. Priests of the church, stationed at the furthest
borders of the two states, conquering and conquered alike,

slave and mistress, owner and serf, formed an im-
measurable complication which did much to bring on the
era which we call that of the Middle Ages, and formed the
cornerstone upon which feudalism rested. The various
degrees of servitude produced in their turn divers degrees
of vassalage. So difficult was it to annihilate slavery, an
institution having its deepest roots in the faith and
manners of the conquering nations and in the laws of the
peoples conquered, that the very monasteries themselves
were slaves, in the larger meaning of the term.

The classes with whom we are especially concerned in
our researches, the innkeeping and tavern-keeping
classes, had, notwithstanding their infamy, come to play
a major part and exert a powerful influence in prolonging
the existence of pagan rites, and in aiding in their celebration, and the determined opposition which Christianity
encountered amongst the slaves and the vilest of the
rabble, may be accounted for by this fact. The tavern-
keepers acted as the trusted agents for pagan cults and
their establishments became the refuge of believers in the
older religions. In fact, these Roman hosts were the born
enemies of Christian austerity, they were the priests and
ministers of the gods of gluttony. They saw themselves
menaced in their vital interests by a religion which en-
joined abstinence and fasting upon their best customers.
Paganism, with its sensual divinities, its orgies, its
sacrificial feasts, its libations in temple or tomb, was the
only religion which they could embrace to their advantage
and, in defense of it, they were prepared to devote themselves, soul and body. Not only did they profit from the
debaucheries which they furthered, but the sacrifices were
also highly advantageous to them. The popa, as we have
already had occasion to remark, was always predaceous,
and generally an innkeeper. We ought not, therefore,
manifest surprise when we find a man of such keen

intellect and convenient principles, for the interests involved in this double calling required both, turning a cold shoulder to the compliments of the first Christians. He would be among the last to hold friendly intercourse with a sect whose purpose was to crush paganism, and, in crushing it, to annul his usefulness to society.

As we have said above, open warfare between the Christians and the innkeepers was waged under Alexander Severus, and the Christians were so weak in influence at court and in the means of defense that only with difficulty could they resist the vile mob of roisterers gathered against them. The cause of this crucial difficulty was a piece of land which they had taken possession of for the purpose of building a church. The corporation of innkeepers laid claim to this land, on what titles we do not know. The affair attracted much attention on account of the malignant and animated clamors of the tavern-keepers, to which, without doubt, the Christians opposed a countenance grave but firm. The case came at last before the tribunal of the emperor. Luckily for the Christians it was Alexander Severus, the first prince whose heart had ever opened itself to the sentiments of Christianity other than to malign and curse them. Lampridius, his biographer, has reported the trial:

"The Christians had taken possession of a site which, in former times, had been public; the innkeepers laid claim to it, and the decision of Alexander Severus was that it would be better in every way to consecrate the site to the cult of some god than to let it fall into the hands of the tavern-keepers."

Having thus gained their cause, through the impartial judgment of the emperor, the Christians were left in possession of the disputed property and proceeded to build their church. Thus was the first church built in Rome. It was erected on ground which, up to that time, had been used by tavern-keepers and claimed by them; a tradition little in keeping with a foundation so pious.

The good fathers of the church waxed bitter and eloquent on the subjects of inns and taverns, but they still would have us believe that the early progress of Christianity brought about the downfall of the debauchery, of the divinities dedicated to libertinage and orgy, and that chastity and the symbol of the Virgin took their place. One may well believe that primitive Christianity was, if anything, a true forerunner of socialism, a precursor of a sort of communism spreading to branches through the inferior classes of the Roman world, and coming finally to dominate them. And why not? Was not its chief appeal directed at the social strata which have from the beginning of organized society formed the real basis of power? In a remarkable passage in the "Destruction of Paganism" the learned author has this to say: "One may repeat habitually that Christianity was the religion of the plebes, the poor, the sad. In fact, it was the refuge universal in its scope of all those suffering from the imperfect organization of Roman society; and that which was true of that epoch was not less so in the fourth century, for, as Jerome remarks, 'The church of Christ is a congregation of the plebes.' "

The growth of the new sect was rapid, but its members could with difficulty reconcile themselves to the necessities of military life, and the dissensions with which the Empire was divided reached their climax under Julian, the Apostate. The social cosmos, distracted with class hatreds and religious dogmas, became gradually less and less able to contend on equal terms with the savage barbarian hosts of the north, and when we reach the age of Arcadius and Honorius, we find Italy overrun with the hordes of Aleric, and a great official, Rutilius Numatianus, to visit his paternal estates in Gaul, was forced to make the trip by boat, as the country had been so ravaged and devastated that there were no inns left in the north of Italy. Commerce and trade languished and finally ceased almost altogether; travel was dangerous and was only undertaken under the most pressing necessity; and the religious monasteries were forced to take upon themselves the burden of hospitality, a burden not destined to be lifted permanently until the rise of guilds, and the necessity of marketing their products had revitalized the inert intelligence of baronial and municipal authority. Then mine host comes again into his own, and may his just reward be out of all proportion to his virtues.

[THE END]

INDEX